The Four

SEASONS

THE LIVING COUNTRYSIDE

A Reader's Digest selection

THE FOUR SEASONS

First Edition Copyright © 1986
The Reader's Digest Association Limited, Berkeley Square House,
Berkeley Square, London W1X 6AB

Copyright © 1986
Reader's Digest Association Far East Limited
Philippines Copyright 1986
Reader's Digest Association Far East Ltd

Second reprint 1990

PRINTED IN SPAIN

Front cover pictures: Beeches and bluebells in spring, with, from
left to right, chaffinch chicks and one of their parents in the nest,
flaming summer field poppies, an autumn harvest of blackberries
and a grey squirrel feeding in the snow.

ISBN 0 276 39661 8

The Four
SEASONS
THE LIVING COUNTRYSIDE

PUBLISHED BY THE READER'S DIGEST ASSOCIATION LIMITED
LONDON   NEW YORK   MONTREAL   SYDNEY   CAPE TOWN

Originally published in partwork form
by Eaglemoss Publications Limited and Orbis Publishing Limited

Consultant

Bob Gibbons

Contributors

Carolyn Boulton	**Paul Freeman**	**Ernest Neal**
John Burton	**Martin Gardner**	**Malcolm Ogilvie**
Tom Cairns	**Tony Harman**	**Jane Ponti**
Michael Chinery	**Jeanette Harris**	**Bob Press**
William Condry	**Stephen Harris**	**Hilary Soper**
David Corke	**Sabina Knees**	**Ian Spellerberg**
Steve Downer	**David MacDonald**	**David Sutton**
Euan Dunn	**Nigel Matthews**	**Barry Tebbs**
Chris Feare	**Chris Mead**	**John Waters**
Jim Flegg	**Barbara Midgley**	**Alwyne Wheeler**
Pamela Forey	**Pat Morris**	**Anthony Wootton**

Contents

The Four
SEASONS

Introduction

In Britain the four seasons are usually strongly marked, and we are very aware of them. Despite the vagaries of the weather, and the likelihood of something unexpected, there is little doubt as to whether the season is spring, summer, autumn or winter, and each of these seasons lasts roughly for its allotted span of three months.

The main cause of the changing seasons is that the earth's angle to the sun alters in the course of a year, giving us more and stronger sun in summer and the reverse in winter. At the same time, the weather patterns themselves alter. Spring is a time of unsettled weather, with alternating warm and cool temperatures, and alternating wet and dry conditions. Summer tends to be more settled, with high pressure extending on into September and early October, but later in the autumn the weather is dominated by mild, wet, windy weather. Then, in winter, the weather is dominated by cold, dry Continental air.

Britain is not a large island, yet the timing and even the character of the seasons vary enormously throughout the country. We are strongly influenced by the sea, and particularly by the warm Gulf Stream from the west, so there is a marked difference between coastal areas and inland areas, with coastal areas being milder. Similarly, the whole west of the country is milder and generally damper than the east, with warmer winters and cooler summers – in other words, a more equable, less Continental climate.

But perhaps the main variation is from north to south – it is rather like going slowly up a mountain! Spring arrives up to two months later in the north than the south, summer is shorter and winter comes earlier and is harsher. Yet, plants and animals are well adapted to life in all these varying conditions.

Left: Beeches in glorious autumn colour – a last fling before all the leaves fall and winter arrives in earnest.

SEASONS AND CYCLES IN NATURE

The survival of all living things is dependent on how they cope with the conditions imposed on them by the cycles of night and day and the four seasons.

The changing seasons, the inevitable rhythm of night and day, the intricate webs of survival and interdependence—each has a profound effect on the wildlife of Britain.

The seasons Most plants and animals are sensitive to changes of daylight and temperature. These two key factors regulate their life cycles and habits, preparing them for the abundance of summer and rigours of winter. Longer hours of daylight and warmth in spring encourage many flowers to open when insects are around to pollinate them. These same triggers make insect eggs hatch and prompt birds and mammals to moult at appropriate times of year, ensuring that a thick coat is present before the arrival of winter and shed again before summer comes. Shorter days and colder weather signal to swallows, for example, that it is time to migrate. Hibernators are forewarned of winter and begin to accumulate food stores or fat.

A delicate balance The countryside depends for its survival on a delicately balanced pattern of life and death. Natural disasters such as the drought of 1976 can affect this precarious cycle drastically (many trees died as a result). When man interferes, he threatens this balance too.

If you look at the simplified food chain (illustrated on the right, under the heading The cycle of survival) you can imagine how even more widespread use of pesticides would affect those birds that feed on insects and other invertebrates; how diseases such as myxomatosis (introduced by man) affect not only rabbits but also the animals – such as foxes and birds of prey – that depend on them for food.

As you read about the changing seasons, bear in mind that Great Britain is over 700 miles long, so the precise timing of seasonal events varies greatly from one area to another. When the south of England has spring flowers and nesting birds, the north of Scotland may well still be in the icy grip of winter. Years vary too. In warmer years spring may come early, for example. This means that exact dates cannot be attached to the seasons, so where months are referred to they are only approximations.

Spring Many woodland plants, such as violets and primroses, flower early before the tree canopy blankets them in shade. Hours of daylight are longer in spring (eight hours in mid-December, $13\frac{1}{2}$ hours by mid-April) and this photo-periodic (light-time) switch triggers plants into flowering and trees into unfurling their leaves.

Summer The warmth of summer ensures that plenty of insects are available for birds, such as this skylark, to feed to their young. Long summer days (17 hours in mid-June) provide more time for birds to forage supplies for the extra mouths. But an early dry spell can mean a disastrous drop in numbers of insects— and so fewer chick survivors.

Autumn Small mammals, like this bank vole, are most numerous in early autumn. But once the glut of berries, nuts and seeds is over there is too little food for all to survive, and within a few weeks the population may be halved. Only the fittest survive the rigours of winter.

Winter Broadleaved trees lose leaves before winter. Otherwise water would be lost through the leaves at times when the soil may be frozen and fresh supplies of water cannot be taken up by the roots. Frost and rain help to break down the leaf litter, returning nutrients such as nitrates to the soil.

The cycle of survival

In the simplified food cycle illustrated here, everything depends on the energy radiated by the sun. Plants use this energy to combine water with carbon dioxide from the air to form carbohydrates such as sugar and starch. These combine with nutrients from the soil to make plant tissues. Along come herbivores (plant eaters) such as snails, rabbits or cows. Their digestive systems transform the carbohydrates, using them for growth and fuel in the creature's body. Activity burns up the fuel, releasing carbon dioxide back into the air through exhaled breath. The herbivore may die and return directly to the soil, or may be eaten by an insectivore (insect eater) or by a carnivore (flesh eater). This animal in turn either dies or it may be eaten by another carnivore such as fox or badger which is at the top of the food chain. Eventually all carcases and droppings decompose with the aid of maggots, fungi and bacteria. Trees and plants die and rot, leaves break down and all these nutrients feed a new generation of plants.

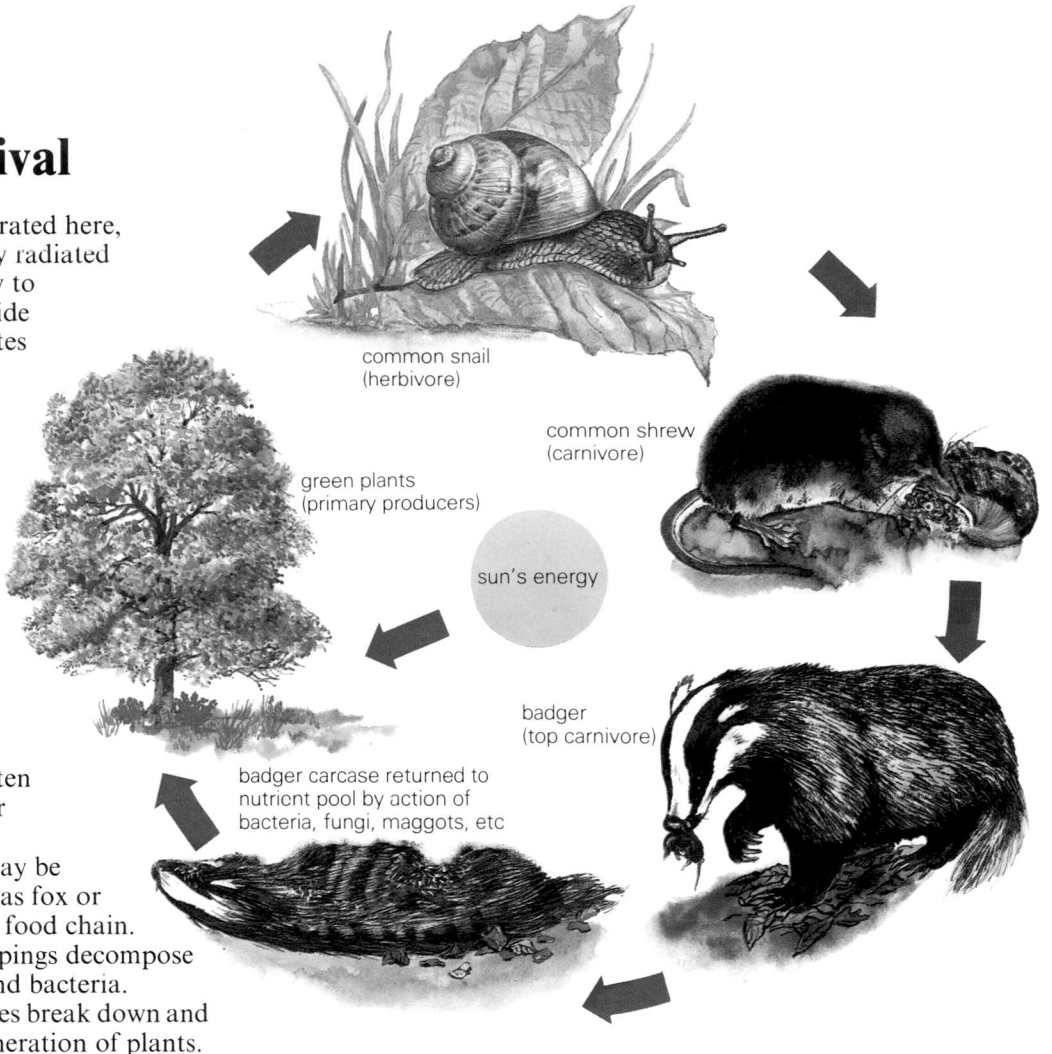

common snail
(herbivore)

common shrew
(carnivore)

green plants
(primary producers)

sun's energy

badger
(top carnivore)

badger carcase returned to
nutrient pool by action of
bacteria, fungi, maggots, etc

The cycle of night and day

The 24-hour rhythm of night and day divides nature into two distinct communities. While one set of interdependent groups is busy during the day and resting at night, others become active only during the hours of dusk or darkness. In each case, the level of light acts as the trigger. Under cover of darkness mice and shrews can move around unseen, whereas during the day they would easily be spotted by predators. The eyes of many nocturnal animals such as the tawny owl are adapted to pick up as much light as possible, while the day-flying kestrels have exceptional focusing powers for long-distance hunting. Coloured flowers attract butterflies by day, while in a nocturnal partnership, moths pollinate the night-flowering catchfly, which attracts them with its perfume.

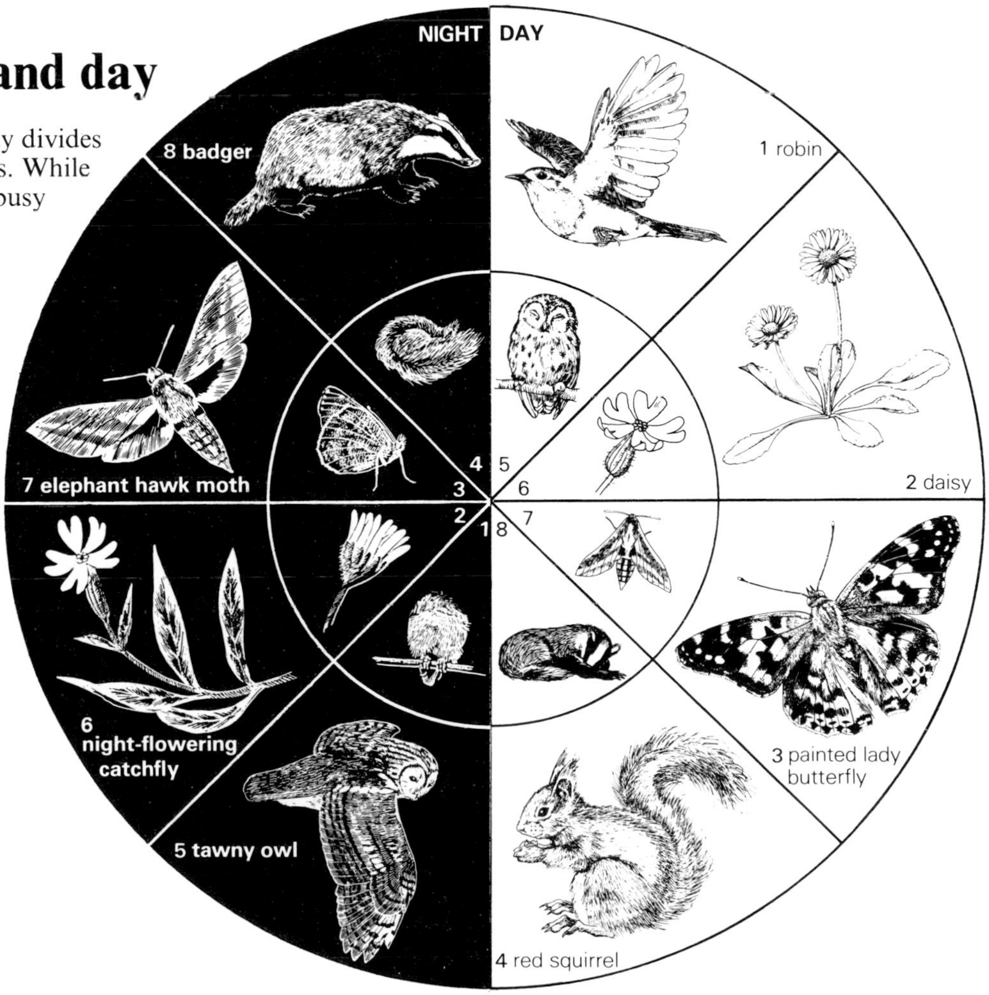

NIGHT DAY

8 badger

1 robin

7 elephant hawk moth

2 daisy

6 night-flowering catchfly

3 painted lady butterfly

5 tawny owl

4 red squirrel

9

WILDLIFE AND THE WEATHER

Weather is one of the most powerful factors influencing the lives of animals and plants. Heat and cold, rain, snow and wind can save life or destroy it, and nature has evolved ingenious responses to the weather's mixed blessings.

Above: A storm gathers over Loch Ness. Storm winds uproot trees and blow migrating birds off course, while the rain drowns insects and small animals, and floods mountain streams, causing perilous rock falls.

From the windswept Shetlands to the English Channel, and from Ireland's moist Atlantic coast to the dry arable lands of East Anglia, the British Isles experience a wide range of climatic conditions. Within the span of nine degrees of latitude, the climatic range encompasses Arctic and Alpine conditions (in relatively small areas) in the mountains of Scotland; high rainfall of over 100 inches a year on the mountains of western England and Scotland; and a dry climate in the east of England where rainfall is below 25 inches a year. And, in the south-west of Ireland, and in parts of England's West Country and the western shores of Scotland, the Gulf Stream brings its warming influence, creating an environment congenial to Mediterranean species such as palm trees.

This variety, however, stops short of the extremes seen in other parts of the world. Our islands are under the moderating influence of the sea, which is always slower to cool or warm than either land or air. We enjoy a temperate, maritime climate, the mildness of which is clearly seen when we compare the British winter–for all that we may dislike it–with the far colder winters experienced in such places as Moscow, which is on nearly the same latitude as southern England but far from the sea.

Crucial for the wildlife of these islands is the fact that our climate consists of a cycle of four strongly contrasting seasons, which

is not the case everywhere in the world. Plants and animals living in a seasonal climate need not only to be adapted to cope with the alternation between warmth and cold, but also must be able to take advantage of the unfailing regularity of those seasons by evolving life cycles that take their timing from them.

While the climate, or long-term range of weather conditions, has played its part in selecting the animals and plants of the British Isles, their life-cycles and day-to-day fortunes are determined by the ever-changing conditions of the moment, in other words the celebrated British weather. This chapter describes the ways in which the behaviour of animals and the growth of plants are geared to take advantage of the changing pattern of weather and, too, how they can be imperilled by the sudden devastating and unexpected tricks the weather can produce.

Temperature governs all The most visible effect of the change of seasons is the appearance of plants. The bursting buds of spring, the profusion of blooms in summer, the fiery colours of autumn and the bare trees of winter each in turn transform the landscape.

Above: A robin takes advantage of a sunny spell to soak up some of the sun's warmth. Often you can almost see the sheer enjoyment of the sun's warmth in the bird's ecstatic movements.

Animals fit neatly into this pattern of plant activity, for they are dependent on the ability of plants to utilise the energy of the sun, and so provide food for all.

Temperature is the most important trigger of seasonal change, and initiates the successive stages of life-cycles. Plants stop growing when average temperatures drop below 6°C (43°F). In the south-west of England this does not happen often, and so grass usually continues to grow all through the winter, though more slowly. The rising temperatures of spring cause sap to rise, plants to make leaves, birds to find mates and build nests, insects to lay eggs and larvae to hatch – all timed so that the young of most creatures can be fed on the bounty of spring and summer. Blue tits have hungry chicks to feed just at the time when the greatest number of caterpillars are about; hedgehogs produce young when worms and grubs are most abundant. For virtually all of Britain's wildlife, spring is the time of breeding.

The success of a breeding season can depend on whether the temperature remains

Above: Wind is useful to birds in more ways than one: besides speeding their flight, it can support them. Here a gannet hovers some way off the rock, in a suitable mid-air position from which it can swoop and catch fish with a minimum of delay as soon as the prey is sighted.

Left: Strong wind has a harmful effect on plants: it dries out the leaves and prevents new ones from growing. This yew on the Anglesey coast is exposed to a constant westerly wind which has prevented new growth on the upwind side.

on a steady upward trend in the early spring or fluctuates sharply – a cold snap at this time of year can be a disaster; for example, it can sometimes kill whole populations of such birds as the goldcrest. This is not to say that birds are ill-equipped to withstand low temperatures – compared with most other creatures they have a high metabolic rate, which is the rate at which they convert food into body tissue, energy and warmth. For added protection, they can improve insulation by fluffing out their feathers; and some tuck their bills and feet into their plumage, to prevent heat loss from these extremities.

Hot and sunny weather, apart from bringing the welcome opportunity for birds to indulge in a little sunbathing, can threaten them with overheating. Their skins do not perspire as ours do, so they lose heat by exaggerated, rapid breathing, or else by lifting their wings to expose the underwing surfaces: these have few feathers, and so they get rid of heat by radiating it directly from the skin.

Rain and high water Rain is a mixed blessing. Moisture is vital for plants and they often send down roots to great depths to obtain it; some species are particularly well equipped to conserve water, having thick and fleshy leaves, inrolled leaves or waxy surfaces. Heavy rain in spring, on the other hand, can destroy seedlings by washing them away. Rain can also benefit a plant by transporting a seed ripe for germination to a suitable spot in which it can grow. When a raindrop strikes a mature puffball or earth ball, it sends a puff of air out through the opening in the top of the fungus, rather like the action of a pair of bellows; this blows the tiny spores into the air, to be dispersed by the wind.

For animals too, rain is sometimes a help and sometimes a hindrance. It can wash away insect eggs from leaves, flood or drown pupae in the soil, chill or drown baby birds or mammals in the nest or home, yet provide welcome puddles where birds can bathe and all animals can drink.

Ice and snow The temperature determines whether moisture in the air will fall as rain or turn to hail, snow or, when on the ground, to ice. The moisture which is welcome as rain may have disastrous results for some bird species when it turns to ice. Birds must bathe, even in the depths of winter, to keep their plumage in good condition. So, when fresh water is frozen over and they cannot bathe, many die of cold because their feathers no longer operate to full effect. Birds which depend on water for their food also suffer in a hard winter. Large numbers of king-fishers and herons, for example, starve to death during severe winters when they cannot fish their usual freshwater reaches.

A blanket of snow makes foraging very difficult for most creatures, and many plants suffer too – branches of conifers often break under the sheer weight of snow, and buds of

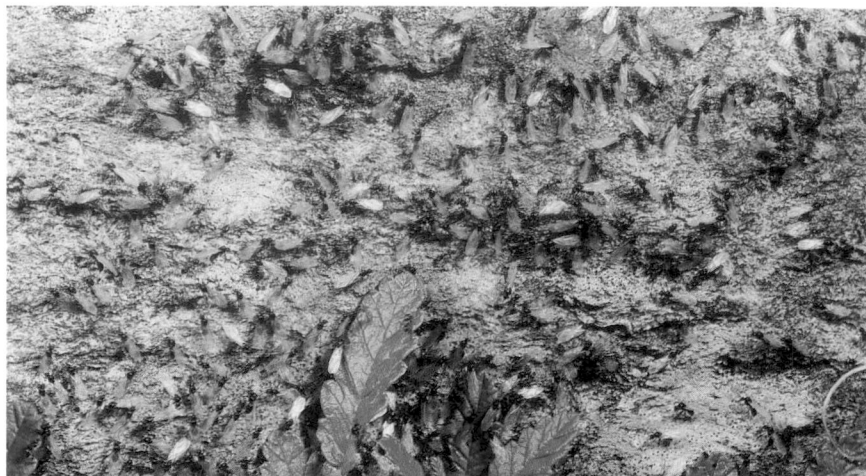

broadleaved trees may freeze and then fail to open in spring. On the credit side, however, snow provides a blanket of insulation under which mountain and other plants can safely grow buds.

Snow makes most birds and mammals more easily noticeable and therefore more vulnerable to their predators; species that have adapted to overcome this disadvantage, evolving winter coloration that matches the white of the snow, are the mountain hare, the ptarmigan and the stoat.

The wild wind Besides being the bringer of changes in the weather, wind has a significant effect in its own right. In particular, it dries up plants. In areas exposed to constant

Above: Garden ants (these are *Lasius niger*) emerge from the nest and take off for their mating flight between July and September when a particular combination of weather conditions occurs – a warm day with still and sultry air.

Below: House martins are able to evade winter altogether – by flying to the sunny south. Here they are gathering in preparation for their departure for Africa.

winds from the same direction, especially on the coast, you can often see deformed trees and shrubs that grow only on the downwind side, producing lop-sided shapes.

But the right wind at the right time can benefit plants, particularly at seeding time. A dandelion clock is really a mass of seeds, each attached to a parachute designed to catch the wind and whisk them away as far as possible from the parent plant. Winged fruits, such as those of sycamore trees, drift down and away, rotating like small helicopters and travelling far with the help of the wind.

Young spiders, too, spread away from the parent colony in autumn by climbing to the top of a grass stem or a fence post – and then facing into the wind and secreting long silken threads which are caught by the wind, and drawn out until there is enough drag to lift the spiders up and away.

Migrating birds are greatly affected by the wind. The epic journeys from Arctic to south polar regions undertaken every year by terns, for example, are achieved by making the most of favourable winds. Winds generally increase with height, which may explain why birds fly at their highest when migrating. Unusually violent winds can blow parties of migrating birds off course and so, after a stormy day, birdwatchers look out for exotic species that have made a forced landing on these islands.

Evasive action If conditions become in-

Above: A hedgehog disturbed in winter, hibernating among dead leaves.

Right: The hoopoe comes to England when favourable winds extend its migratory flight further north than usual.

Below: While conifers stay evergreen, deciduous trees respond to shorter days and cold by changing colour and dropping their leaves.

tolerable for an animal or plant, it will die, perhaps leaving eggs, seeds or spores to spring to life in its place when more suitable conditions prevail. If conditions regularly become intolerable at the same time every year, various evasive strategies are adopted. Birds, for example, have the enviable power of flight, and many migrate: the swallow, for instance, departs in October for South Africa, while the whitethroat leaves for Spain and West Africa.

Migration is less practical for land-bound animals – indeed, for the British land-bound fauna, the sea is an insuperable obstacle; instead of leaving altogether, several mammals – hedgehogs, dormice and bats – hibernate. Other creatures go into a similar dormant state for the winter, without experiencing such profound bodily changes as hibernating mammals: reptiles lie in their burrows, snails creep into shelter among roots of plants, and various moths such as the herald moth remain motionless in caves or buildings, until the return of spring.

WILDLIFE AND OUR CHANGING CLIMATE

Britain's climate over the past two thousand years has been far from unchanging. There have been long periods of alternately warm and cold weather. Even today, each change in climate has an important influence on Britain's wildlife.

People have been keeping reliable weather records only for about the last 300 years. To find out what our climate was like before that we may look at indirect evidence, such as contemporary writing and human activities. More scientifically, investigations into lake-bed sediments and peat bogs reveal the plants and animals living at different times in the past. Some of these now live far to the north, or far to the south, of us, and so we can assume that the weather at that time was distinctly colder or warmer than it is now.

When the Romans invaded Britain about 2000 years ago our climate had just about recovered from a cool wet period which had lasted some 2000 years. The Romans enjoyed warm, dry conditions–warm enough to enable them to cultivate grapes successfully at such northerly latitudes. Their departure soon after the year 400 coincided with a deterioration to cooler, wetter weather which affected the whole of Europe, especially the north.

Some centuries later the weather began to improve again and, from about 800 to 1300, there was a long period of considerable warmth. Winters were mainly wet and mild and summers were, on average, 1-2°C (1.5-3°F) warmer than they are today. Vineyards in Britain prospered to such an extent that during the warmest phase they rivalled those of both France and Germany in quality. Little is known about the effects of this long, very warm period on Europe's wildlife, but it seems highly likely that many species associated with cold conditions retreated well to the north while more southerly species advanced northwards to replace them. The literature of the time suggests that such warmth-loving birds as the hoopoe, golden oriole and quail were then familiar birds in Britain.

The Little Ice Age The beginning of the 14th century saw a deterioration in the climate. By 1350 it had declined so much that our vineyards were no longer viable: the Little Ice Age had arrived and another 500 years were to pass before it relented. This was the period when the Thames and other European rivers often froze during the severe winters, particularly during the 17th and 18th centuries, which were the coldest periods of the Little Ice Age. Yet it was not all a time of unrelieved gloom–the climate often brought hot, dry summer spells.

Again, there was little systematic observation that would have enabled us to deduce the effects the Little Ice Age had on our wildlife. Nevertheless, we do know that birds, seals and whales from the Arctic region ventured further south than previously. The same was true of Eskimos. Between 1682 and 1701 they were often encountered off the coast of Orkney. We began to lose some of the

Above: The serin's fortunes during this century's climatic warming have been spectacular. Once, this finch was confined to the western Mediterranean but it has now colonized much of Europe, including Russia. In Britain, a few pairs have nested here irregularly since 1967.

Opposite page: Frensham Little Pond, Surrey, iced over in winter. The recent run of colder winters suggests that such sights may become more common in the future.

Below right: During the mild first half of this century the lizard orchid spread out from Kent to colonize other areas of south-east England. Since then, however, its range has contracted as our weather has become colder.

Below: The Thames frozen at Richmond in 1855, at the end of the Little Ice Age. The number of times such scenes were depicted suggests that they made a great impression on contemporary artists.

butterflies that had apparently been well established here during the warm weather of the Middle Ages. They included such attractive species as the purple-edged copper and the scarce copper.

Warming up Although there were some short-lived improvements early in the 18th century the Little Ice Age did not end until the middle of the 19th century. Even then the gradual improvement, which affected the whole Northern Hemisphere, was interrupted by brief returns to cooler weather. A general warming up (which climatologists call an amelioration) began in earnest at the beginning of the 20th century.

Nobody is sure why this amelioration occurred but it resulted in Britain, and indeed the whole of north-west Europe, coming under the influence of warm, moist, westerly winds blowing from the North Atlantic. Moreover, their increased prevalence and strength, often in the shape of deep depressions, combined with a tendency to take a more northerly track, meant they carried warm air (and also warm water) far into the

Two millennia of climatic changes

DATE

butterflies lost

| 0 AD | 400 | 800 | 1000 | 1100 | 1200 | 1300 | 1400 | 1500 | 1600 | 1700 | 1800 |

warm summers
wet, mild winters

sunless summers
cold winters

Romans grow vines **English vineyards flourish** **Thames frozen** **Arctic seals and Eskimo**

Above: The recent cooling of the climate has so far been felt more in the Arctic than in temperate regions, with the result that many Arctic species are retreating southwards. The snowy owl, for example, used to be confined to northern Scandinavia and other Arctic regions but, over the last 20 years, it has been seen more regularly further south and has attempted to colonize Shetland.

Left: A male peacock butterfly basking. Since the early part of this century this species has spread northwards and can now be found well into southern Scotland. This was due solely to an improvement in the weather since the butterfly's larval food plant, nettle, occurs throughout Britain.

Arctic. Not surprisingly the ice pack retreated northwards.

Britain's weather became increasingly maritime in character, with mild winters and wet, dull summers, particularly between 1896 and 1939. Nevertheless, when the amelioration reached its height in the 1930s and 1940s the summers were generally very warm and sunny. The 1940s also saw a run of cold winters, notably that of 1946-7, which was to signal the end of the mild weather.

Effects on wildlife The effects of this climatic warming on our wildlife have been considerable. About a dozen species of birds have either colonized Britain from the Continent or attempted to do so, and a number of others already breeding here extended their range northwards. The first group includes some spectacular successes such as Cetti's warbler, a species previously confined to the Mediterranean region but which began to expand northwards soon after 1920 and, by 1970, had colonized southern England. Even more astonishing is the spread of the collared dove, which first arrived in Britain in 1952 and now has a population of about 100,000 pairs.

During the same period more than 40 species of moth have appeared here for the first time from Continental Europe and, as with birds, many species already here have pushed their breeding ranges northwards.

Among plants it is difficult to point to

examples because they are obviously much less mobile than animals and are therefore slower to take advantage of favourable changes in climate to move into new areas. The quickest plants to respond are those with very light, wind-borne seeds like the lizard orchid, which spread between 1900 and 1940 from Kent northwards and westwards over the calcareous soils of south-east England to an astonishing extent.

The climatic trends of the first half of the present century did not suit all our species. Birds of cooler climates, such as the whimbrel and the red-necked phalarope, moved north, the whimbrel being slowly replaced by its southern counterpart, the curlew, as it did so. On the other hand the wetter, cooler summers adversely affected some summer migrants—such as wryneck and red-backed shrike—which depended upon plenty of warm sunny days to catch enough adult insects to sustain them. Both birds withdrew south-eastwards; up to 1900 they had bred regularly and quite commonly in southern Britain but had virtually ceased to do so by 1980. Likewise,

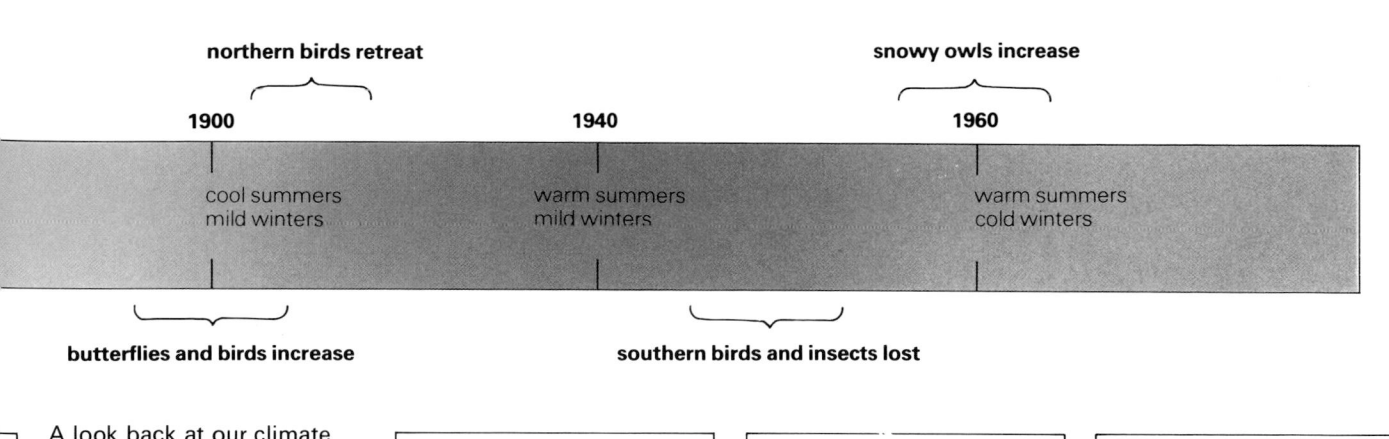

northern birds retreat

snowy owls increase

1900 **1940** **1960**

cool summers
mild winters

warm summers
mild winters

warm summers
cold winters

butterflies and birds increase

southern birds and insects lost

A look back at our climate over the last 2000 years shows long periods of alternately warm and cold weather. This pattern is reflected in the distribution of species: the white admiral butterfly spread as summers became warmer in the 1940s; the red-backed shrike has declined because of a long-term trend towards milder summers; and the lizard orchid, which spread out with the climatic improvement of the early 20th century, has now declined again with the deterioration in our weather.

Distribution of white admiral

■ 1900-1910
□ 1940-1950s

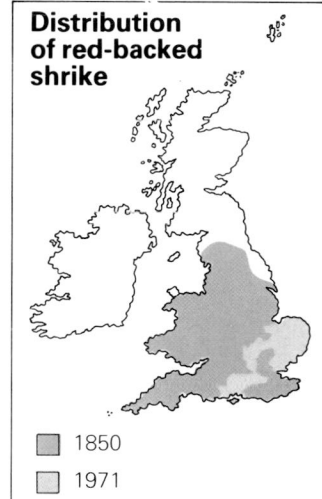

Distribution of red-backed shrike

■ 1850
□ 1971

Distribution of lizard orchid

pre 1920
• 1960s
■ max extent 1920-1950

insects have retreated south-eastwards. The field cricket, for example, has almost disappeared from Britain.

Present climate The harsh winter of 1946-7 was a sign of things to come for, by 1950, the climatic amelioration was waning with a decline in average temperatures and a weakening of the atmospheric circulation. This was most pronounced in the Arctic, and as it started to bite further south one expected to see a reversal of the processes that took place in the first half of this century. Arctic and sub-Arctic species moved southwards in response to the increasing cold and reoccupied territory they last held at the end of the Little Ice Age. Thus snowy owls, redwings, buntings and purple and wood sandpipers began attempting to colonize northern Britain.

A feature of the present weather is the occurrence of long spells of the same type of conditions, for example, the drought summer of 1976, the severe winter of 1978-9, the wet autumn of 1976 and the wet spring of 1983. These were all caused by a stationary area of high pressure. The persistence since the 1960s of such a blocking 'high' in spring over Scandinavia appears to have deflected some migrant birds away from southern Scandinavia to eastern Britain; the few breeding pairs of wrynecks in eastern Scotland and the golden orioles breeding in East Anglia are believed to have originated in this way, as is the recolonization of the

Below: During the Little Ice Age, which ended around the middle of the last century, Arctic seals such as this bearded seal were often seen off the coast of northern Britain. Today they are once again sighted in our waters—a sign that foretells a change in our future weather.

Scottish Highlands by the osprey.

The future It is difficult to predict what will happen to Britain's climate over the next century or so. By the middle of this century it had begun to look as if we could expect a return to the climate experienced during the 18th century. But, in more recent years, the earth's climate seems to have been warming – either as a result of natural climatic changes, or because of atmospheric pollution.

NOCTURNAL WILDLIFE

As dusk descends over the countryside a great change-over takes place – the animals and plants of the daylight hours disappear while the nocturnal species stir into activity.

There are two main reasons why some animals are active at night rather than in the daytime. The first is that many animals (mainly invertebrates) lack a waterproof skin to prevent desiccation, and so have never been able to move about in the drying daytime sunshine. They can, however, survive on land in the coolness and humidity of the night. The second is that nocturnal life offers better chances to many animals of finding food and evading predators.

Nocturnal activity also reduces competition for available resources. This can be seen in the fact that there are certain close parallels between the day and the night 'shifts' of animals, in which the role of the daylight animal is taken over by the one that is active in the dark. Hawks and harriers, for instance, are replaced by owls; butterflies give way to moths; and the swallows and martins make way for bats and nightjars.

The danger of desiccation A hedgehog comes out at night because that is when slugs and other small invertebrate prey are about. But why should the slugs pursue a nocturnal existence? Most of them are vegetarians and so their food is available both day and night.

The fact is that they have probably never been anything but nocturnal. The earliest land mammals in existence were certainly nocturnal. Aquatic animals do not need waterproof coats to preserve them from desiccation, but the first animals to crawl out of the water lacked any efficient waterproof covering. Unless they remained in the swampy areas at the water's edge, they would not have been able to move about by day. Only at night, when the air was heavily laden with moisture, and the drying rays of the sun were absent, could they venture into the open without risk of desiccation. Daytime activity would only be possible when they had evolved waterproof skins.

Many invertebrate groups, however, have never developed the waterproof coats necessary for daytime activity and so they remain creatures of the night. They include slugs and snails, millipedes and centipedes, and wood-lice. Frogs and toads also failed to evolve waterproof skins and they too are aquatic or

nocturnal.

The competitive urge The other terrestrial animals – the reptiles, birds, insects and mammals – became fully adapted for life on land, and probably for diurnal (daytime) activity as well, although many have now adopted nocturnal habits. To find out why an animal, which is physically capable of life by day or night, opts for one or the other, we have to look at the biological factors that affect them. These factors can be summed up in a single word: competition. Life is an endless struggle for existence and animals always exploit any structural or behavioural advantage to that end.

Predation is clearly of major importance in the lives of animals and it is likely that many herbivorous mammals became nocturnal in response to continued attacks by predators in the daytime. Those members of a grazing population who preferred to feed in the evening or the early morning and hide during the day thereby escaped the attentions of predators. This advantage would tend to increase

Above: The dusky slug is typical of the many invertebrates that have never evolved a waterproof skin and so, in order to avoid desiccation, can only venture forth in search of food in the relative humidity of the night.

Opposite page: A pair of barn owls. This species has several special adaptations to a nocturnal way of life, including exceptionally sharp eyesight and extremely acute hearing.

Below: The hedgehog is one of the few mammals in Britain that are entirely nocturnal in habit.

al equivalents of the butterflies, evolved nocturnal habits simply to avoid competition for nectar. This may well have been so, but again we cannot be sure. It may have been freedom from birds, rather than extra food, that gave moths the advantage at night. But whatever it was, the moths evolved into very efficient night-time fliers. Many other kinds of insects also fly at night and probably evolved this habit to avoid predation by birds during the day. There are, of course, a few night-flying insectivorous birds, as well as bats, but these are generally far less numerous than the day-flying insect predators.

The bats also pose interesting questions. The insect-eating species obviously could not have evolved until the night air was full of moths and other insects. But did they evolve nocturnal habits in response to competition from day-flying birds? This seems to be the most likely explanation.

Signals in the night Navigation, food-finding and communication all require special systems in the darkness (although it is never absolutely dark at night). Some animals can see perfectly well in the dark with the aid of extra-sensitive eyes. One common method of increasing the eye's sensitivity is to have a reflective layer just behind the retina. Known as a tapetum, this layer sends the light back through the light-sensitive retina, which thus gets twice as much stimulation from a given amount of light. The tapetum is particularly well developed in cats and foxes, whose eyes shine brightly in artificial light.

The senses of smell and touch are also well developed in nocturnal animals. The sense of touch, for instance, is often centred in the sensitive whiskers of mammals. The sense of smell is especially useful at night because odour molecules dissolve in the atmospheric moisture and are held there. They are then more easily detected than in dry air. The hearing of nocturnal animals is also very sensitive and nowhere is it better developed

Like mammals, insects often have distinct peaks of activity, few of them being out and about throughout the night. The privet hawk moth for example, seen here (above) feeding on nectar from a flower, is usually on the wing half an hour or so after the sun has gone down. Birds such as owls, and also bats, are the only night predators it has to fear. Life in the dark often requires special signalling and communication devices. The female glow-worm (left) produces a greenish or yellowish glow to attract a male for mating.

the numbers of such animals at the expense of their diurnal relatives, until the whole population showed nocturnal tendencies.

In due course predators would have evolved nocturnal habits, too, in order to catch their nocturnal prey; in fact, all our carnivorous mammals are primarily animals of the night.

The fox is a typical night-time prowler, but we cannot say exactly why it has opted for this way of life. Possibly it evolved nocturnal habits to avoid competition with the wolf, an extremely successful daytime hunter, but it could just as well have become nocturnal in response to the nocturnal habits of wood mice and other prey. (Not all the fox's prey is nocturnal, however; it eats a good number of voles which, like shrews, are active in short shifts by day and by night.) Rabbits have not been established in Britain long enough to have affected the fox's behaviour, although they may have been involved in its behavioural evolution on the Continent – becoming nocturnal themselves and thus 'encouraging' the fox to do likewise.

It is easy to assume that moths, the nocturn-

Below: Limpets are night-time foragers, rasping algae and detritus off rocks by means of a special feeding organ called a radula.

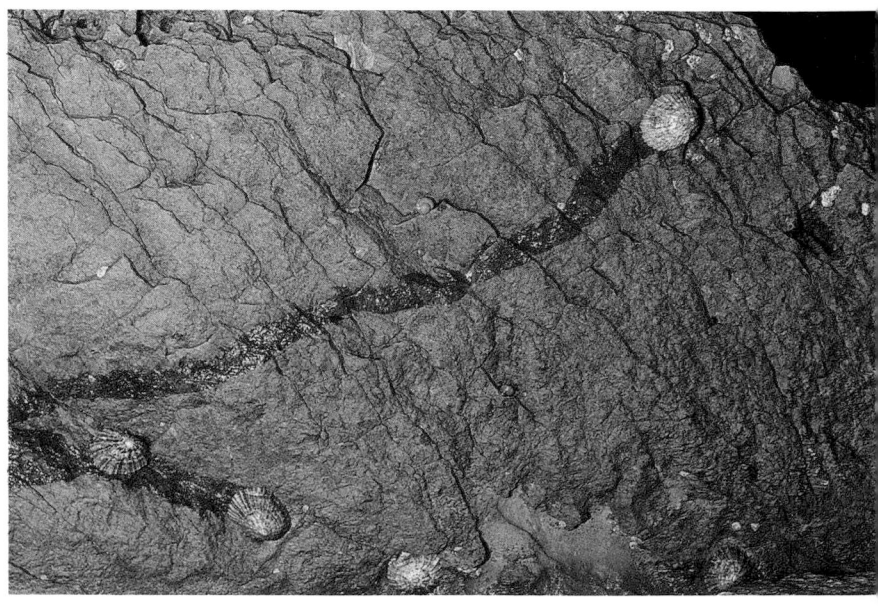

nocturnal birds, are so well adapted for hunting at night that they have been called cats with wings. They may have passed through a diurnal phase, however, during which they were in direct competition with hawks and related birds. Some ancestral owls, by virtue of their better eyes and ears, probably began to hunt more at dusk. They would have been more successful, because of reduced competition, and so would have reared more young. Thus began their evolutionary path towards almost complete nocturnal activity. Their eyesight and hearing are incredibly sharp, and they fly almost without sound – a useful asset for swooping on to unsuspecting prey.

Nightjars, summer visitors to Britain, feed in the early part of the night, swooping through the air on long wings and scooping up moths and other insects. The nightingale, another summer visitor, is famous for its nocturnal song. Unfortunately, we do not know why the nightingale feels the need to defend its territory by song so vigorously at night.

Among other birds at least partly nocturnal are the lapwings, which often roam fields and make a lot of noise on autumn nights. Some sea birds too, such as the shearwaters, normally bring food to their young only under cover of darkness. They are slow and clumsy on land and easy targets for predators. Many small birds normally active during the day choose to migrate at night, calling continuously to keep their flocks together. These night flights enable the birds to land and refuel with food during the day.

Night life in the water Although physical conditions in the water differ much less between day and night than they do on land, there are still some marked changes in the activity and distribution of animal life. Both in the sea and in freshwater lakes, planktonic animals tend to swim up to the surface layers at night to feed on drifting plants; they then swim down to the lower layers to rest during the day. Among the fishes and other water animals, there are both nocturnal species and diurnal ones, just as there are on land and in the air. It is unfortunate that they are rather difficult to see by night.

than in bats. These animals emit high-pitched sounds through the mouth or nose and listen for the echoes with their large ears. The period between sound and echo tells the bat how near it is to an object.

Signals are also necessary for waking the nocturnal animals in the evening. Many species rely on an internal 'clock' to govern their daily cycle of sleep and activity, although this 'clock' can be regulated and even overruled by external influences, such as changing day length. Falling temperatures and increasing humidity are responsible for waking some animals, such as slugs and snails, while the darkness itself may wake others.

Nocturnal insects Many insects lead nocturnal lives, although most are physically able to cope with a daytime existence. Examples include bush crickets, whose varied songs often continue far into the night, earwigs, most moths, lacewings and many mosquitoes and beetles. Some spiders are also active by night rather than by day.

Like the mammals, many nocturnal insects have distinct peaks of activity. The elephant hawkmoth is often on the wing as soon as the sun sets in May and June; and within half an hour it may be joined by privet, poplar and eyed hawkmoths. The buff ermine moth, however, usually waits for another hour, while its relative, the white ermine, frequently waits until midnight before taking to the air.

Night fliers Owls, the best known of the

Above: A badger out and about for a night's foraging. Like most of our nocturnal mammals, badgers are most active just after dusk and just before dawn.

Below: Night-blooming flowers like these evening primroses are pollinated by night-flying insects such as moths. Such flowers are often pale in colour – usually white or yellow – so that they can be seen easily in the dark.

Spring ~
new life in the countryside

The arrival of spring in March is eagerly welcomed after the long, dark days of winter. The lengthening days and warmer temperatures trigger plant growth; from early dawn birds proclaim their territories, and all kinds of other animals are revitalised as the new year begins.

In spring the strengthening sun begins to release winter's grip on the countryside. To the meteorologist, spring is from March to May, and it is a period of instability. This is because the ground is warming up but the air is still quite cold, producing a bittersweet mixture of squally showers, fine spells and cold, frosty nights. Just when the days appear to be improving, a deep depression can whip moisture-laden air down from the polar seas, hurling it on the countryside as sleet and snow. Thus, after warm March days, when the blackthorn comes into bloom, there is often a sting in the tail of the month – the blackthorn winter of March 29-31. Thereafter, the setbacks are steadily fewer as the unsettled weather develops into the milder, showery pattern of April – just what is needed to stimulate dormant vegetation into action.

Plant growth is triggered and can be sustained whenever the mean temperature rises to 6°C (43°F), which, in the British Isles, is regularly reached in March. It is the variation around this critical threshold that makes spring such a fickle period for plants. While a north-facing roadside verge may sleep on in the chill until late March, the south side, basking in the sun, may produce celandines as early as January. Even so, celandine flowers have a short day, barely opening before 9am and closing up by 5pm.

While rising temperatures promote general growth, the lengthening days have special significance for the flowering process itself. Some plants flower only when the daylength falls within certain limits, and spring flowers are therefore in the category of 'short-day' plants, requiring less than 12 hours of daylight to bloom.

The celandine, in common with many other spring flowers such as snowdrops and daffodils, has an underground cache of nutrients in the form of bulbs, which can galvanise the plant into action as soon as the soil begins to warm. Long after the flowers have died the leaves continue to manufacture nutrients.

Many spring plants, the primrose for instance, form cushions or clumps which conserve the sun's frugal warmth, hastening growth. Decaying plant litter is also a good insulator which generates some heat of its own. Beneath a thick bed of litter, therefore, spring effectively begins a few days earlier for plants such as ground elder and ground ivy, the rosettes of rosebay willowherb and the spear-shaped leaves of lords-and-ladies (also known as arum and cuckoo-pint). A few

Left: Misty green, newly opened beech leaves – Ashridge Park in the spring.

Below: Primroses are one of the earliest flowers to appear in the woods in spring.

hardy trees, such as elder, also respond quickly to the first hint of mildness, and sprout tentative leaves in January and February. One of the earliest to leaf, the horse chestnut sheathes its swelling buds in sticky resin against damage by frost. The leaves of most deciduous trees are vulnerable when they first emerge; initially lacking the woody compounds called lignins, which are built up over the summer to resist attack by insects, the nascent leaves of the beech, for example, are beautifully tender and transparent. The new leaves of some other species, such as the oak and the sycamore, are diffused with red pigment which may act as a protective filter against intense spring sunlight, and especially against ultra-violet radiation.

Several trees flower well before they leaf, giving us one of our most cherished symbols of the advancing year – the 'pussy' willow. Tree species adopting this pattern include hazel, poplar, aspen, alder and hornbeam. The male and female flowers are often borne on separate trees and the pollen is wind-dispersed. Because most of it falls by the wayside, pollen is produced in vast amounts, frequently in long, pendulous catkins; in addition, each pollen grain is typically provided with an air sac, helping it to remain airborne for up to 20km (12 miles). Larch is also wind pollinated and flowers early (for a conifer) at the beginning of April.

The willows, well-known for their attractive early catkins, differ from these other species in being insect-pollinated. They provide an eagerly sought-after bonanza of pollen and nectar, at first for queen bumblebees newly emerged from hibernation and later on for other sorts of bees and flies. By flowering so lavishly, the willows are guaranteed a generous stream of insects, even in March, and so are efficiently pollinated.

The great majority of spring flowers also depend on insects to carry pollen from one to another. The primrose and the deadnettles are very attractive to bumblebees and, since the primrose stays open at night, it welcomes moths as well. For many primroses, however, the pollinating agent is the bee-fly, a robust furry fly with a remarkably long proboscis capable of tapping the flower's deep nectaries.

The fact that many spring flowers are pollinated not by bees, which emerge relatively late, but by moths, flies and beetles, explains why, compared with summer, red and blue flowers are much less common in spring than, say, white and yellow ones. The vision of bees, but not of the insects listed above, is especially sensitive in the red-blue (and ultra-violet) spectrum, so summer flowers, by evolving these colours, attract the bee multitude to them.

The brimstone, first of the butterflies to emerge from hibernation, flutters from the evergreen where it has spent the winter. The male is lemon yellow, the female greenish white. Another early flyer, the orange-tip seeks its crucifer food-plant, notably jack-by-the-hedge, in which to lay its eggs.

Scores of less exotic insects are also on the move, and the annual cycle begins in earnest. Ladybirds begin hunting for aphids, their staple diet; queen wasps scrape laboriously at fence-posts and shed doors to furnish wood-pulp for nest-building. Others pounce on the barely wakened trees, leaves and buds, gall-wasps attacking buds from the outside, sometimes to meet newly hatched caterpillars munching from within. On warm March days a host of March-fly pupae hatch in squadrons of rather sinister-looking black insects. Slow flyers, with dangling legs, March-flies are snapped up by birds.

Some ground-beetles have a special bonus diet – the spores of a select band of spring fungi. Of these, the best known, though by no means the most common, is the morel, unmistakable with its bizarre honeycombed cap; it is found in open woodland, hedgebanks and sometimes gardens, notably on chalky ground. Morels are highly palatable, not only to man but also to squirrels and badgers.

Also edible, but less tasty, is the St George's mushroom, so-called for appearing around the Saint's day on April 23. It forms striking

'fairy rings' on chalk grassland as, however, do some closely related poisonous species, so identification here is best left to the experts. St George's Day is also traditionally the time to collect dandelions, then at their best, for wine-making.

The moist March night that favours the growth of morels is just the sort awaited by toads to converge on their spawning ponds. If you sit by a pond as daylight is just failing, everything is still and nothing out of the ordinary seems about to happen; but suddenly all the toads which have been laid up for the day near the pond emerge from hiding and begin advancing purposefully towards it. Around the pond's edge there is mayhem as ardent males compete to waylay the females even before they reach the water.

A similar mating urge pervades the entire cold-blooded kingdom of amphibians and reptiles. Frogs resort to water from late February onwards, and newts quit their winter quarters in March. Reptiles need higher temperatures to stir from their underground retreats. In mid-April vipers, which have overwintered communally in a tangled mass, slither dozily out to bask and moult together in the sun. When the females surface a couple of weeks later there is a mad scramble for mating rights. The males are now highly mobile in search of mature females, and they indulge in ritual combats in efforts to gain supremacy over their rivals. Some fall prey to recently awakened hungry hedgehogs.

Badgers, being omnivorous, are quite capable of despatching a hedgehog – the rarity of hedgehogs in some woods is attributed to the healthy badger population there. Badgers dig out bumblebee nests for the juicy bee grubs inside. Ever busy, the badger also tends to domestic chores, cleaning the soon-to-be-needed nursery in its sett. A tell-tale litter of dried grass and leaves around the entrance reveals that the badger has been hauling out the soiled winter bedding to replace with a fresh lining.

High in the trees in late March rooks are busy repairing nests with a great deal of squabbling over choice twigs. They are preceded only by tawny owls, which may already be sitting on eggs in late February. Many insectivorous birds, such as tits and robins, cannot begin nesting until April or May when their diet of caterpillars is accessible from opening buds. Each species starts nesting at an allotted time, when its particular kind of food becomes abundant enough to meet the extra energy demands of laying eggs and raising a brood.

To meet these special needs, birds are prepared to travel enormous distances. Spring is therefore a time of frenzied reshuffling as many, such as redwings and fieldfares, now return to breed in a northern Scandinavian spring in May and June. Meanwhile, hordes of migrants pour into the British Isles from the tropics. Many waders, such as the knot and grey plover, pass hastily through en route to Arctic breeding grounds.

For many others, however, Britain is the goal. The arrival in late March of the chiffchaff heralds the immigrant influx of warblers, while the sand-martin leads the tribe of swallows and martins. The coastline, too, is filling up with flocks of terns and skuas from the far south, the Arctic tern journeying 12,000km (7500 miles) from Antarctica. Gulls and auks, which have been dispersed offshore all winter, also assemble at traditional breeding colonies. Puffins prospect old nest burrows or work furiously to dig new ones.

Ringing studies have shown that, notwithstanding the complexities of navigation, most migrants, if they survive the winter, return to the very spot they occupied the previous year, often the self-same nest. Competition among breeding birds for space and food, heightened by this invading army, is reflected in one of our best-loved phenomena, the dawn chorus – a lusty proclamation of territorial ownership, often started by the dunnock and the robin well before sunrise. Within half an hour their duet is swelled by a torrent of song. Come late April, a new voice is added – the measured fluting notes of the cuckoo, signalling summer.

CATKINS: BLOWING IN THE WIND

Late winter and early spring is the time of year when most catkins start to open out. On many trees, particularly willows, poplars and hazels, they emerge before the new season's leaves to take full advantage of the wind to disperse their pollen.

Most of us are familiar with the soft, grey, silky catkins of pussy willow that are picked at Easter time, or the long, hanging catkins, known as 'lamb's tails', that appear on hazel trees. Yet, there are other trees whose flowers are described by botanists as catkins, even though in some cases their flowers are quite different from the familiar tasselled catkin shape.

What is a catkin? A catkin is a structure consisting of many extremely small flowers in which the petals and sepals (bud scales) are usually absent. These structures are necessary to insect-pollinated flowers since they help to attract insects. But they are not needed by catkins which are mostly wind pollinated – if present, petals and sepals would only hinder the process of wind pollination.

Most catkins consist of either male flowers or female flowers. Only on a few trees, notably the sweet chestnut, are both sexes found on the same catkin. Male and female catkins can be borne on the same tree, as with oaks and alders, or they can be borne on separate trees, as with willows and poplars. To confuse matters, some species occasionally have male-only trees among a population of trees bearing both male and female catkins. An example is hazel.

All male catkins have the familiar tasselled catkin shape, as do some females. But many female catkins are quite uncatkin-like in their appearance. The female catkins of the English oak, for example, are minute and bud-shaped. Similarly, female hazel catkins consist of small bud-like structures with feathery red stigmas protruding out.

Pollinated by wind Because catkins are wind-pollinated they usually ripen early in the year before the leaves have emerged to hinder the process.

Catkins are formed at the end of summer. By the beginning of the following year they are still small and tightly closed, but with the coming of longer days and higher temperatures they begin to ripen rapidly. The male catkins elongate as they grow, no doubt to ensure that there is plenty of space around each individual flower to allow the pollen to escape – hence the typical shape of the male

Right: The catkins of most trees mature early in the year, often before the leaves emerge. The earliest catkins to appear are those of hazel; they can be seen from January through to the spring.

Below: Male catkins of the silver birch dispersing pollen. Most catkins, including those of birches, are wind pollinated.

catkins. Male catkins produce copious amounts of pollen since wind pollination (which depends on the strength and direction of the wind for success) is much more random than insect pollination. Anyone who has collected pussy willow catkins in spring and brought them indoors will have noticed the great amount of yellow pollen.

The pollen grains released by wind-dispersed catkins are, in most cases, much smaller and lighter than pollen grains distributed by insects since they have to be carried on the wind for long distances. They also have smooth surfaces so that they do not stick together but separate freely, again to ensure that they are distributed over a wide area. Insect-borne pollen grains are rough-surfaced and sticky to help them adhere to the insects.

Female catkins have a greater range of shapes than male catkins but they all have large feathery stigmas which increase their chances of trapping pollen.

Insect-pollinated catkins Not all catkins rely solely on the wind to disperse their pollen. Sweet chestnut catkins are insect pollinated and therefore mature much later in the year when there are plenty of pollinating insects available. Willows utilise both wind and insects. Their catkins mature early, often before the leaves have emerged, to aid wind pollination, but they also produce nectar to attract early insects such as bumble bees.

Catkin evolution

Catkins are mostly wind-pollinated, and it used to be thought that they were more primitive than insect-pollinated flowers, but this is now known to be false. Catkin-bearing trees belong to a large group, the Angiospermae, consisting of all the flowering broad-leaved trees, herbs and shrubs. Almost all angiosperms are insect pollinated and, since insects evolved before angiosperms, catkin-bearing trees must once have been insect pollinated too. Only later did they become adapted for wind pollination.

Right: The catkins of all species within a particular genus have roughly the same shape and colour. Shown here are male and female catkins of representative species from each of our commonest catkin-bearing genera.

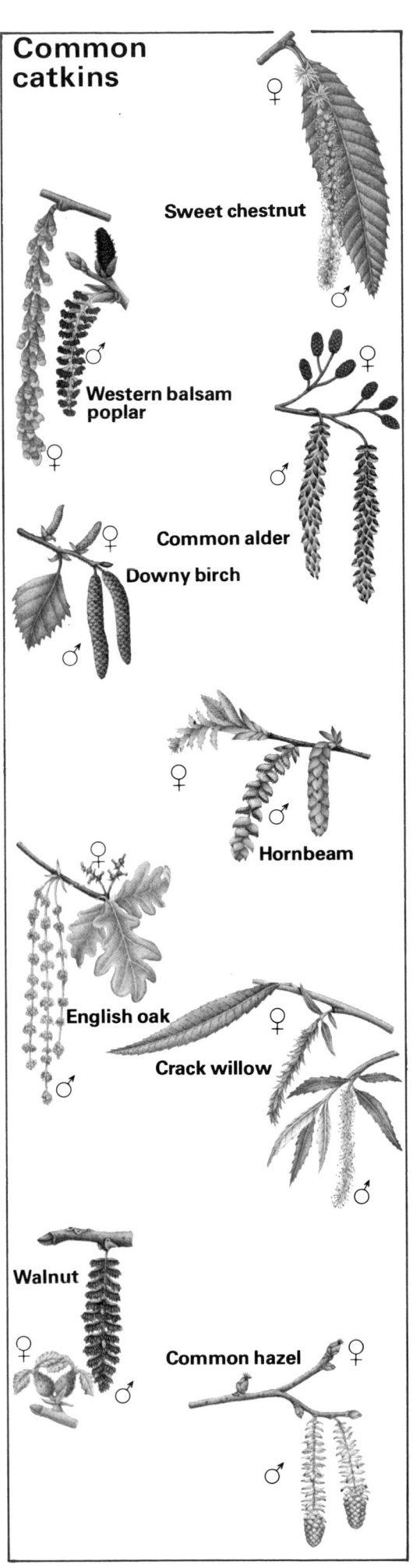

Common catkins

Sweet chestnut ♀ ♂

Western balsam poplar ♀

Common alder ♀ ♂

Downy birch

Hornbeam ♀ ♂

English oak ♀ ♂

Crack willow ♀ ♂

Walnut ♀ ♂

Common hazel ♀ ♂

Catkin families

Catkins are much less common on trees than petalled flowers. They are borne on just a few genera of broad-leaved trees within an even smaller number of families. The following are the most common catkin-bearing genera found in Britain, grouped into families.

The Beech family: Oaks The male catkins are yellow-green and drooping; the female catkins are small and insignificant. Both sexes occur on the same tree. Flowers April to May.

Sweet chestnut Catkins are yellow and borne erect. Each contains male and female flowers. The male flowers are borne at the tip and ripen before the females to prevent self-pollination. Pollination is by insects. Flowering period is June to July.

The Birch family: Birch Male and female catkins are borne on the same tree and are tassel-shaped. They flower in April or May.

Alder Male and female catkins are borne on the same tree. Male catkins are green; female catkins are brown and smaller. They flower in February and March.

The Hazel family: Hazel Male flowers occur in long drooping catkins known as 'lamb's tails'. The female catkins are tiny, with red styles. Both sexes are borne on the same tree and flower from January to April.

Hornbeam Male catkins are greenish; the females develop a three-lobed bract. Both occur on the same tree. Flowers April to May.

The Willow family: Willow Male and female catkins borne on separate trees. The males are usually elongated but may form rounded heads. Pollination is by wind and insects. Flowers usually appear in spring.

Poplar Male catkins are usually red and are borne on separate trees from females. They flower in February or March.

The Walnut family: Walnut Male catkins droop; females are small and borne on short spikes. The flowering period is June.

Above: The only catkins to rely solely on insects for pollination are those of the sweet chestnut. They develop in early summer, to take advantage of greater insect activity at that time of year.

Above: Few people associate catkins with oak trees, yet the male flowers are distinctively catkin-like in shape. The female catkins are extremely small and borne in the terminal axils. Both catkins develop in April and May, at the same time as the leaves emerge. Shown here are the catkins and foliage of a sessile oak.

Left: The familiar male catkins of the goat, or pussy, willow. When they first develop the male catkins are grey or silver but soon become yellow as the anthers become covered with pollen. The female catkins are greenish-white and borne on separate trees. Traditionally, twigs bearing male goat willow catkins are used to decorate churches on Palm Sunday.

WOODLAND ORCHIDS IN THE SPRING

Some of Britain's most beautiful orchids are to be found in deciduous woods. The time of year to go looking for them is the spring, before the trees have had a chance to cast the woodland floor into deep shade with their dense canopy of leaves.

Below: The narrow-leaved helleborine is by far the more attractive of our two species of early-flowering woodland helleborines, the other being the large white helleborine. But it is also the rarer and its numbers are decreasing. The flowers of both species are similar—white petals with the lip marked with several orange-yellow ridges, though the flowers of the narrow-leaved helleborine are always more widely open than those of the large white helleborine.

A woodland habitat, like any other, imposes its own restrictions on the species growing within it. In summer the centre of a dense wood has very few species growing beneath its canopy, simply because the light is not strong enough for most plants to thrive. Nevertheless, many plants do grow in woods. Some survive by flowering early in the year before the trees have developed their canopy; or they may occupy favourable open areas of the wood—the margins or places where trees have fallen or are less closely packed.

Among Britain's orchids there is a small group that is characteristic of woodlands, particularly of beechwoods on the chalk of southern England. Most members of this group flower early in the year, while others grow in clearings and margins. The woodland orchids are at their best in the months of April, May and June.

First to flower The early purple orchid is the first of the woodland species to flower. This is a handsome plant with flowering stems up to 60cm (2ft) tall. The flowers, which are at their best in April and early May, have a three-lobed lip and a blunt spur. The glossy leaves are usually covered in purple-black blotches on the upper surface—an old folktale states that these were caused by the blood of Christ dripping on to the leaves, which accounts for its nickname of bloody butcher. (This orchid probably has more local names than any other. Shakespeare noted a West Country one—long purples—which is both more sympathetic and more fitting.)

The early purple orchid is fairly common in many woodlands, although it particularly favours chalky soils.

Lady-like orchid A species related to the early purple orchid is the lady orchid. Seen in full flower through a sun-dappled beechwood in May and early June this is one of our most striking orchids. Its broad, glossy green leaves surround a flowering stem that may be almost 1m (3ft) high and bears some 25 individual flowers. These have a complicated arrangement of parts that make them look like a caricature of a woman in a long skirt—hence the common name.

height of twayblade (20cm/8in) and has smaller, heart-shaped leaves. Like twayblade it is a woodland plant, but its natural habitat is the open pine forests of Scotland. It is a rare species and, because of its size and inconspicuous colouring, much overlooked.

White-flowered helleborines Several orchid species bear the name helleborine, some of which flower early in the year and others later. Two early-flowering woodland species are the large white helleborine and the narrow-leaved (or sword-leaved) helleborine. Both produce white flowers from late May to early June, although the narrow-leaved helleborine finishes flowering a week or so later.

The large white helleborine can grow to a height of 60cm (2ft), with 15 flowers on a stem, though this number fluctuates greatly. The flower segments are arranged to form a tube, which gives the flower the appearance of not having opened out. The lip of the flower bears several orange-yellow ridges. This species tolerates fairly deep shade. For example, it can be found growing on the almost bare ground under a dense tree canopy. It also grows outside woods, where it seems to favour sites under large isolated beech trees.

The narrow-leaved helleborine is a far more attractive plant. Its flower spike is much more distinct from the rest of the plant and its flowers open wider. Both these helleborines are found on similar soils and in similar conditions – beechwoods on chalky soils – yet the narrow-leaved helleborine is becoming rarer. There is no obvious reason why this species should have declined in recent years, but there may possibly be some small climatic differences that have tended

Regrettably the lady orchid is not a common species. Its stronghold is the beechwoods of south-east England where, as a result of reasonable maintenance and the fact that it is a protected species, it still occurs in some numbers.

Two twayblades At the same time of year, and in the same habitat, an altogether more modest orchid can be seen flowering. This is the twayblade, its name coming from the pair of large, broad, flat leaves placed opposite each other a short distance up the stem.

Although it is perhaps our most common orchid, many people will not have noticed it in a wood because it is also one of the most inconspicuous of our larger orchids, with dull greenish-brown flowers. This species is capable of growing in deep shade, such as that produced by young pine trees. But, as with the other species, beechwoods are its favourite habitat. Occasionally it has been known to grow on chalk downland rather than in woodland.

The twayblade has a smaller and even less conspicuous relative, the lesser twayblade. This plant usually grows to only a third of the

Above: The early purple orchid is the first of the season's woodland orchids to come into flower, in April or early May.

Right: The twayblade is perhaps Britain's most common orchid and it is also one of our most inconspicuous. The flowers have dull greenish-brown petals, apart from the long lip, which is divided into two and usually a bright yellowish-green. This lip is smeared with a trail of nectar. A visiting insect is attracted to the nectar and follows the trail up the lip until it makes contact with the pollinia (the yellow organs shown here). These deposit pollen on the insect's back which is then transferred to the stigma of the next flower the insect visits, thus effecting pollination.

Left: The flowers of the aptly named lady orchid look exactly like a Victorian lady, complete with a bonnet and crinoline skirt. Each flower consists of three flower segments formed into a tight hood, two more segments arranged one on each side of this hood, and finally a large, broad lip in between. Much of the effect comes from the contrast between the purple-brown hood and the much paler lip.

the lesser butterfly they remain parallel.

The future These orchids, many of them rare, face an uncertain future. All can be seen in one comparatively small wood in southeast England. Fortunately it is protected by the local County Naturalists' Trust, so its future seems assured. But other woods are not so safe. There is always the risk that the wood's indigenous trees may be destroyed and replaced by aliens, especially conifers. Worse still, the trees may be grubbed up and the land used for arable or building purposes.

Once a wood has disappeared a unique community dies, and every time that occurs all woodland plants–and especially orchids, which are vulnerable–become scarcer.

o favour the decline of one rather than the other species.

Butterfly orchids Of all our woodland orchids, the butterfly orchids look most like the exotic tropical species. The greater butterfly orchid is a handsome plant, growing up to 60cm (2ft) tall, with glossy leaves and large white flowers appearing from May to early July. The flowers bear some resemblance to a butterfly, having widespread side petals and a long narrow lip with a long, backward-pointing spur. The presence of this spur, which is full of nectar, and the fact that the flower is at its most fragrant in the evening, indicates that its purpose is to attract evening-flying butterflies and moths.

The greater butterfly orchid is a fairly common species in woodland communities. It grows best in oakwoods and does particularly well where the woods are managed by coppicing (a process by which the trees are cut back regularly). Where this is done to a wood for the first time in many years the following spring often reveals numbers of greater butterfly orchids in flower, which until then had remained dormant in the soil. Sadly, however, coppicing and wood management are dying arts because they are too labour intensive and no longer economic.

The other woodland species in this group, the lesser butterfly orchid, is usually a smaller plant and more characteristic of acid moorland. However, it also grows in woods along with the greater butterfly, usually being a larger plant there than in the open and therefore looking very much like its relative. The two species are best told apart by the pollinia (pollen masses) inside the flower. On the greater butterfly the two pollinia diverge away from each other, while on

Identifying woodland orchids

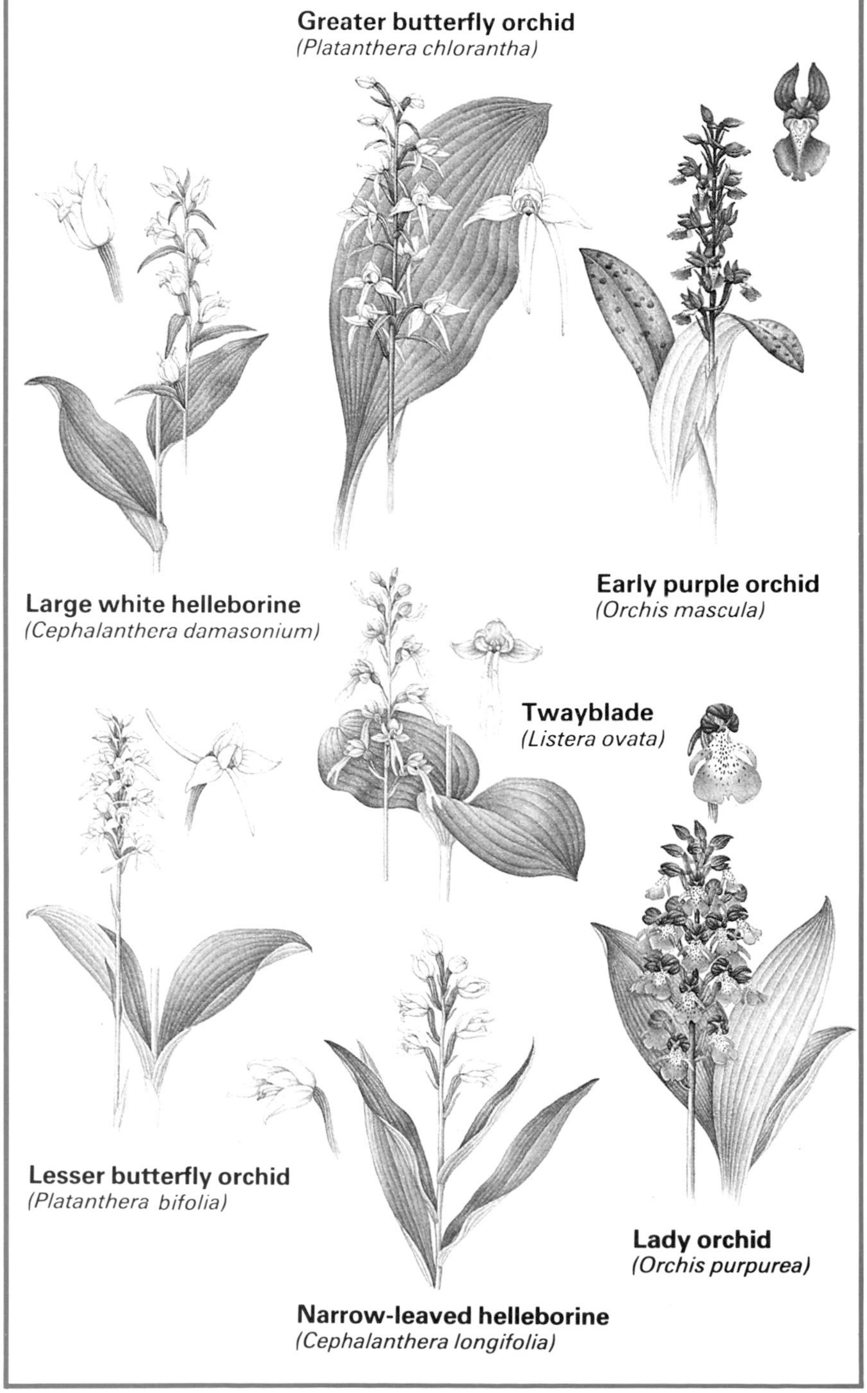

Greater butterfly orchid
(Platanthera chlorantha)

Large white helleborine
(Cephalanthera damasonium)

Early purple orchid
(Orchis mascula)

Twayblade
(Listera ovata)

Lesser butterfly orchid
(Platanthera bifolia)

Lady orchid
(Orchis purpurea)

Narrow-leaved helleborine
(Cephalanthera longifolia)

VIOLETS AND WILD PANSIES

From early March our hedgerows and woodlands are brightened by the lovely hues of violets and pansies; sadly only one violet, however, gives off a scent to match its beauty.

Thirteen species of violets and pansies are native to the British Isles and all belong to the family Violaceae. Both our common wild pansies are classed as weeds because they grow among crops, although you would be hard pressed to find two more attractive weeds.

Violets all tend to be low-growing plants, often producing clumps of distinctly heart-shaped leaves and lance-shaped stipules which sprout from the root-stocks. Wild pansies tend to have more erect stems. Their leaves usually grow from the stem in groups of three and are variable in shape. The lower leaves tend to be rounded, whereas the upper leaves are more lance-shaped. The leaf stalks are often fringed with fine leaf-like stipules. (See illustration right.)

Similarities The flowers of violets and pansies have a similar structure: both consist of a pair of upper petals, a pair of side petals and one lower petal which extends backwards as a hollow tube (spur) in which nectar is secreted. The nectar is only available to insects, such as bees, moths and butterflies, with a tube-like tongue (proboscis) long enough to reach right into the spur. The lower petal and, to a lesser extent, the side petals are

Why plants have Latin names

The Swedish botanist Karl von Linné revolutionised the botanical world in the 18th century by devising a method of naming plants that was both simple and accurate. He gave each plant two Latin names. The first, written with a capital letter, showed the genus into which it and other closely related plants were grouped; the second was its species name, by which it was distinguished from Its relatives.

For instance, speedwells are placed in the genus *Veronica*. The grey speedwell's Latin name is *Veronica polita*, for its shining flowers look almost as if they have been polished. The ivy-leaved speedwell is *Veronica hederifolia*; the Latin word for ivy is *hedera*, so this literally means the speedwell with ivy foliage. In this way the species name usually gives you some extra information about the plant.

Many people find Latin names initially rather off-putting, but they can be less confusing than English plant names. The bluebell is a good example. In England the fragrant bluebell inhabits woodland: its Latin name is *Endymion non-scriptus*. But in Scotland the 'bluebell' is a scentless plant of heathland, a completely different species named *Campanula rotundifolia*, which in England is known as the harebell.

Many Latin names recur. For instance, the Latin word for medical workshop, *officinalis*, often turns up in the names of plants used in medicine – *Borago officinalis* for borage, once used as an aphrodisiac, and *Althaea officinalis* for marshmallow, which was thought to cure many diseases. The word *vulgaris*, meaning common, is given to many widespread species, such as the primrose–*Primula vulgaris*. Names indicating the habitat of a plant also crop up frequently, such as *nemorosa*, meaning a woodland plant – as in *Anemone nemorosa*, the wood anemone – or *arvensis* meaning a field species – like *Viola arvensis*, the field pansy.

This system of classification makes it easier for scientists all over the world to communicate accurately exactly which species they are referring to. They are constantly reclassifying species in the light of new research, and the names they choose are words and parts of words borrowed from many languages which they then latinize. Karl von Linné even latinized his own name to Carolus Linnaeus.

Left: There are numerous references to violets and pansies in literature. In Shakespeare's *A Midsummer Night's Dream* Oberon squeezes the juice of wild pansies (seen here) on to the sleeping Titania's eyes so that she will fall in love with Bottom on awakening.

streaked with dark lines radiating from the nectar source. These 'honey guides' strongly reflect ultra-violet light which is easily recognised by bees – the most common pollinators.

The colour of the violets' petals varies enormously from deep purple to blue, mauve, pink and white; the spur is usually pale, often yellowish. The more rounded petals of the wild pansies are tinted with a mixture of white, yellow and mauve.

Reproduction An interesting feature of the violet family is that its members do not rely solely on insects for fertilisation. In a cold spring there are few insects around and, as the season progresses, violets tend to become submerged under the foliage of taller plants; so their flowers are hidden from view. Their reproductive chances are not lost, however: they grow a second cluster of flower buds in summer which never open. The pollen inside fertilises the flower which then produces good seed. This self-pollinating mechanism is called cleistogamy. The sweet violet can also reproduce a third way – by vegetative reproduction; it throws out long stolons that root at the tip when they touch the ground and make new plants.

Fruit and seeds The fruit capsules which lie on the ground are divided into three boat-shaped pods containing the seeds. As the pods ripen they dry and shrink, clamping tightly on to the seeds inside. When the tension becomes too great the pods split lengthwise and eject their contents. The system is effective; the tiny, almost weightless seeds of the field pansy have been thrown up to 2m (6½ft) from the parent plant.

The seeds of some violets are joined to a fleshy stalk rich in oils. Ants eagerly collect the seeds, carry them to their nests, and later discard them once they have eaten the fleshy stalks. This is why hairy violets flourish on grassy hillsides, where ant hills are often abundant.

The sweet violet may be the only scented British species of violet, but it is widely regarded as the most fragrantly perfumed of any native wild flower. In medieval times it was grown in gardens for use in both herbal medicine and cooking; the petals were added to meat and poultry dishes. The scent seems particularly quick to fade – and not just because it evaporates quickly. The reason lies with the chemicals that make up the scent; one constituent temporarily numbs the sense of smell of the person sniffing the flower.

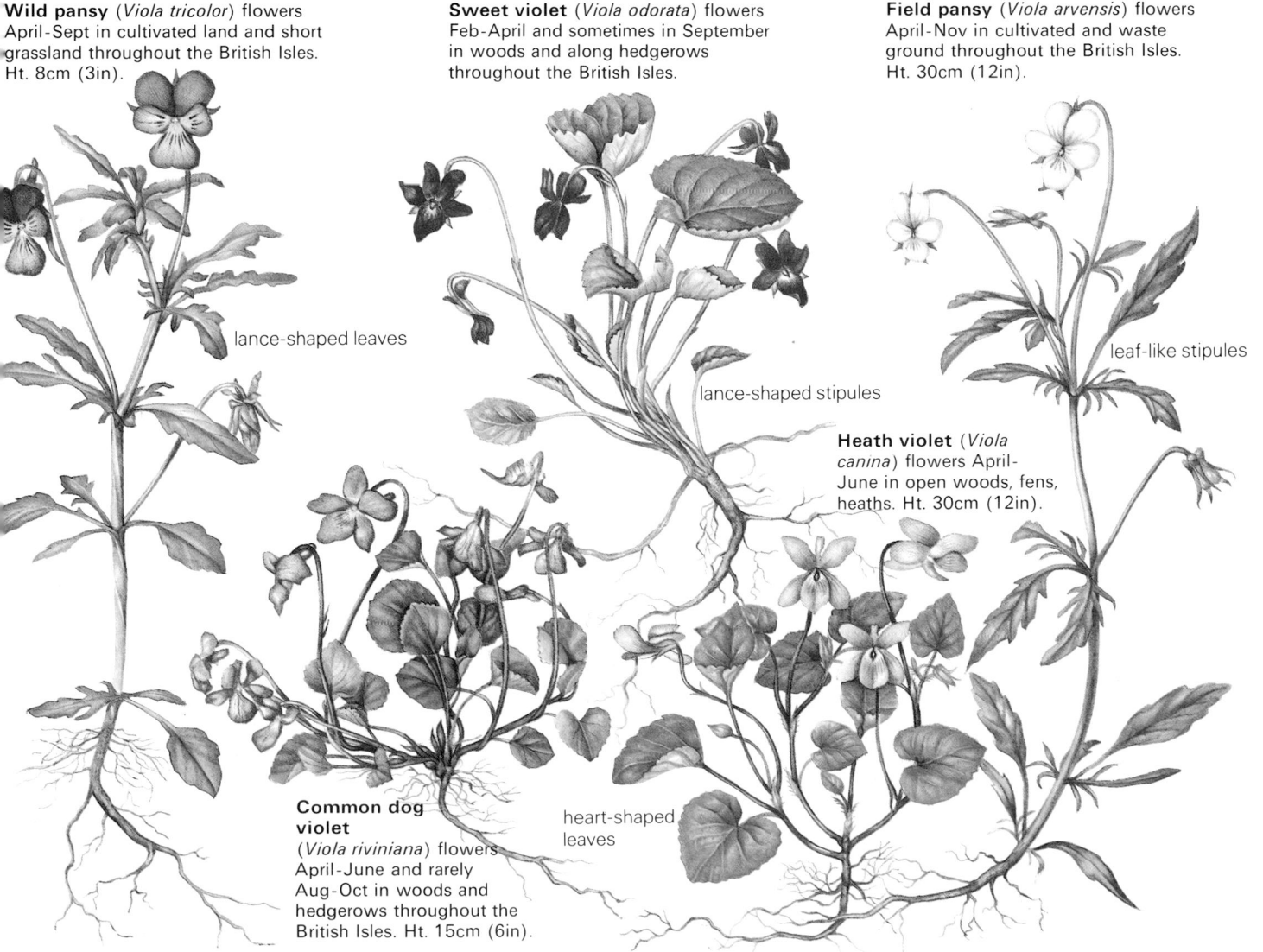

Wild pansy (*Viola tricolor*) flowers April-Sept in cultivated land and short grassland throughout the British Isles. Ht. 8cm (3in).

Sweet violet (*Viola odorata*) flowers Feb-April and sometimes in September in woods and along hedgerows throughout the British Isles.

Field pansy (*Viola arvensis*) flowers April-Nov in cultivated and waste ground throughout the British Isles. Ht. 30cm (12in).

lance-shaped leaves

lance-shaped stipules

leaf-like stipules

Heath violet (*Viola canina*) flowers April-June in open woods, fens, heaths. Ht. 30cm (12in).

Common dog violet (*Viola riviniana*) flowers April-June and rarely Aug-Oct in woods and hedgerows throughout the British Isles. Ht. 15cm (6in).

heart-shaped leaves

FRITILLARY MEADOWS

In late spring the delicate blooms of the snake's-head fritillary are at their best, flowering in profusion amid the other wetland plants of our ancient flood meadows.

Fritillaries, like so many other members of the lily family, have captured the imaginations of gardeners for centuries. About 85 species exist in the genus but there is only one British representative among these exotic bulbous perennials.

Snake's-head fritillary and snake-in-the-grass are the most common names for our native species, but in areas where it was once very common local names such as oaksey lily, chequered daffodil, drooping tulip and mourning-bells-of-Sodom were used to describe this charming yet curious plant.

In common with many bulbs, snake's-head fritillary blooms comparatively early in the year so seed production is over by July when hay-making traditionally begins in its favoured habitat, flood meadows. The fruit capsule is spherical but slightly three-sided, and contains numerous flattened winged seeds. Fritillary flowers are usually solitary and borne on slender stems reaching about 50cm (20in) in height, each stem having three to six long, narrow grass-like leaves that are arranged alternately along its length.

Vanishing flood meadows Sadly, the snake's-head fritillary is no longer a common plant. The grazing or picking of plants has been partly responsible, but the main cause of its dramatic demise in numbers–and even entire populations–can be attributed to changes in land management. Fritillaries thrive exclusively in our ancient flood meadows and it is these very meadows which are suffering from the modern agricultural practice of land drainage. Although the loss of water makes the land more manageable for farmers, it has a drastic effect on the habitat, and the first to suffer are such plants as snake's-head fritillary which depend on damp conditions for their existence. Once sufficiently dry the land may be ploughed up for crop cultivation, completing the destruction of the flood meadows which provided such ideal growing conditions for fritillaries.

Another cause for the decline in fritillaries and associated wetland plants is the application of artificial fertilisers to the land. In contrast to farmyard manure, which is a good

Above: The best sites for fritillaries are the flood meadows along the upper Thames and in East Anglia. These meadows have been managed in the same way for centuries: in July the grass is cut for hay, left to regrow a little in August and then subjected to livestock grazing from September to November. The livestock may remain there, if it is not too wet, until the following spring when they are taken off the land, and the grass– along with many spectacular flowers–is allowed to grow. Up to a hundred plant species have been recorded in flood meadows flourishing alongside the fritillaries: cowslip, meadow rue, pepper saxifrage and orchids to name but a few. Sadly, though, the floral composition of these meadows has undergone drastic changes since World War II, partly because of the increasing use of artificial fertilisers, and partly because of land drainage schemes making conditions generally drier.

meadow fertiliser causing no harm to the plants, the high concentrations of chemicals found in most modern fertilisers are highly damaging to the more delicate wild flowers.

A vulnerable species Snake's-head fritillary was known to occur in 27 counties in the British Isles before 1930, but by 1970 its distribution was reduced to nine counties. The Biological Records Centre keeps a watchful eye on changes in the distribution of various plant species in the British Isles and uses 10km squares (tetrads) as its basic reference unit. If a species is found in fewer than 15 tetrads it is considered to be near danger level and is classified as endangered, rare or vulnerable in the *British Red Data Book* for vascular plants. Snake's-head fritillary, along with 300 other British plants, is considered a vulnerable species as, by 1970, its distribution had shrunk from 116 to 15 tetrads.

North Meadow The largest fritillary population has over 50,000 plants and is contained within the boundaries of the National Nature Reserve at North Meadow, Wiltshire. This may seem a large number but it represents 80% of the total British population of fritillaries. The 44ha (109 acres) of land are now owned largely by the Nature Conservancy Council, and they are of particular interest for they consist of ancient meadows, the management pattern of which has remained more or less unchanged for the last 800 years.

Traditionally the meadow is laid up for hay annually on February 13 and left until early July before it is cut. Lammas Land, as the area is known locally, is sectioned into lots which the local people buy for hay. On August 12, known as Lammas Day, the meadow becomes common pasture and an ancient system of land tenure ensures that any resident of Cricklade can graze 10 horses, 10 head of cattle and 20 head of sheep from September 12 until the following February 12.

It is largely because of the existence of common rights that North Meadow has developed its uniquely rich flora. The system is a very effective stabiliser of land use as no individual could obstruct the rights of others by, for example, ploughing his lot.

White fritillaries Although North Meadow supports the largest population of fritillaries, other sites with smaller populations are equally interesting since no two meadows are ever identical. Variations in altitude, aspect, topography, substrate and (ultimately) management all play their part in creating a unique habitat. A similarly well-balanced meadow to North Meadow, found where Berkshire and Hampshire share a common boundary, is well known locally for its fritillaries. Large numbers of white-flowered forms are common, often appearing to be in the majority because of their conspicuous brightness. The meadow is privately owned, but managed in conjunction with the local naturalists' trust.

Fritillary sites

This distribution map shows how the sites where fritillaries occur (represented by a dot) have declined dramatically since the 1940s. Nowadays the flood meadows in which they thrive are located mainly along the banks of the upper Thames and in East Anglia, but prior to 1950 they occurred throughout much of southern and central England.

● since 1950
○ before 1950
✕ garden escapes

Right: The fritillary flower, similar to an inverted tulip at first sight, comprises six petals, each with a shiny nectary at its base. Its six stamens are a golden yellow. Fritillaries are often pollinated by bumble bees, but should the insects fail to visit, the flowers can pollinate themselves.

Below: A white-flowered form of fritillary can sometimes be found. Here it is growing in a meadow along the Berkshire/ Hampshire border.

THE FUNGI THAT FRUIT IN SPRING

Most of our astonishing assortment of mushrooms and toadstools appear in the fields and woods in autumn, but a few surface in the spring. Mushrooms are the fruiting bodies of fungi. Often colourful, and sometimes deadly, they are nature's dustmen, feeding on debris and rotting wood.

The emergence of the colourful and often grotesque fruiting body of the fungus is the climax to a rather unobtrusive existence that can only be properly observed with the aid of a microscope. A fungus has one of two main life styles: a saprophytic fungus digests the compost of decaying plant remains that accumulate throughout the year; a parasitic fungus feeds directly from living plants and animals. A fungus cannot manufacture food as green plants do and its main body, which consists of a web of delicate threads called hyphae, infiltrates its food supply.

Saprophytes play a vital role in nature's waste disposal system. Over one ton of plant rubbish (leaves, twigs, branches, etc) per acre

Below: **Jew's ear** (*Auricularia auricula-judae*), usually found in spring on dead branches of elder trees. It is edible.

falls each year over a woodland floor. The fungi help to break the pile down and if it were not decomposed from year to year our woodland would gradually become buried in its own waste. In addition, saprophytes help to recycle raw materials that would otherwise be unobtainable for green plants, which need new soil minerals as well as sunlight for their growth.

The majority of fungi produce mushrooms and toadstools–the fruiting bodies full of spores–in summer and autumn, often after heavy rain. Most mushrooms and toadstools are killed off as winter approaches; because they are composed of up to 90% water, they are quickly destroyed by frost. However a few species can be found in spring, either because they are tough enough to survive the winter or because their fruiting season begins in spring.

If you inspect dead elder branches you will, sooner or later, come across the jew's ear. It forms a brown, flabby, fruiting body which looks like an inverted cup and measures up to 8cm (3in) across. The outer surface is smooth and velvety, while the inside is wrinkled with shallow folds rather like an ear. You only need to squeeze it to see why it is classified as a jelly fungus. When fresh it is limp with a soft, rubbery texture; as it dries out it becomes shrivelled and leathery. The name that has been adopted for it is somewhat inappropriate; it was originally known as Judas's ear,

Above: **Scarlet elf-cup** (*Sarcosypha coccinea*), found in late winter and early spring on hazel. Poisonous. It is one of the easier species to identify because of its distinctive colour and shape.

Above: **King Alfred's cakes** (*Daldinia concentrica*) found all year on dead ash trees and occasionally beech or elder.

Above: **The morel** (*Morchella elata*) is found on chalky ground which has been disturbed. The species reaches about 10cm (4in) in height and appears from January to April. Like most morels, it is not easy to find, and it may not appear regularly from one year to another.

Left: **Common morel** (*Morchella esculenta*) is found in spring in clearings and beside hedges. It is edible, with a good flavour.

Bottom left: **Common ganoderma** (*Ganoderma applanatum*), found all year round on many broadleaved trees. Note how the surrounding leaves are covered in spores. Poisonous.

stemming from the ancient belief that Judas Iscariot hanged himself from an elder tree after betraying Jesus. Jew's ears are considered a great delicacy in China, where they are cultivated on stacks of oak logs.

The common morel is a particularly odd-looking fungus that appears during spring in woodland clearings and under hedges. Its extraordinary cap varies in colour from dirty white to pale brown and resembles a bath sponge. It belongs to the Ascomycete group of fungi, the spores of which are formed in special cells called asci; these line the surface of the honeycomb pits. The pale yellow stems are squat, hollow and very brittle. The fungi are edible and can either be cooked fresh or dried and added to soups and stews.

The striate birds nest fungus first appears in spring and continues fruiting until autumn. It grows on woodland debris such as fallen branches, sticks and cones, often in dense colonies. The red-brown cups, about 1cm ($\frac{1}{2}$in) across, are grooved: the outer surface is clothed in fine bristles, but the inside is smooth and glossy. The spores are contained in small bodies called peridioles which lie in the 'nest' just like a clutch of eggs. The spores are dispersed when raindrops splash into the cup, knocking the 'eggs' over the side.

A number of species form 'fairy rings' as the fungus gradually spreads through the soil, like a drop of ink on blotting paper, getting wider each year as it produces mushrooms at the edge of the ring annually. One of these is St George's mushroom, so called because it springs up around St George's Day (April 23). The creamy-coloured cap up to 10cm (4in) across is silky smooth on top and fleshy. The margin of the cap is usually wavy and turned in on itself. The stems are rather stocky and pale brown or creamy yellow in colour.

The common ganoderma is an example of a hardy species of bracket fungus that can be found throughout the year clamped tightly on to tree trunks, especially those of beech. It is a parasite which slowly drains the life out of its host. It has an extremely hard, rusty-brown cap with a white margin and undersurface covered in tiny pores from which literally billions of spores rain down in summer. It grows a new layer of pores each year and if you cut a cross-section you can count these layers and tell its age.

Another unusual fungus that is easy to find in spring is King Alfred's cakes, which grows mainly on ash trees. It owes its name to the fact that it resembles lumps of charcoal – the legendary result of King Alfred's disastrous episode in the kitchen. In many country areas it is also called cramp balls and used to be carried by older villagers to ward off rheumatism.

One of the most colourful fungi found in winter and early spring is the scarlet elf cup, which grows on sticks and brushwood. It is particularly common in the West Country. During the Christmas season it is sometimes brought indoors on twigs and used as a table decoration with mosses and dried flowers. The pale outer surface of the cup, which is stalked like a tiny goblet and covered with fine down, contrasts sharply with the rich scarlet interior. The spore-containing asci are embedded in the brilliant red lining of the cup. When the spores are ripe they are pushed to the surface and then dispersed by the wind or rainwater.

Although a number of fungi growing in the British Isles are edible – and some are even delicious – it is not worth your while to try even the smallest morsel unless you are quite sure you know what you are eating. Choose fully grown species because they are easier to identify and, to be safe, try a little at a time.

BUZZING BEE FLIES

Early in spring, as soon as the bright yellow primroses begin to flower in hedgerows and woods, bee flies make their appearance. We have 12 species of these pretty little insects that look just like bumblebees–and buzz like them, too.

Above: *Bombylius major*, seen here feeding on bugle, is the most common of the 12 species of bee fly in the British Isles. It has six long thin legs, a very long proboscis, and a rounded furry body covered with tawny orange hair. It also feeds on the nectar of ground ivy, dandelion, violets, lungwort and sallow blossom, and many other spring flowers including such garden species as the grape hyacinth.

Although rarely seen in the north, the bee fly *Bombylius major*, a member of the Diptera (true flies), is common in southern parts of the British Isles. You can often see this tiny insect flying low and hovering over flowers; occasionally it makes a light landing on one pair of legs, with wings still rapidly vibrating, and pokes its long tubular tongue into the flower to sip nectar. To watch a bee fly you need to approach it carefully and make sure your shadow does not fall on it; if you make any sudden movement, it will be gone.

A parasitic life cycle The female bee fly lays her eggs on the ground near the nest holes of various species of solitary bees. On hatching, the young bee fly larva, despite having no true legs, quickly wriggles its way into one of these holes and takes up residence inside. At first it feeds on the pollen and honey stored by the solitary bee for its own larva. After its first moult, however, the bee fly grub changes from a vegetarian into a carnivore

and attacks the bee's own larva, first eating the non-vital organs and finally, when it is fully grown, killing its unwilling host.

Bee fly pupae have been extracted from the nests of solitary bees, so it seems that bee flies grow to maturity within their host's home, only emerging as adults in spring.

This sudden switch on the part of the bee fly larva from a vegetarian to a meat diet is remarkable, and unusual among insects, especially since the bee fly returns to a diet of nectar as an adult.

Round-bodied bee flies *Bombylius major* has the characteristic rounded, furry body of most bee flies. It is 12-18mm ($\frac{1}{2}$-$\frac{2}{3}$in) long and can be identified by the irregular but broad and clearly defined brown margin running along the front surface of its wings, from the tip to where they join the thorax. *B. discolor* is much the same size, but has spotted wings with variable brown patches. Its pupa has conspicuously large hooks and bristles, by means of which it works its way to the surface of the soil, where its old pupal skin can sometimes be seen sticking out of the surface after the adult fly has emerged.

There are four other species of the genus *Bombylius*. *B. canescens* is slightly smaller than *B. major* and, as in most species of this family, the female is slightly longer than the male. The species shows a readily recognisable external difference between male and female. The wings of the female are normally quite clear, whereas with the male they are suffused a dark greyish-brown from the thorax outwards for about half their length, and mainly towards the front edge. The body hairs of both scxcs are generally dark, but interspersed with some yellow hairs which give this fly a rather greyish appearance in some lights. Both sexes have a fringe of black hairs behind the eyes. They are thought to parasitise larvae of *Andrena* and *Colletes* bees and are widely distributed as far north as Scotland.

Bombylius minor is about 22mm (⅞in) long; the wings of the male are usually darker than those of the female. There are orange hairs on the ends of the legs nearest its body and white hairs on the upper part of its face. The two other species, *B. venosus* and *B. ater*, are uncommon and very difficult to tell apart from each other.

Hairy bee flies The three species of the genus *Villa* (meaning 'hairy')– *V. cingulata*, *V. circumdata* and *V. modesta*–are not easy to distinguish either. They are among the larger species of bee flies and have somewhat square-ended bodies, unlike those of *Bombylius* species, which are markedly rounded. They are not conspicuously coloured and rarely attract attention. There are a few dark markings on their wings.

The larvae of *Villa* bee flies parasitise caterpillars of moths as well as the larvae of ichneumon flies. Some *Villa* larvae also attack the grubs of true flies of the tachinid family. (Tachinid larvae are internal parasites, mainly of other insects.) We thus havc the interesting situation of a parasite (the *Villa* larva) parasitising another parasite (the ichneumon larva). In fact, they belong to a very small group of insects that are known as the hyperparasites.

Above: *Thyridanthrax fenestratus*, a dark-coloured bee fly, is found on sandy heaths.

Below: *Bombylius minor* has a southern distribution and is particularly common in south-west England. Here it is feeding on bell heather. Its long, thin larvae parasitise the nests of *Colletes* bees and feed on the honey and pollen stored by the host. When the larvae moult, however, they become carnivorous and prey on the bee larvae within the nests.
The name *Bombylius* means 'the buzzing one'.

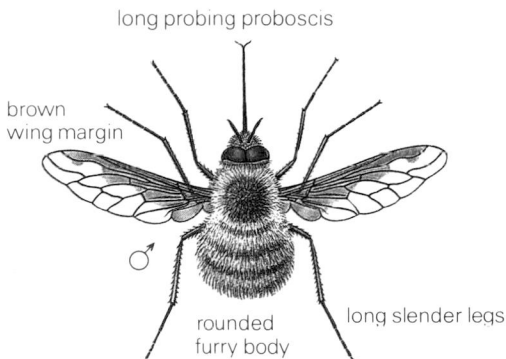

long probing proboscis

brown wing margin

rounded furry body

long slender legs

Bombylius major

Like those of *B. discolor*, the pupae of *Villa* bee flies are heavily armed with hooks and bristles–no doubt essential since the pupae must break out of the host's dried larval or pupal skin before the adult flies can emerge. As with other members of this family, the *Villa* species are sun lovers, preferring the warm sandy heathlands of the south. *V. modesta*, in particular, seems to be a typical fly of coastal sand dunes.

Some other species Our three remaining bee flies all belong to different genera. *Thyridanthrax fenestratus* is usually associated with bare patches of ground on sandy heaths. It is about the same size as *B. major* and has a narrow black body adorned with a few conspicuous white tufts of hair. Its wings are mottled on the inner two thirds with a vague brown U-shaped pattern.

Phthiria pulicaria, a very small species little more than 3mm long, is yellowish-grey and conspicuously hairy. The proboscis through which it sucks up nectar from flowers is rather long for the size of the bee fly. This species seems to prefer coastal regions where it can occasionally be seen in large numbers on composite flowers such as ragworts, hawk-weeds, sowthistle and sometimes sea-aster.

Anthrax anthrax is our last species of bee fly. As its name emphasises ('anthrax' means coal or carbon), it is a dark-coloured insect. It is slightly smaller than *B. major* and is rather rare.

SURFACING FOR SPRING

In spring snakes, lizards, frogs, newts and toads emerge from the various hiding places into which they retreated five or six months before –and sometimes in mixed groups—to survive the winter cold.

Reptiles and amphibians are cold-blooded creatures. This does not mean that they are immune to the cold but that their internal temperature fluctuates considerably depending where they are, the time of year and how much food is available. In summer they alternate between basking in the sun to keep warm (although if it gets too hot they will seek the shade) and foraging for food to keep up their energy levels. Lizards feed on insects, grasshoppers and spiders; frogs, toads and newts eat slugs and snails and a variety of insects.

In the tropics snakes, lizards and amphibians can stay active all year round. In the British Isles where winter brings little warmth and dwindling food, they become increasingly sluggish and therefore vulnerable to predators. In order to survive they must spend the winter in shelter or underground in a dormant state, to conserve their energy. If they stayed exposed above ground over a long period they would certainly freeze to death.

The length of this period of inactivity varies with the species and also differs from place to place. Adders in western Scotland for instance start to seek shelter in early October, whereas adders in the south of England (where it is generally warmer) do not become inactive until late October or early November— almost a month's difference. Common lizards, slow worms and grass snakes usually go underground about mid-October, while sand lizards and smooth snakes probably disappear a little earlier. Frogs, toads and newts usually suspend activity in October or November.

Choosing a hideout The common lizard capitalises on the remaining days of summer to build up substantial reserves of energy-rich fat, storing much of it in its stocky tail. Thus fortified it seeks its winter retreat.

The adult females are the first to retire, followed by the males and lastly the juveniles. Sand lizards may dig their own winter hideouts, but other reptiles search out disused burrows or other dry holes in a bank or settle under stones, logs or the roots of a tree. Overwintering reptiles are therefore hard to find. In Scandinavia where the ground freezes hard in winter, adders have been found up to 2m (6½ft) below ground.

The entrance to a reptile's retreat will often have a sunny aspect and usually adjoins a habitat which will provide the first meal in spring. Underground the reptile's body temperature, heart rate and respiration drop dramatically. With these functions only just ticking over, precious fat reserves can be eked out over the long winter. Even so, in unusually

Amphibians
Frogs, toads and newts are amphibians, which means they can live on land but have to breed in water because the young (tadpoles) only take in oxygen through gills. Our six native species are: the common newt, crested newt, palmate newt, common toad, natterjack toad and common frog. The edible frog and marsh frog were introduced from Europe.

Reptiles
Snakes and lizards are reptiles and have a protective scaly coat which they can shed—or slough. There are six native species: the three lizards are the slow worm, sand lizard and common (viviparous) lizard. The snakes are the adder, grass snake and smooth snake.

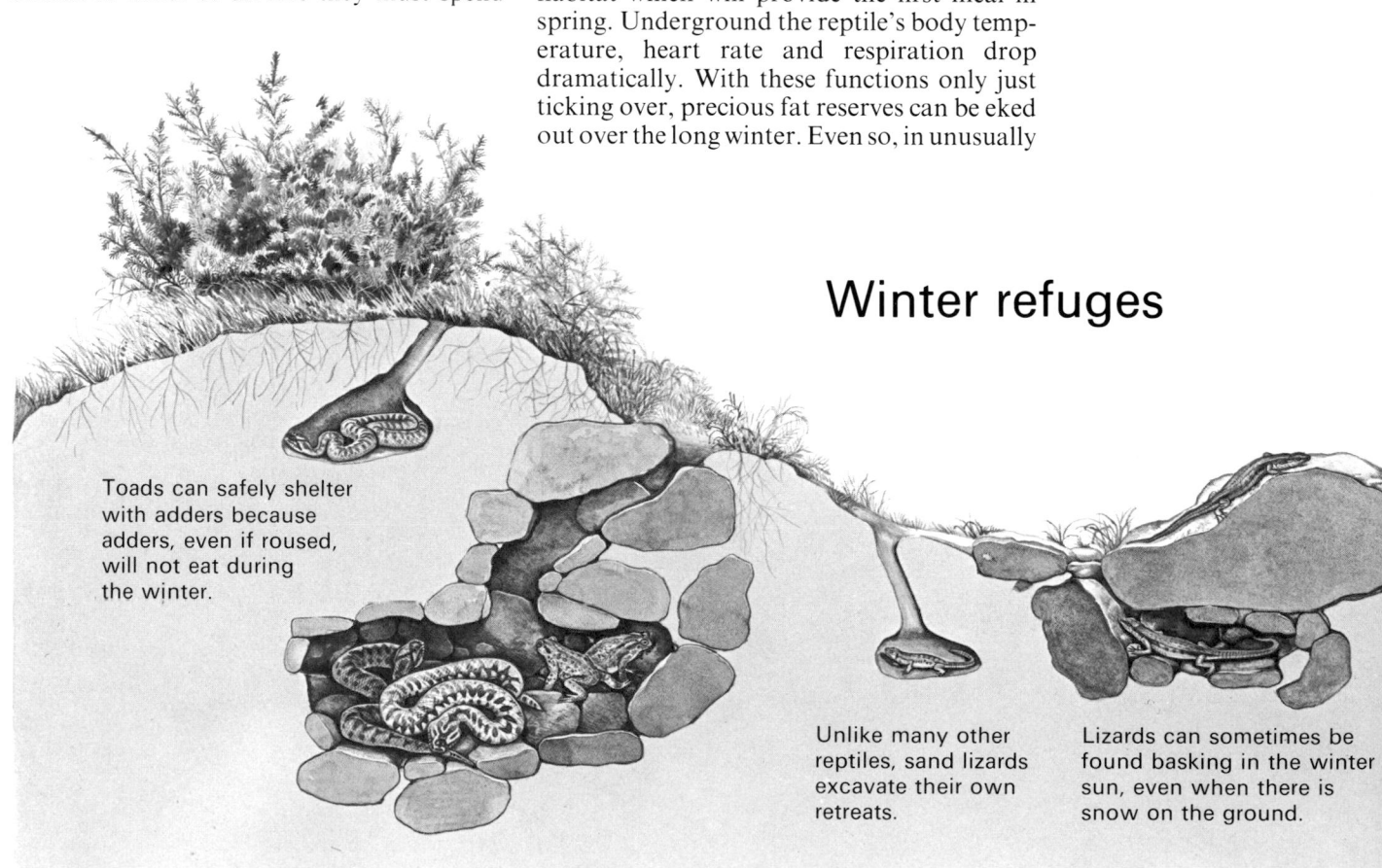

Winter refuges

Toads can safely shelter with adders because adders, even if roused, will not eat during the winter.

Unlike many other reptiles, sand lizards excavate their own retreats.

Lizards can sometimes be found basking in the winter sun, even when there is snow on the ground.

harsh conditions many reptiles and amphibians die.

Most frogs (and some newts) submerge under water and bury themselves in the muddy bottom of a pond or ditch. Frogs have lungs; when on land they can breathe in air through their nostrils, but underwater they have to absorb sufficient oxygen through their skin. All toads, some newts and a few frogs look for a dry land refuge, such as a mouse burrow, the warmth of a compost heap or even a dark cellar or garden shed.

In Britain, winter withdrawal is rarely uninterrupted; both reptiles and amphibians can shake off their torpor to surface and bask on a sunny day, even with snow on the ground. Where the occupants are a mixture of species they may sunbathe together, but they do not look for food. The adder, for example, has no appetite for the lizard which, in the middle of summer, it would regard as fair game.

Spring awakening Emergence, which takes place in early spring, is a gradual process, initially confined to the middle of the day when the sun is hottest. At first reptiles and amphibians do not stray far from their winter retreat and their sorties are brief and laboured. Common frogs usually surface in March, but this can vary from January in Cornwall to as late as April in the high moorland regions of the northern Pennines. They sometimes get an unwelcome shock when they wake up in a late cold spell and, emerging from the mud and leaves at the bottom of the pond, find that the surface is still frozen over. The ice-covered pond may cause these frogs to die from lack of sufficient oxygen.

Marsh frogs appear in early April, while some edible frogs may not emerge until mid-April or even early May; perhaps they require more sun and warmth to stimulate them because of their southern European origin. Toads and newts stay hidden until March or April. Natterjack toads do not emerge from their sandy burrows (where they escaped the frosts and freezing winds) until the weather is warm enough in March and April. Slow worms, adders and grass snakes start to flourish again in early March, while sand

lizards and smooth snakes emerge a little later.

Shared slumber Reports of reptiles converging on the same spot to overwinter communally—entwined, in the case of snakes and slow worms—are not unknown. Adders are particularly sociable, often gathering in spectacular numbers; at Kirkcudbright, in Scotland, a tangle of 40 was once unearthed, together with ten toads and some common lizards. Perhaps this strategy helps them conserve body warmth, or it may be simply a shared attraction to a highly favourable site. More surprising than the numbers is the fact that different sorts of reptiles and amphibians are discovered together.

Above: This common frog has found some rotten wood to lie under for the winter. Frogs usually prefer to bury themselves in the muddy bottom of ponds.

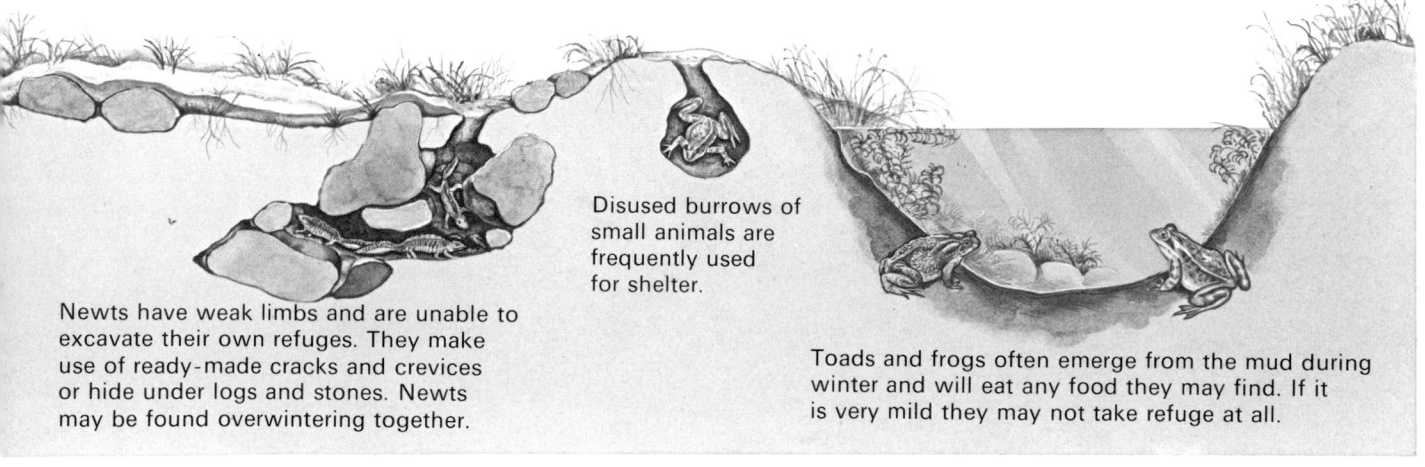

Newts have weak limbs and are unable to excavate their own refuges. They make use of ready-made cracks and crevices or hide under logs and stones. Newts may be found overwintering together.

Disused burrows of small animals are frequently used for shelter.

Toads and frogs often emerge from the mud during winter and will eat any food they may find. If it is very mild they may not take refuge at all.

BIRDS IN SPRING: A NEW START

The frosts are over, and food is plentiful: you can see signs of new energy and excitement in bird life, as the breeding season draws near.

For many bird species, the beginning of spring is an easy time of year and a welcome relief from the savage influence of winter. Ice no longer freezes up the food supply, whether it be invertebrates in the soil or fishes in the water. Darkness, cold and damp are on the decline, and with easier foraging there is more time to enjoy the sunshine. At the same time, while this is true for the majority of birds, there are a number of species for which a mild winter, at least, is the easiest time of all. Mallard and the small gulls, for example, can often be seen enjoying very leisurely days in mild winter weather. Their food is abundant and it is easy to collect a day's supply in, say, an hour; no time has yet to be devoted to pairing or breeding activities; and so even the short daylight period of winter has to be whiled away with long roosting and preening sessions on quiet lakes. But they are the exceptions, not the rule.

Buds, flowers and insects One of the first beneficiaries of spring is the bullfinch, whose sharp-edged, rounded bill makes short work of swelling flower buds from fruit trees and bushes, extracting only the nutritious central tissues otherwise destined to become flowers, and eventually fruits.

Both flowers and the insects which come to feed on their pollen and nectar provide food for birds. Attacks by house sparrows on nectar-rich crocuses (most often yellow) and plum blossom are perhaps the best examples of the first. Birdwatchers always make a point of visiting ponds, lakes and other damp areas from the beginning of March onwards, for the pussy willows come into flower in these places in spring and attract a host of insects – which in turn attract birds. Here you can count on seeing the first chiffchaffs and sand martins to return from southern Europe and N. Africa.

Seed eaters Of all land birds, it is probably the seed eaters which benefit last from spring, for fresh seeds must, by definition, follow some time after the flowers. For some species, such as the greenfinch and siskin, early spring is therefore the time of greatest food shortage, and this explains the high frequency of spring visits to peanuts in gardens by such birds.

The dawn chorus Song and display provide

Above: A kingfisher holds its catch. This is one of the birds most likely to find spring an enormous relief, for iced-over rivers and ponds spell starvation.

Opposite page: With the new canopy of protective leaves appearing in the woodlands, nesting and egg-laying can begin.

Left: The long-tailed tit's chances of survival increase dramatically as soon as spring brings a new crop of insects.

Sights and sounds in spring

Song thrush

Chaffinch
winter

spring

House sparrow

Swallow

Dawn chorus: the first half hour of a spring day is often astonishing for the sheer volume of birdsong.

Feather abrasion: by late February the male chaffinch's head feathers have worn into breeding colour.

Feeding on flowers: to birds, certain flowers can be particularly nutritious–like these yellow crocuses.

Migrant arrivals: as soon as flying insects become plentiful, Britain is habitable for swallows.

Above: A sedge warbler singing among newly opened willow leaves, soon after arrival from migration. Birdwatchers find willows and sallows rewarding trees to watch at the start of spring, largely for the sake of sights–and sounds–like this.

Below: The male bullfinch is one of the perennial delights of spring, with a bold display of black, wine-red and grey plumage–and a flashing white rump.

clear and effective communication between individuals of the same species–essential if the available resources are to be shared between adjacent pairs without resorting to mass fights. Britain has a number of excellent songsters including some, like the song thrush and robin, which can be found even in city centres. In the dawn chorus, each aspiring territory-holder declares his presence to all who listen.

These loud exchanges travel farthest on cold, calm mornings when a temperature inversion forms (when a layer of cold, dense air is topped by warmer, light air), since some sound waves are reflected back towards the ground instead of passing up into the atmosphere. Such conditions therefore prompt the greatest number of birds to partake in the dawn chorus. Birds also sing in a chorus at dusk; another reason for singing at these times may be that the early or late hours of daylight may be too gloomy for feeding.

Return of the native As a general rule, birds keep or reclaim the same territories in successive years whenever possible. This is hard to prove since different individuals usually look so alike, but it does explain the recurrence of particularly tame robins, or blackbirds that are recognisable by their complete or partial albinism, in the same garden for several years running.

Furthermore, ringing studies have shown that even migrants return each year to exactly the same spot. Given that they themselves were reared successfully, it is logical that they should return to breed in their native locality. On the other hand, even adjacent territories may vary considerably in their 'suitability', so some jostling for the best position can be expected.

Coming into plumage Breeding plumage, so important in displays and mate selection, is often most marked in spring, and to achieve this some species, like the ruff, grow feathers specially for this purpose in late winter and early spring. At their communal lekking grounds their extraordinary colours are displayed to the full. Other species retain their breeding plumage all year round–the black grouse, for example, another species with remarkable communal displays, moults only in autumn each year.

Still others make effective use of feather abrasion, the process whereby the tips of feathers wear away during the winter months. The male chaffinch is one such species; when first grown (in autumn), his head feathers are broadly tipped in buff, and only when the buff tips have worn away is the blue-grey breeding coloration visible.

The earliest eggs The task of laying eggs and rearing young is essentially a summer activity, but some species regularly reach this stage of the breeding cycle before even March has ended. Mistle thrushes sometimes lay eggs at the end of February, and their peak laying

Starling

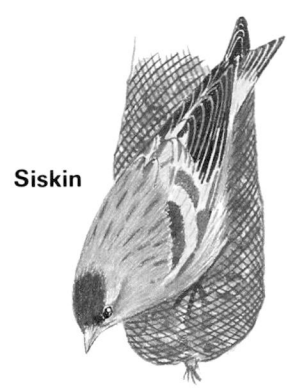

Siskin

Common terns

Nest building: the male starling starts building a nest early in April, before it has found a mate to occupy it.

Garden visitors in spring: siskins tend to run short of seeds in the wild, and turn to garden peanuts if available.

Mating begins: common terns return to their colonies, pair and mate. Eggs are laid only a few days after mating.

season is the end of March and early April.

However, the earliest nesting attempts of each bird species often fail, either because of subsequent cold weather, chilling the eggs or nestlings, or because there are too few leaves at this time to conceal the nests from predators.

Flying north Many species of birds migrate from, through or to the British Isles in spring. Departures of winter visiting birds, like redwings and fieldfares, may easily go unnoticed, and recording last dates of sightings requires studious, ideally daily, notes of all the birds seen.

Perhaps even more easily missed are departures of numerous finches, starlings and other small birds which swell the resident numbers here in winter. Many seabirds, waders and wildfowl also head north from our coasts, and from inland wetlands, to their breeding grounds inside the Arctic Circle.

Arriving from the south Arrivals of summer visitors are more easy to see and record, and it is an interesting exercise to compare first dates of different species. Among the earliest are the chiffchaff, swallow, sand martin, wheatear, Sandwich tern and black redstart, while the swift and spotted flycatcher arrive very late – rarely before the end of April. Males often precede females, and adults usually precede juveniles, so that, for example, the first yellow wagtails are conspicuously bright yellow, while later birds of the same species are more brown. Most migrants, eager to set up territory, fly direct to their breeding grounds, but a proportion, tired from the journey, land as soon as the opportunity arises.

For this reason coasts, especially in the south, are always worth a look in spring. Headlands, and patches of bushy scrub in otherwise open terrain, often attract a variety of species. Sea watching can be rewarding if waders like whimbrels and godwits are flying past, and you could see small passerines coming in; or perhaps a rarity such as a red-necked phalarope on its way to the Scottish Islands or beyond. Some of these exciting waders stay in Scotland for the season, but many pass through in spring and continue north to Iceland and Scandinavia.

Right: The Sandwich tern arrives among the earliest migrants in spring, at the beginning of March. This one is still in winter plumage: by the end of March it will have a shaggy black crest of feathers extending back from the base of the bill.

Below: Among British birds, the whimbrel is the curlew's northern replacement, occupying a breeding range that extends northward from Sutherland and the Hebrides into Orkney and Shetland. The migration journey is long, for the bird winters in tropical Africa. Therefore whimbrels do not reach their breeding grounds until late April or May. They are often seen breaking their long journey with stops on headlands on the southern and eastern coasts of England.

THE TIRELESS AND TIMELY SWALLOW

Every spring, swallows make an astounding journey from their winter quarters in South Africa. They travel nearly 5000 miles in one month, arriving here in early April to nest and breed and take advantage of our plentiful supply of insects.

Above: Young swallows about to receive a few welcome morsels of food from an assiduous parent. In their nest high up in the corner of an outbuilding, the young are generally fairly safe from predators; the adults warn of the presence of an inquisitive cat (or human) with a series of loud, sharp alarm calls, but use a longer, shriller and more penetrating cry if a bird predator—such as a hobby—appears.

According to the proverb, one swallow doesn't make a summer, but to many people the return of this bird each year is a sure sign that winter is at an end and summer just round the corner. As the weather gradually warms up in spring the flight paths swallows take on their migration journey north from South Africa can be mapped right across Europe. The first swallows appear in southern Britain on or around April 10, but the north of Scotland may have to wait until early May before the breeding birds arrive.

Food supply is the vital factor controlling both arrivals and departures. Swallows feed by catching insects on the wing, and in good weather you can often see them flying low over water meadows or skimming along a river, above a hayfield or even the local cricket pitch. In cold, wet or windy weather they gather in large flocks to concentrate on places where insect food remains available, often down-wind of large bodies of water where insects may be hatching, or in the lee of a wood or hedge where there is shelter. In temperate northern areas such as Britain where the birds breed, the summer supply of food is very good and is fully exploited by the migrants arriving from the south. In winter however there are few if any flying insects and any swallows rash enough to remain would soon starve to death.

A question of identity There are four species of fork-tailed, aerial-feeding birds which come to Britain for the summer months and which, at first glance, may be confused with each other. One, the sooty-black swift with its sickle-shaped wings, is not closely related to the swallow. The other two, the house martin and the sand martin, are members of the same family group as the swallow—the hirundines. The house martin has a patch of white on the back at the base of the tail while the sand martin can be distinguished by its dark brown upper parts and small size. The swallow has a longer and much more deeply forked tail than the other species, and the sleek, burnished blue of its head, collar and back, rusty red chin and pale pinky-brown undersides make it unmistakable.

Right: The angle between rafters in a barn or shed is a favourite nesting place for the swallow, providing a firm base for the cup of mud reinforced with dried grass. A lining of hairs and feathers makes a soft bed for eggs.

Swallow (*Hirundo rustica*), also known as the barn swallow; 19cm (7½in) from beak to tip of tail; distribution widespread throughout the British Isles from spring to autumn. Summer visitor.

Spring visitors
The swallow is the best known spring/summer visitor to Britain, but there are more. This list gives some of the other bird species that appear regularly each year.

Arctic skua
Arctic tern
Blackcap
Chiffchaff
Common sandpiper
Common tern
Cuckoo
Dotterel
Garden warbler
Grasshopper warbler
Great skua
Hobby
House martin
Lesser whitethroat
Little ringed plover
Little tern
Manx shearwater
Marsh warbler
Montague's harrier
Nightjar
Osprey
Pied flycatcher
Red-backed shrike
Redstart
Reed warbler
Roseate tern
Sand martin
Sandwich tern
Sedge warbler
Spotted flycatcher
Swift
Tree pipit
Turtle dove
Wheatear
Whimbrel
Whinchat
Whitethroat
Willow warbler
Wood warbler
Yellow wagtail

Raising a family The first swallows to arrive – the males – are quick to establish their nesting sites; females arrive soon after. Pairs are formed with aerial display flights, mutual preening and exploration of the chosen site. Swallows show a very positive preference for buildings as breeding places, choosing a variety of barns, sheds, garages and porches. The main body of the nest is made with pellets of wet mud cemented together and is lined with hair and feathers and sometimes dried grasses.

The first clutch of four or five white eggs with reddish markings, laid fairly quickly, is incubated by the female and hatches after 14 or 15 days. The youngsters are fed by both parents for about three weeks, until they fledge, and then for a few days more while they fly around the nest site. After that, the young birds disperse and the adults set about raising a second brood. Some assiduous pairs manage to rear three broods successfully.

The birds you see gathering in flocks on the telephone wires for the autumn migration are generally young individuals. These birds do not have the pressing family responsibilities of the adults and spend their time gener-

ally making themselves familiar with the area to which, if they survive, they will return the following year to breed. Young birds are also the main occupants of the massive autumn roosts that form in reed beds throughout the country.

Migrating millions For centuries it was believed that swallows hid themselves in mud at the bottom of ponds throughout winter. People found it difficult to account for the sudden disappearance of the species every year in any other way. Even Gilbert White, the 18th century Hampshire naturalist famous for the accuracy of his observations, did not dismiss this idea completely. By the end of the 19th century, however, the migration of birds was established as fact, proved conclusively by the tracing of ringed birds. The 10,000 miles that swallows fly on migration to South Africa and back each year is a fact every bit as astonishing and marvellous as the supposed six month hibernation period under water.

Migration starts as early as the end of July in some years, and is in full swing from mid-August to the end of September. An early cold snap in October may catch lingering

How to tell adults from young

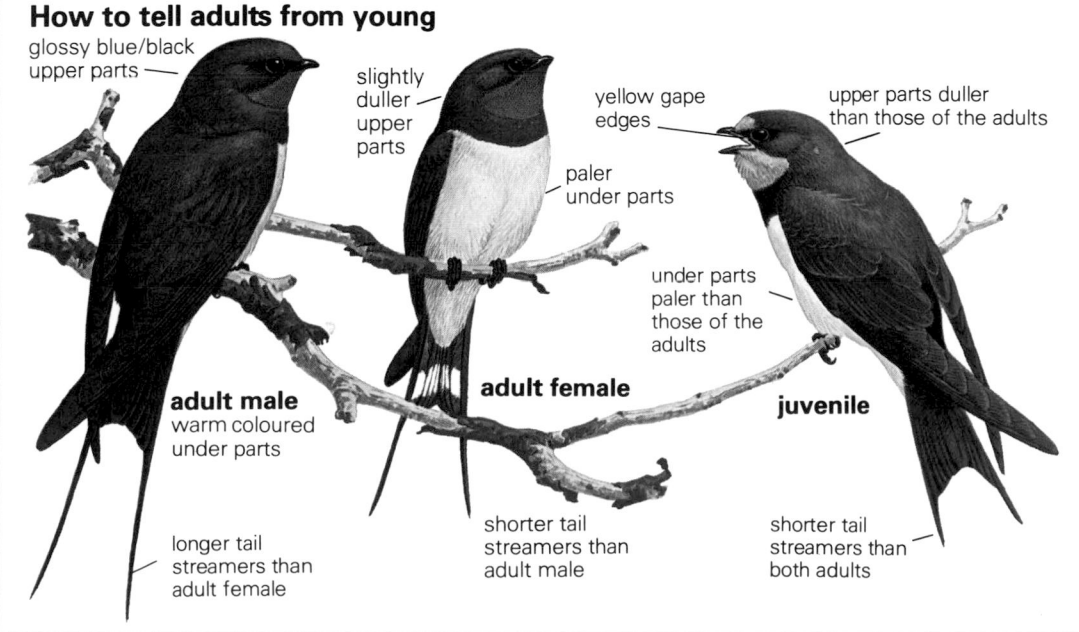

glossy blue/black upper parts

slightly duller upper parts

yellow gape edges

upper parts duller than those of the adults

paler under parts

under parts paler than those of the adults

adult male
warm coloured under parts

adult female

juvenile

longer tail streamers than adult female

shorter tail streamers than adult male

shorter tail streamers than both adults

At first glance, male and female swallows look very similar. But the male has much longer, thinner-tipped outer tail feathers than the female; also the male's chestnut or rust-red forehead and chin is often richer and darker than the female's. Both sexes share the glossy, deep blue upper parts, pinky-brown underside and white spots on the inner tail feathers. You can distinguish the juvenile in autumn by the short, blunt outer tail feathers and very pale forehead and chin.

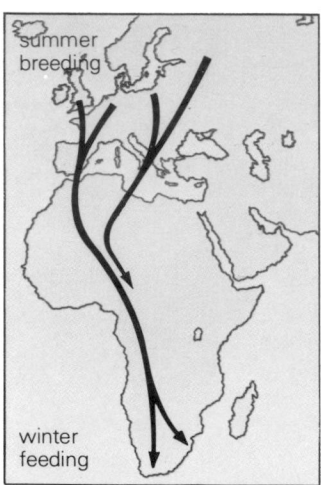

Above: The route taken by swallows on migration to South Africa is a direct one, passing over western France, the east coast of Spain and Gibraltar. British swallows are joined en route by birds from Russia.

Below: Swallow drinking on the wing. The low, skimming flight over land or water is characteristic of this bird, which flies nearer the ground than any other in its search for insects.

swallows unawares and inflict heavy casualties. In such circumstances thousands of weak and torpid birds have sometimes been gathered up from north of the Alps and flown in a plane further south where they have revived in the warmer conditions and continued their journey. This is a worthwhile gesture, but not one on which the European population of swallows relies for its continued existence – there are probably as many as ten million individuals migrating south each autumn from Britain alone.

The swallows' passage south is generally fairly leisurely – taking up to two months; the northward spring trip is much faster, often being accomplished in just one month. The birds travel by day in large flocks, feeding as they go so they do not have to put on a great deal of fat before the journey to use as fuel. At sunset the flocks settle for the night in roosts – usually in marshy reed beds where there is adequate shelter. Young birds find their way south by instinct; they do not have to be taught which route to follow by their parents.

Hazards en route The greatest barrier the swallows face on their journey is the Sahara desert. They can rely on favourable winds to assist them on the autumn crossing but they must nevertheless be in good condition, and with reserves of fat, before they can set out across the Sahara with any hope of survival. On the return trip in spring the winds are not always favourable, and the area to the north may itself not be very hospitable. This part of the northward journey is therefore particularly risky and in some years there are mass fatalities in the desert and on its northern edge. Totally exhausted – and doomed – birds have been found still alive but weighing as little as 10g ($\frac{1}{3}$oz); their normal weight is about 20-22g ($\frac{3}{4}$oz).

Winter in the sun Swallows find an abundance of food and warmth in South Africa to keep them in good condition throughout the winter. The British population has shifted its wintering area at least once in the last 20 years. Up to 1961, only one British ringed swallow had been found in the south-western area of South Africa, but since then about a third of all records have come from there. Different populations of European and Eurasian swallows wintering in South Africa are quite well segregated. For example, German birds are generally found over 1000 miles north of the British birds, spending their winters in the Congo basin.

A few of our swallows are tempted to stay in South Africa all year round to nest and breed; but since there are 15 other native species to compete with for food, the majority undertake the incredible journey northwards each year to rear their chicks on the summer bounty of British insects. In a cold spring or summer with a subsequent lack of insects, the birds do not breed in the same numbers.

CUCKOO: THE NEST SQUATTER

The cuckoo, whose call is so familiar in early summer, comes here to breed, but it neither builds a nest nor cares for its young – other birds do that for it!

The cuckoo is frequently heard but, being a shy bird, is seldom seen. The one British breeding species is extremely vocal from the moment it arrives here from Africa in mid-April. It sometimes calls on the wing, but usually waits until it alights before uttering the familiar, far-carrying 'cu-coo'. Occasionally the cry is 'cu-cu-coo' which, with other variants (and contrary to popular belief), can be heard at the start of the season as well as near the end. A much lesser known call is a comparatively subdued liquid bubbling sound. It is likely that most of the 'cu-cooing' comes from the male and most of the bubbling from the female, but both sexes can make these calls. Both also use a deep 'grow-ow-ow' sound. Strangely enough, cuckoos often seem to call with their beaks closed.

The only view you're likely to have of a cuckoo is as it hastens by on a direct, level course, its rapidly beating wings held mainly below the body, or as it glides the last few yards to a perch. It is a long-tailed, hawk-like grey bird with barred underparts and bright yellow eyes, and often perches horizontally with wings drooping. Cuckoos' feet, which have two toes pointing forwards and two pointing backwards, like those of a parrot, are adapted to make perching and scrambling about in branches easy, but it makes the birds clumsy waddlers on the ground.

The cuckoo is insectivorous, feeding on the

Above: A young cuckoo about two weeks old. Juveniles are often reddish in colour and can be further distinguished by a pale patch on the nape. Occasionally, when two cuckoo eggs have been laid in the same nest, the foster parents find they have two chicks to rear because neither has succeeded in evicting the other.

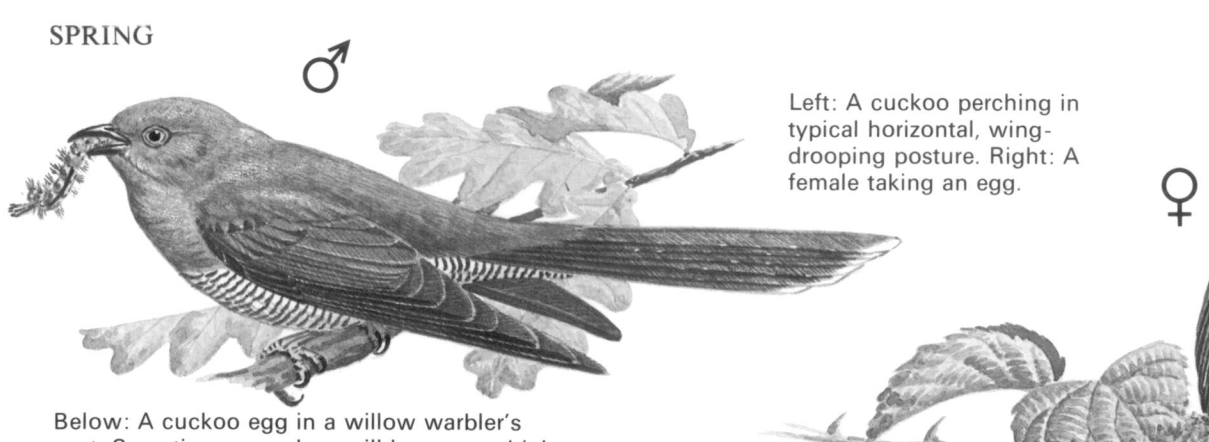

Left: A cuckoo perching in typical horizontal, wing-drooping posture. Right: A female taking an egg.

Below: A cuckoo egg in a willow warbler's nest. Sometimes a cuckoo will lay eggs which very closely resemble the eggs of its host; for example, blue eggs which match those of the dunnock, a frequent host species.

caterpillars of magpie moths and the larvae of sawflies and other insects; it is also unusual in being an avid devourer of hairy caterpillars and brightly coloured ones which warn of an unpalatable taste–insects normally avoided by birds.

Take-over bid The breeding season begins as soon as the cuckoos arrive in Britain. The males display excitedly, sometimes several of them together: calling loudly, they sway from side to side, bobbing up and down and even spinning round, their large, decorative tails raised and fanned out.

While the males display, the female cuckoo keenly defends her own territory, at the same time observing possible host species–birds smaller than herself such as willow warblers, meadow pipits, dunnocks or even robins. Her aim is to find out where they are building and when they start laying their first eggs. After days of careful watching, the female chooses a nest with an incomplete clutch of eggs– usually with just one egg–where incubation has not yet started. Between mid-afternoon and eight in the evening–a time when her victims are likely to be away feeding (because their eggs were laid in the morning)–the female cuckoo flies straight to the nest, ignoring any small birds which mob her in mistake for a hawk. She takes an egg out of the nest and holds it in her beak while she quickly lays one of her own in its place. Finally, she eats or discards the egg.

Cuckoos' eggs have been found in the nests of over 50 different British birds. Some of these nests–such as the hole type–seem rather unsuitable. Where the nest is in a hole too small for the cuckoo to enter, she clings with outspread wings and tail against the opening and ejects her egg into the nest. If this fails and her egg rolls aside she abandons it, making no attempt to pick it up.

Most small birds lay an egg a day, but the cuckoo lays every second day, presumably to give herself time to find all the nests she needs, for she may lay a dozen or more eggs. When her final egg is laid the female cuckoo's task is over, and she takes no further part or interest in her progeny's future. Nor does the male. He stops singing by the end of June and then he, and all other adult cuckoos, are free to fly back to Africa. They leave in July, the earliest of our summer birds to go.

Fooling foster parents An intriguing feature of the story is the foster parents' generally willing acceptance of the cuckoo's egg. Occasionally the put-upon fosterers react by burying the alien egg under a fresh layer of nesting material; a very few species, such as the blackcap and the spotted flycatcher, seem to have become cuckoo-resistant, readily deserting the nest if a cuckoo lays her egg in it. Most cuckoos avoid the nests of these species. The female cuckoo's biggest risk is that her egg may be rejected. Perhaps her main reason for removing an egg before depositing her own is to minimize suspicion in the fosterer's mind. Sometimes two or even three cuckoo eggs are found in one nest, but they are almost invariably laid by different birds–something which is easy to check since the eggs of each cuckoo are individually marked and can be recognised from year to year.

Whenever possible a female cuckoo, all her life, lays in the nest of only one kind of host species. The females are grouped into various clans–such as the meadow pipit cuckoos (probably the commonest clan in Britain), hedge sparrow cuckoos (mainly in woodlands and hedgerows) and reed warbler cuckoos (in aquatic habitats). Such fixations seem to go back to the cuckoo's earliest days: a meadow pipit cuckoo is one which was born in a

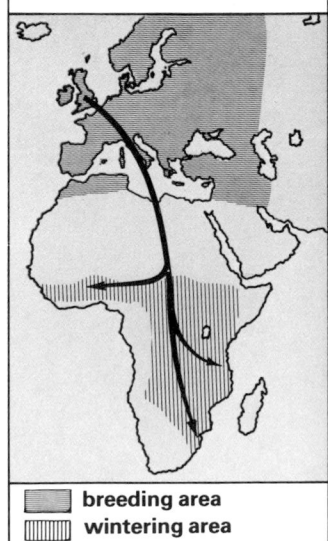

Above: A newly hatched chick ousting the host's egg from a nest. The instinct to do this is very powerful and lasts for about four days.

Migration route
Adult cuckoos leave in late July, flying through Italy and across to Africa. The young follow in late August, finding their solitary way by instinct only.

breeding area
wintering area
route

meadow pipit's nest and becomes permanently imprinted to pipits. It is thought, however, that male cuckoos do not become imprinted.

Room for one only The cuckoo's egg is incubated with the host's eggs and hatches about the same time, or even earlier. The cuckoo chick is immediately faced with an acute problem of survival: to grow into a much larger bird than its foster parents it needs far greater quantities of food than would be given to each of the bona fide young. It must therefore eliminate all competition. So, when it is about eight hours old, the chick is seized by a powerful urge (lasting about four days) to get rid of any eggs or young sharing the nest with it. To do this – though tiny, blind and naked – it crawls beneath the eggs or nestlings one at a time, manoeuvres them into a hollow in its back and, using its legs and featherless wings, climbs up the side of the nest and heaves them out.

The parent birds take no steps to prevent this, nor to retrieve ejected eggs or feed any young that are thrown out. Eventually the cuckoo has the nest to itself and the entire attention of the foster parents. These birds feed the cuckoo as if it were their own, never abandoning it as long as it goes on begging for food and no matter how huge it becomes.

The rapidly growing cuckoo frequently utters a wheezy hunger cry – 'chi-chi-chi' – and this persuades not only its foster parents but sometimes other birds (occasionally even a passing cuckoo) to drop food into its gaping mouth. At about four weeks old the young cuckoo reaches independence, and in August or September it flies off to find its solitary way to Africa for the winter.

Nest parasitism The large output of eggs – ensuring that a fair number are likely to survive – is the chief advantage of the cuckoo's remarkable life style. It is difficult to say how nest parasitism evolved. Only some of the world's many cuckoo species have become parasites. The most interesting and significant is the American yellow-billed cuckoo which does build a nest and rears its own young: the nest is usually only a very flimsy structure and the eggs often fall out of it, so the female frequently usurps the nests of other birds and uses them to bring up her family. Occasionally she leaves her eggs to be incubated in the nests of other birds. The yellow-billed cuckoo may therefore be a species hesitating on the brink of nest parasitism.

It seems likely that nest parasitism may have originated in birds which first got into the habit of appropriating the nests of other species for their own use. The sight of the eggs in the usurped nest might well have stimulated the newcomer to add another to the clutch. Eventually, the laying of eggs in other birds' nests could have become habitual. One mystery not yet fully understood is why the host species have not become more resistant to such victimisation. The survival value of a bird being a nest parasite is also questionable – it seems very risky for a species to entrust all its eggs to foster parents. However, it is a life style that is very successful: the cuckoo is a numerous bird with a breeding range that spreads across Europe and Asia

Cuckoo (*Cuculus canorus*); 33cm (13in) from beak to tail; distribution widespread in woodland, heaths, commons, marshes, fields with hedgerows and coastal dunes; a summer visitor.

Below: A young cuckoo develops rapidly; in three weeks it is far larger than its foster parents and has usually outgrown its nest; so it has to perch nearby to be fed. When it begins to fly a little, the fosterers accompany it and continue to stuff its insatiable beak with insects.

WATCHING BADGER CUBS GROW UP

You can have a lot of fun watching badgers – particularly cubs at play – during the warmer nights of late spring. With time and patience, you will find the cubs learn to tolerate your presence and may even come up to snuffle at your shoes.

Badger-watching takes you out into the countryside at night and is both exciting and unpredictable. The dramatic and successful watches make up for the disappointing and frustrating ones and you are spurred on to go again and again.

When planning to watch a sett for the first time, or after a long interval, it is useful to make a reconnaissance first. The morning is a good time, since any scent you may leave will have dispersed by the time the badgers emerge. Try not to disturb the vegetation and avoid stamping about near the entrances and on the main badger paths.

Watching cubs Any time of the year can be interesting, but late spring is probably the

most rewarding since cubs are then likely to be above ground. Wear inconspicuous, warm clothes which do not rustle – and don't smoke or use scent. Make your way slowly and quietly to your watching place, checking that you are downwind of the sett to avoid detection. In May and June you should get into position before sunset in secluded places. It is much better to get there on the early side than to arrive after the badgers have emerged. Binoculars can be useful, as is a torch. Make sure the torch switches on silently and has a red filter; badgers take little notice of dim lights, particularly red ones.

The time waiting for the badger to appear is always interesting. Birds may be seen going to roost, rabbits appear from their burrows and you may glimpse a fox or the antics of a squirrel as it makes for home. Then comes the thrill of that first sight of the black and white head at an entrance, nose sniffing for any scent of danger. If you remain quiet and still and the wind is right, the badger may emerge and will probably begin scratching itself; this is a good sign that it is at ease. Soon it may be joined by others and if cubs are about, you should see them play.

Best viewpoint If you have a choice of setts to watch, choose one which shows signs of recent use and does not have too many entrances. Footprints, bits of fur caught on brambles or twigs, and regularly used latrines all indicate a sett. A few trees or bushes 5-10m (16-33ft) from the hole affords good cover for watching. Too much vegetation immediately around the holes, however, makes observation difficult.

The ideal place from which to watch badgers is from a tree or bush about 10m (33ft) from a well-used hole; check your view is uninterrupted. You can be up a tree or standing or sitting with a tree or bush at your back to break up your outline.

Play among badger cubs is an important part of growing up. It helps them to develop co-ordination, strengthens the muscles and trains the cubs for adult activities.

When cubs are first seen above ground their movements are tentative and their sense of balance on steep slopes not well-developed. They keep near to each other or their mother. If one wanders away, it is soon called back again. As they grow older, the cubs play more boisterously, usually near a sett entrance, and

the ground becomes hard and smooth with all this activity. Adults often join in the fun and the cubs keep up a continuous 'whickering' noise which rises intermittently with excitement.

Cubs become more adventurous as they mature and their play patterns grow more recognisable. A popular game is 'tag', when they chase each other around a tree trunk or in and out of holes. When one is caught and bitten, it turns round and chases the others. Cubs also make use of old logs or steep banks when playing a type of 'king-of-the-castle'. One takes up a higher position and the others try to dislodge it and take its place.

In between bouts of play the cubs explore the neighbourhood of the sett and snuffle among the vegetation. Every object is carefully investigated and they soon become familiar with food items and various types of vegetation, largely through sense of smell. Sight plays little part in learning since the first two months or more of their lives are spent in darkness below ground where smell, hearing and touch are more useful.

Even at three months old, when they have

Above: This badger is using its nose and forefeet to grub for food among leaf litter. Before the end of summer the cubs are weaned and can then forage for themselves.

boar scratching

Social behaviour among badgers

Right: Badgers take considerable care over their grooming, often after they emerge from the sett. Vigorous scratching (right, above) helps remove fleas and may also be used to mix scents from other badgers. When playing, the cubs chase each other; if one is caught and bitten (far right) the roles reverse.

grooming

young badgers at play

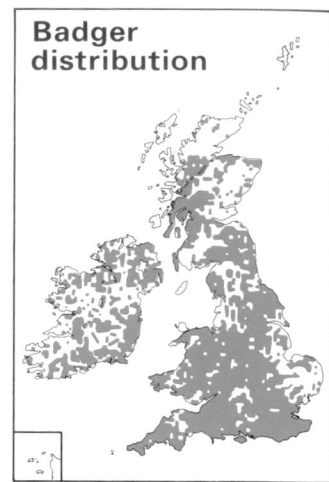

Left: The badger's latrine is never far from the sett. Droppings are deposited in a shallow pit and left uncovered. You may also find latrines strategically placed at the edge of a group's territory.

Badger distribution

been used to light for some weeks, the cubs are still very short-sighted. Their hearing, on the other hand, is good, and they react to sudden, unaccustomed noises by bolting for a hole. They soon learn, however, to discriminate between the normal sounds in their environment and those that spell danger.

Gradually they extend their knowledge of the habitat beyond the vicinity of the sett until all the trees, bushes and main paths are familiar landmarks. These give them a scent picture of the whole area, which helps when sudden danger threatens; then they automatically bolt for the nearest hole by the easiest route. By following the example of their parents, the cubs also learn to use the 'latrines' sited near the sett.

Setting scent The process of growing up does not include just play, exploration of the habitat and learning whether things are edible, harmless or dangerous. It also involves becoming part of the social group and scent plays an important part in this process.

The sow, on leaving the sett, often squats for a moment near the entrance or on one of the main paths. She is leaving a tiny smear from the musk glands under her tail; this reinforces the scent trail she is following. But setting scent also has a social function. Adults will set scent on each other and the cubs, and cubs on each other. In this way the distinctive scent is shared with all the others in the group to form a composite smell characteristic of the whole community. This smell will be different from that of neighbouring groups and helps recognition of friends and strangers.

Individual grooming is another characteristic kind of behaviour often seen soon after emergence from the sett. This usually involves scratching, when every part of the body is given most vigorous treatment. This may well be a reaction to fleas, but it is also likely that scratching helps to blend the scents received from others. Sometimes mutual grooming takes place, usually between adults, when each gently nibbles the other's fur with its teeth. This appears to be a pleasurable occupation which strengthens the bond between adults in the group.

Weaning usually begins when the cubs are at least three months old. During this time they feed on some solid food, particularly earthworms or the occasional dead bird, and follow the mother when she goes off to feed herself. But weaning can be delayed for a further month or so if food for the cubs is scarce. After weaning, cubs tend to forage independently.

Adults are at their lowest weight in the spring as territorial behaviour by the boars and suckling by the sows will have reduced their stored fat to a minimum. So during the summer and autumn the adults are mainly pre-occupied with feeding to restore their condition ready for the winter.

Opposite page: A family of badgers emerges from the sett to begin foraging.

Below: Cubs soon find their way round the territory, scenting various landmarks such as trees.

Summer~ season of replenishment

Summer, with its long hot days and short nights, sees the entire countryside buzzing with life. Many animals are raising a second brood of young, taking advantage of the season's abundance of food and protective luxuriant growth. As autumn nears, the days become sultry, birdsong dies and only the buzz of insects is heard.

No season is hailed with more pageantry and merriment than the birth of summer on May 1st, for summer is above all the season of replenishment. May-day rituals, of great antiquity, reflect a bygone time when our own prosperity and survival were more intimately entwined with the quickening of nature.

The maypole symbolises many things, but none more than the hub around which the seasons revolve. For plants and animals, this hub, in turn, is the sun which has been progressing northwards with the unwinding of spring. The movement heralds a weakening of the vigorous storm track which has dominated the weather pattern in winter and spring. As April passes into May, high pressure steadily asserts itself over the Azores in the mid-Atlantic, wafting warm, clear weather to the shores of Europe, and the troublesome low pressure region centred over Iceland begins to flag, enhancing the growing stability of the Azores high.

With the welcome improvement in the weather, May sees a swift conclusion to April's tentative unfolding of woodland foliage. In many places the pinnate leaves of the ash are the last to appear, in early May. The sudden opulence of deciduous woodland tends to obscure the quiet stirrings of the conifers. Because they are adapted to the fleeting summers of northern climates, spruces and pines concentrate their growth between May and July, with the dramatic eruption of a candle-like spire from the topmost bud.

As the tree community spreads its canopy, a deep shade engulfs the woodland floor, and the flush of flowers which thrived in the spring sunlight filtering through the bare branches begins to wane. A second generation of shade-tolerant herbage flourishes, dominated in many English woods by a green sea of dog's-mercury. The new emergent flowers, like woundwort and bugle, have a deceptive lustre in this muted light, none more so than the carpets of bluebells which attract man and other animals alike by their heady fragrance.

High in the mountains a choice variety of alpine flowers nestles close to the ground and between crevices. Species such as roseroot and mountain avens add a dash of colour to the rocky slopes, and colonies of golden yellow globe flowers thrive down in damp gullies. On clifftops and on rocky shores patches of pink thrift and various orchid species blossom. With a rich brew of colour, scent and shape, the summer flowers vie among themselves for the favours of passing insects.

Left: A meadow left fallow is a delight in summer with poppies and scented mayweed.

Below: In summer the fox shelters from the heat of the day among long grass.

Flowers and insects have had such a long evolution of mutual benefit – the giving of nutritious nectar and pollen in exchange for pollination – that the majority of summer flowers are oases, purpose-built to satisfy their guests. Some, such as roses and poppies, produce only pollen which is sought by beetles and hoverflies, as well as by the better-known bees and butterflies. Many, such as the orchids, fumitories, and flowers of the pea family, are so constructed that bees, in seeking the nectar source, cannot help but brush against the pollen-bearing stamens as they enter and leave the flowers.

Flowers help bees in various subtle ways to recognise them as targets. In hedgebanks, the spikes of foxgloves and viper's bugloss, for example, are luminous to bees whose vision is finely tuned to their mauves and blues. Similarly, reds and mauves are especially attractive to many butterflies.

Bees and some other insects see ultra-violet light which is invisible to us. Not surprisingly, some flowers have evolved ultra-violet markings which help the insect to home in on the nectar source. The evening primrose, for example, which appears to us a uniform yellow, has a striking ultra-violet patch at the centre which glows to night-flying moths.

Just before dark we may see one of the most typical moths of June and July. Jigging about over the grass, as if on the end of an invisible thread, the male ghost swift moth performs an aerial dance to attract females. Like the fragrant honeysuckle (and for ultimately the same reason – self-perpetuation), it too leaves a telling trail of odour in the night. In this case, however, it is a specific attractant – a pheromone – which the female can follow up-wind before mating. Once mated, the female lays her eggs in a somewhat unorthodox manner (compared with other insects).

Most moths lay directly on the foodplant of the caterpillars-to-be, and exercise great care in doing so. The cinnabar moth, for example, seeks ragwort for its black and yellow banded larvae to devour when they hatch. The female ghost swift moth, however, just drops her eggs into the grass as she flies. When they hatch, the caterpillars crawl into the soil to feed on roots.

In the tree-tops, caterpillars of a host of relatively inconspicuous moths have been gorging themselves on the foliage and flowers since the buds burst, and are now ready to pupate in June. Some, such as the green oak tortrix, cocoon themselves in a nearby leaf; others, such as the winter moth caterpillar, lower themselves to the ground on a silken thread. Exceptionally, a large oak may play host to half a million winter moth caterpillars alone, and in such outbreak years the effect of this and other leaf-eaters can be devastating, stripping the tree of its leaves and even sometimes killing it. If you walk through such a wood in early June there is an audible and incessant whisper of frass – the residues of the caterpillars' activities in the canopy – raining down on the woodland floor. Oaks, and other deciduous trees, however, are usually capable of countering such attacks, producing new buds to compensate; as late as July, there may be a resurgence of growth, the so-called Lammas leaves. The new foliage is virtually devoid of caterpillars which, having eaten themselves out of house and home in June, seal their own fate.

These caterpillars which, even in average years, are enormously abundant, are the life-support of most of our woodland birds, and often the resource which regulates their breeding success. Not only do they sustain our resident species, but also a huge immigrant population of warblers. We often suppose that birds breed throughout the summer, but for many the season is relatively short-lived, and over by the end of June when all the caterpillars have pupated and are less accessible. This means that the birds have to start nesting before the caterpillars emerge *en masse* to ensure their young are in the nest at the caterpillar peak.

Most great tits and blue tits, for example, squeeze all their breeding activities into the eight weeks of May and June. Once the young

hatch, the parents' work-load is formidable. A pair of blue tits may transport about 10,000 caterpillars to the nest in 18 days, about the time it takes for the young to fledge. There is much debate about how much impact such an onslaught has on woodland caterpillars, but in the long term the moth populations are as resilient as the mother oak. For the blue tit this onerous hunting schedule would be impossible without the bonus of extended summer daylight. Birds and other animals breed in the summer not only because food is most abundant then but also because there is sufficient time to find it.

Though caterpillar stocks are largely exhausted by the end of June, the peak of flying insects occurs later, and times the breeding effort of some other insectivorous immigrants, notably the spotted flycatcher and the nightjar. Many birds which normally feed from the ground become more adaptable at this time, and we may see such species as starlings and gulls hawking for swarms of flying ants. Indeed, relatively large birds often resort to preying on insects if they are sufficiently numerous or large to warrant the chase. A substantial and clumsy flyer like the cockchafer (or Maybug) then becomes fair game for the rook, the little owl, and even the tawny owl.

The feverish activity of birds–singing, fighting and foraging for food–makes them highly vulnerable to predation in summer. Hole-nesting tits are often discovered by keen-eyed weasels, needing sustenance for their own hungry young. Many fledglings and eggs likewise fall prey to roving foxes and other mammals; even the grass snake marauds nests by scaling trees such as the willow.

By the end of July most birds are moulting their dishevelled breeding plumage. Drake mallards moult in a particularly drastic fashion, dropping all their primary and secondary feathers at once; they take refuge in reed beds and play no part in raising their own offspring. The duck tends them alone, leading her charges to the shallows where frog tadpoles are still easy prey.

In the open countryside, which is starting to brim with ripening seeds and fruits, the change in the tempo of bird life seems somehow almost too sudden and premature. It is signalled by a virtual cessation of song and often July finds the yellowhammer sawing out his lazy notes unchallenged. This is summer's most indulgent time when, with luck, it is too hot for us to do anything except listen to nature's other sounds; by the pond there is the thin clattering of the hunting dragonfly's wings, broom seeds cracking in the sun, and grasshoppers singing down below. It is not quite the sound of the jungle, though the closest we ever get in the British Isles with our only cicada insect species, the rare *Cicadetta montana*.

In the wood, the undergrowth has become rank with bracken, nettles and willowherb–too tall to make watching badgers and fox cubs worthwhile any longer, and dense enough to offer good protection to mice, dormice and voles. The first half of August brings the 'dog days' when the brilliant Dog Star Sirius rises and sets with the sun. It is characteristically a time of hot, sultry, weather when warm air towers over the newly harvested stubbles and thunderstorms descend on them. Harvest mice scuttle for safety away from the rain and the combine harvester. Occasionally the heat even becomes uncomfortable for some animals such as lizards which temporarily go underground to 'aestivate' for a while. If we have a prolonged dry spell, earthworms also aestivate deep in the ground to remain moist, well away from the strong sunlight.

It can be a particularly trying time for birds such as rooks, which are dependent on soil invertebrates for food. Many, especially inexperienced young birds, resort then to roadside verges to glean the insect casualties of passing traffic. For an enormous number of others, there are clear signs of the bonanza ahead: the scarlet berries of the rowan ripening early in August and the darkening blackberries have already given the thrushes and blackbirds a foretaste of the season to come.

THE HORSE CHESTNUT: SUMMER SPLENDOUR

The dazzling flowers of the white horse chestnut are a sure indicator of summer. Perhaps more than any other tree, the horse chestnut vividly reflects the changing seasons: the fat sticky buds of winter open in spring to reveal downy green leaves, and shiny brown conkers litter streets and parks in autumn.

Below: The horse chestnut in early summer — a cascade of brilliant white flowers. The tallest specimen in the British Isles — 39m (128ft) high — is at Ashford Chase, Hampshire.

White horse chestnut
(*Aesculus hippocastanum*)
Deciduous, introduced,
grows to more than 30m
(100ft), lives up to 100
years. Cultivated in parks
and gardens, occasionally
grows wild, on rich well
drained soils.

The white horse chestnut is an impressive tree at any time of the year—and in flower it is truly magnificent. With its wide-spreading branches and typically rounded crown it presents a towering mass of luxuriant foliage throughout the summer and a glorious blaze of colour in early autumn.

Growing wild in hilly regions of Greece, Bulgaria and Iran, the horse chestnut was introduced into Great Britain early in the 17th century. Since then it has been widely planted as an ornamental tree in gardens, parkland and often in long avenues. The horse chestnut avenue in Bushy Park, Teddington, is a fine example which in Victorian times drew large crowds to admire the trees in flower. It is also planted in and around fields to provide shade for farm animals. The foliage is palatable to cattle and horses who stretch to eat all the leaves they can reach while sheltering beneath the tree. The base of the crown of a tree eaten like this forms a straight line parallel to the ground.

A curious feature of the horse chestnut is its slowness to establish itself in the wild, despite its apparent adaptability: it is a hardy tree able to grow on most soils and its seeds (or conkers) germinate freely, yet it seems unable to compete easily against many of our native plants which often crowd it out. This is in stark contrast to other introduced species, such as sycamore, which spread rapidly into woods and plantations.

It is impossible to confuse the white horse chestnut with any other tree, including other chestnuts. The red flowered horse chestnut, which is less widespread, is a result of a cross between the common species and red buckeye, a native of North America. It differs by having red flowers, smoother fruits and generally smaller leaves. The totally unrelated sweet chestnut is clearly distinguished by its yellow flowers, spirally-twisting bark, long saw-edged leaves and more spiny fruit cases.

Bark and timber The horse chestnut's grey-brown bark, which is initially smooth, becomes rough and scaly with old age; the oldest dated specimens in this country were planted in 1664. The tree itself is of little

Left: The horse chestnut bears up to 100 male or bisexual flowers on each candle. The centres of each flower change from yellow to red after pollination.

Below: Under the spreading horse chestnut in autumn you find golden leaves — the largest of any tree in Britain — and conkers that children use in the game originally known as 'conquerors'.

practical value. The cream-coloured wood is soft and weak, making it unsuitable for most purposes, although it is used to make toys and trays. It does not burn well; but in medieval times its charcoal went into the manufacture of gunpowder.

Sticky buds The fat buds, which form during the previous summer and are so prominent in spring, are coated in shiny resin; this protects the new season's shoots from attack by insect pests. The sticky resin gums up these insects, immobilising them and preventing them from chewing into the delicate buds.

If you collect the winter twigs in bud and place them in a jar of water, you can watch the buds burst into leaf. In early spring the buds swell and break open on the tree, the bud scales peeling back as the growing tip emerges. The young leaves are pale green and clothed in white, furry down which gives protection throughout the winter, although the down is soon shed as the leaves expand. Large horseshoe-shaped scars are left on the twigs where previous years' leaf stalks were attached.

The leaves are among the first of any tree to appear in spring and also among the earliest to colour and fall in autumn—changing to yellow and deep gold before dropping. Growing up to 20cm (8in) across, the largest leaves of any tree found in Britain—indeed in Europe—they are made up of from five to seven pear-shaped leaflets borne on a long, stout stalk. When the tree is in full leaf it forms a dense, shady canopy which shows beautifully how leaves can be arranged to reap the maximum benefit from incoming sunlight. Moreover, the leaves can twist on their stalks during the day and position themselves to catch the sun, so avoiding being shaded by their neighbours.

Candles The flowering spikes, or candles, blossom in mid-May, although they emerge earlier with the young leaves. Made up of four or five petals, the white flower is tinged with yellow blotches that turn red after the flower is pollinated. Hard-working bees pick up and transfer pollen from the seven red-tipped stamens that protrude from each flower to the stigmas of other flowers. Two other horse chestnuts, the Japanese and the Indian, also have white/yellow candles. The Indian flowers later than the white horse chestnut.

Conkers form inside a tough, spiky capsule and are protected by a lining of soft white padding; as they ripen they change colour from white to rich, glossy brown by early October. If they do not fall with the capsule, or are not knocked down with sticks thrown by children, they will be released as the three segments that make up the capsule dry and peel away from the swelling seeds. During October most playgrounds and classrooms become littered with broken horse chestnuts, the aftermath of energetic conker duels—a game first popular in the 19th century.

It has been suggested that horse chestnuts

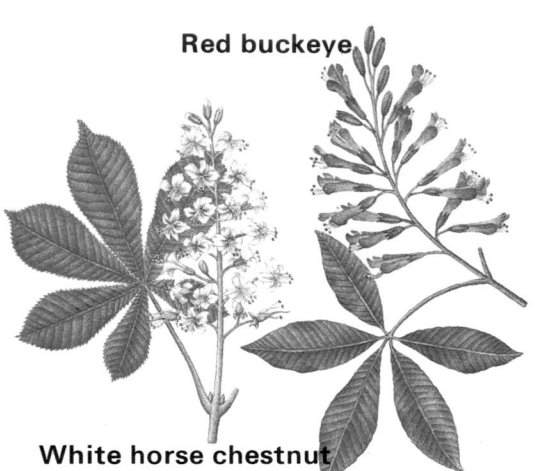

Red buckeye

White horse chestnut

Above: The white horse chestnut and the red buckeye (a North American species) combine to produce a hybrid, the pink horse chestnut. Although both the white horse chestnut and the red buckeye belong to the same genus, their offspring, the pink horse chestnut, is not always fertile.

Above: Apart from the common horse chestnut, you can sometimes find the Indian horse chestnut, an introduced species, in Britain's parks and gardens. The flowers of the Indian horse chestnut are larger than the common form, and also appear later in the summer.

Pink horse chestnut

Above: The pink horse chestnut (*Aesclus* × *carnea*) is deciduous and bears pink flowers and crinkled leaves. It reaches a maximum height of 20m (65ft).

were so called because the conkers were a remedy for horses with a cough. This is, in fact, unlikely, for horses refuse them owing to their very bitter taste; but deer and sheep will eat them.

Protect a tree As has been mentioned above, horse chestnuts may germinate and then soon become overwhelmed by other vegetation. However a sapling usually flourishes if it is moved to deep, preferably loamy, moist but well-drained soil and a sunny position. Keep it free from smothering plants and protected from livestock and it will have a good chance of survival. And you will have contributed another beautiful summer sight for the next generation to enjoy.

SUMMER-BLOOMING SPEEDWELLS

Grassy banks, woodland and watersides are the best places to find the attractive 'bird's eyes' or speedwells. Although the flowers are characteristically blue, with a white 'eye', some are pink or white, making them easier to identify.

Above: The germander speedwell (*Veronica chamaedrys*) is probably our most familiar speedwell species, the deep blue flowers with a prominent white eye often carpeting hedgebanks and grassy places. There may be as many as 20 flowers on a single flower head, and they are in bloom from March to July. A common name shared by many speedwells is 'bird's-eye', the small blue flowers supposedly resembling birds' eyes among the grass.

Speedwells belong to the same family as figworts and foxgloves–the Scrophulariaceae–but their flowers differ from other members of the family in Britain in that they have only four petals, not the usual five. The upper petal of a speedwell flower, which is slightly larger than the others, represents two petals that have become joined. There are over 20 species in the British Isles, many of them rather similar, and a close look may be needed to identify them.

Shades of blue The familiar deep blue flowers, each with a prominent white eye, belong to the germander speedwell. Buxbaum's speedwell has similar, but brighter, blue flowers without such a conspicuous eye, while

thyme-leaved speedwell has almost white flowers with violet lines on all but the lowest petal. The colour variation continues in ivy-leaved speedwell, which has small lilac flowers, and in pink water speedwell where the flowers are, as the name suggests, pink.

The differences between the species are even more apparent on close observation. Some speedwells, such as the ivy-leaved speedwell, have flowers borne singly at the base of a leaf, while in others the flowers are borne in elongated heads. Species such as the brooklime have a number of flower heads towards the end of the stems, each one arising from the base of a leaf, while such species as the spiked speedwell bear numerous flowers in a long spike forming the tip of the stem.

Speed-you-well The flowers' common name may refer to the old parting saying 'Speed-you-well' or 'Speed well', which is equivalent to 'Farewell'. Indeed, in Ireland the speedwell was once sewn on to clothes to protect travellers against accidents. The association between parting and the speedwell probably arose from the way that the petals fall quickly from the plant, often as soon as it is picked. Alternatively, the name may refer to the plant's curative powers, for it was used as a remedy for ailments as diverse as coughs and leprosy, and in the healing of wounds.

Water speedwells Many of the speedwells grow in a wide range of habitats, but brooklime and the marsh, water and pink water

speedwells are found in very wet places. These range from marshy soil to the shallow water of ponds, streams or the sides of rivers and lakes.

All four are more or less hairless plants and have a similar arrangement of flowers, arising in elongated heads branching from the main stems. The pale pink marsh speedwell is the most easily distinguished as its flower heads are on alternating sides of the stem. As its name suggests, it can be found on marshy ground in wet meadows and bogs, although it sometimes occurs in shallow water.

The flower heads of the remaining three species arise in pairs on opposite sides of the stems. Brooklime, often found at the water's

edge, has broad, rather blunt leaves, each with a distinct stalk at its base. The two water speedwells are very similar in appearance and often confused with each other. Both have upright stems, and rather narrow, pointed leaves which clasp the stem at their base. However, the pink flowers of the pink water speedwell are a distinguishing feature, as is the position of the seed capsules when they develop. The stalks of the developing seed capsules of the pink water speedwell spread out at right angles to the flower head stem, while those of the water speedwell are angled towards the tip of the flower head.

Grassland and wasteland species Four annual speedwells–ivy-leaved, Buxbaum's, grey and field speedwell–grow in disturbed soil. They are found in gardens, farmland and other places where the ground has been cleared–usually by man's activities.

They form a characteristic group among the speedwells, with stalked flowers borne singly at the base of the leaves, which are all very similar in size and shape. Those of ivy-leaved speedwell are, as its name indicates, rather like those of an ivy, with five to seven lobes. The leaf margins of the other three species have small, rounded teeth.

The flowers vary in colour and size. Those of ivy-leaved speedwell are tiny and may be lilac or white, with heart-shaped sepals. Buxbaum's speedwell has larger, bright blue flowers measuring up to 12mm ($\frac{1}{2}$in) across.

Above: The two species of speedwell most commonly confused with each other are the germander speedwell, shown here, and Buxbaum's speedwell (*Veronica persica*), shown below left. Although the two are similar shades of blue, Buxbaum's speedwell very often has a much paler lower petal. Another distinguishing feature is the structure of the flower head–Buxbaum's speedwell produces a single, long-stalked flower while the flower spike of germander speedwell consists of several blooms.

Right: The spiked speedwell (*Veronica spicata*) is easily distinguished from other speedwells by its spikes of blue-violet flowers which appear from July to September. However, it is a very rare species, found only in East Anglia and a few counties of western England and Wales, where it is protected by special legislation, making it illegal to take any part of the plant from the wild.

Above: **Water speedwell** (*Veronica anagallis-aquatica*). Flowers June-Aug.

Above: **Common speedwell** (*Veronica officinalis*). Flowers May-Aug.

Above: **Rock speedwell** (*Veronica fruticans*). Flowers July-Aug.

Above: **Marsh speedwell** (*Veronica scutellata*). Flowers June-Aug.

Above: **Thyme-leaved speedwell** (*Veronica serpyllifolia*). Flowers Mar-Oct.

The blue flowers of the grey speedwell (its name refers to the leaf colour), and the white or pale blue flowers of the field speedwell, are much smaller, measuring only 6mm ($\frac{1}{4}$in) across.

Buxbaum's speedwell was first recorded in Berkshire in 1825, having been introduced accidentally from western Asia. It is now widespread throughout the country, and is thought to be our most common species in gardens and on waste ground. Ivy-leaved speedwell and grey speedwell are most common in southern England and rare elsewhere, while field speedwell is scattered throughout the British Isles.

Annuals and perennials The four species described above are all annual, as is the wall speedwell. This species often grows as a weed, but can also be found on heath and grassland. It can also take root in crevices in rocks and walls, growing well in dry, bare places. It has small blue flowers on very short stalks and the leaves become much smaller towards the upper part of the stem.

The many perennial species of speedwells include the germander, common, wood and thyme-leaved speedwells. The small, pale flowers of the thyme-leaved speedwell are borne towards the tips of the main stems. It is a common species on various types of grassland and also grows in damp spots in gardens.

Common speedwell is another plant of grassland, although it prefers drier soils, and it is also found on woodland margins. The individual lilac flowers are carried on very short stalks and packed rather closely in an elongated head.

Germander speedwell is another grassland species, although it sometimes appears in woods as well. It has as many as 10 to 20 blue flowers in each flower head, and paired, often stalkless, leaves.

The wood speedwell bears some resemblance to the germander speedwell, but it has lilac flowers–usually five or less in a head–and paired, stalked leaves. It is common in woodland, usually on damp soils.

Shrubby speedwells Some perennial speedwells are slightly woody at the base–the rare rock speedwell, for example, a species of high

mountains in eastern Scotland. No speedwells are true shrubs, however, but there are some plants known as shrubby speedwells, which were formerly included in the same genus as the British speedwells. These are the hebes, originating from New Zealand but cultivated in gardens here, where they grow vigorously in our relatively mild, damp climate. The plants produce long heads of flowers and set abundant seed, seedlings appearing around the parent plants and often outside the confines of the garden. In this way, several species have become naturalised. The hybrid *Hebe × franciscana* is often planted in seaside towns because of its tolerance of salt-laden winds and it is now naturalised over miles of cliffs.

Above: An illustration of the diversity of colours and forms found among the speedwells if you examine them closely. Although many species are the familiar, characteristic blue, the flowers of others may range from almost white with lilac veins, to the red-eyed, bright blue flower of the rare rock speedwell. In some species the flowers are borne in long spikes, while in others they appear on single stems.

Above: Some speedwells favour watery habitats, growing by ponds and streams and in other wet places. The pink water speedwell (*Veronica catenata*) produces small spikes of pink flowers from June to August. The attractive brooklime (*Veronica beccabunga*), shown left, flowers in similar habitats from May to September. The lower part of its stem, often creeping, rooting and rather fleshy, may extend out into the open water and is sometimes partly submerged.

VETCHES: CLIMBING GRASSLAND PEAS

One of the most familiar sights of the summer along roadsides and on chalk grasslands are the small, brightly coloured, pea-like flowers of vetch, a group of mostly weak-stemmed climbers that hang on to neighbouring plants by means of long tendrils.

Right: The bitter vetch (*Vicia orobus*) is the only member of the true vetches to lack tendrils on the tips of its leaves. A rare species of meadow and scrubland, it flowers from June to September.

A great many plants share the common name of vetches but the true vetches, or tares as they are also known, belong to the genus *Vicia*. This genus belongs to the pea family, Leguminosae, as can be clearly seen from the structure of vetch flowers, which have the same petal arrangement as other pea flowers: a pair of petals called the wings sit below and to each side of the standard petals; below these is the keel, consisting of two petals partly joined together at the base. Concealed within this structure is the stigma, ten partially joined stamens and a nectary–the nectar-producing gland.

In vetches the flowers may be borne in clusters on a stem, in pairs, or on their own, and their colour varies from blue, through shades of red and purple, to yellow. Bees find the attractively coloured flowers, with their scent and sweet nectar, irresistible and land on the keel searching for the nectar. Their weight pushes down the keel, exposing the stamens and stigma, and pollen from the stamens is deposited on their backs. In turn, pollen from a previously visited vetch flower is transferred from the bees' bodies to the stigma, thus effecting pollination.

Robber insects Some insects, particularly a species of bumble bee called *Bombus terrestris*, adopt underhand methods of obtaining the flower's nectar. They alight on the stalk of the vetch and bore a hole in the base of the flower, through which they suck the nectar, thus obtaining the food without pollinating the flower.

Some species of vetch solve this problem by producing nectar both inside the flower and at the base of leaf-like appendages–the stipules –found on the stem. The latter are referred to as decoy nectaries and appear to the naked eye as black spots. Insects which would otherwise steal the floral nectar are attracted instead to the stipules' nectaries.

Leaf arrangement The leaf of a vetch consists of small leaflets arranged along each side of a central stalk–as they are on many pea plants. The number of leaflets on each leaf varies from species to species. The Bithynian vetch, for example, may have as few as one or two pairs to a leaf, while the tufted vetch may

Above: Being members of the pea family, all vetches and vetchlings bear fruits in the form of long narrow pods, which split open when mature to release the seeds. The fruits and flowers shown here are those of the meadow vetchling (*Lathyrus pratensis*).

Right: A red form of kidney vetch (*Anthyllis vulneraria*) found near the coast.

Opposite page: Tufted vetch (*Vicia cracca*) scrambling over a hedgerow.

have as many as a dozen pairs of leaflets.

Unlike many plants in the pea family, vetch leaves do not end in a single leaflet but in a modified leaf called a tendril, which many species use to cling on to other plants. However, there is an exception to the general rule–the bitter vetch, which lacks tendrils.

Vetch habitats Vetches can be found in a wide range of habitats, including woods, grassland, cliff tops, coastal sands and shingle. The majority, however, prefer sunny grassy places, such as roadside verges and south-facing chalk banks. In contrast, the Bithynian vetch and the yellow vetch are more or less confined to our southern coastline where they grow on cliffs; the yellow vetch, in particular, favours coastal shingle.

Two of the commonest species are tufted vetch and bush vetch. Both are perennials with flowers borne in clusters called racemes, appearing along wayside verges and hedgerows from June through to August. The tufted vetch sometimes has as many as 40 purplish-blue flowers in a cluster, while the purplish-pink flowers of the bush vetch are less profuse.

Despite its common name, the wood vetch can be found growing on shingle, but it mainly inhabits woods and also rocky places inland. This handsome perennial may bear as many as 18 flowers on a raceme, each being white and marked with attractive blue or purple veins.

Another species often found in rocky woods is the bitter vetch, a stout-stemmed perennial with between six and twenty flowers on each raceme. The flowers are similar to those of the wood vetch: white with purple veins.

The common vetch, despite its name, is not the most common member of this group

Above: A close-up view of the flowers of tufted vetch shows their similarity to others in the pea family, such as broom, gorse and bird's-foot trefoil.

Right: Yellow vetchling (*Lathyrus aphaca*) lacks true leaves, having instead broad enlarged stipules.

Below: Everlasting pea (*L. latifolius*) colonizing a railway embankment.

–though it is widespread–nor is it a native of Britain. It was introduced here as a fodder crop and is often seen naturalised in waste places and the margins of cultivated fields. Its small, pale purple flowers are usually borne in pairs in the leaf axils. At one time, the seeds were cultivated commercially and sold as food for poultry, doves and pigeons. Ironically, the common vetch is the only British plant in the genus that is at all poisonous, though curiously only the occasional plant is so.

Another species of *Vicia* widely cultivated for many centuries is the broad bean, or horse bean, whose large seeds are eaten as a vegetable. It occasionally escapes to the wild but rarely persists long enough to be considered naturalised in this country.

Annual tares Three closely related species of *Vicia* share the common name of tare: the hairy, smooth and slender tare. The last two are the most closely related of the three. Both have pale blue flowers, unbranched tendrils and relatively long leaves. They are found mainly in the south of Britain, the slender tare having a more local distribution and being most common in East Anglia.

The hairy tare is noticeably different from

the other two, with its dirty white to purplish flowers, shorter leaves and branched tendrils. It is often seen as a tangled mass in hedgerows and, as a rampant weed of cornfields, it used to be known as strangle tare. It has a scattered distribution throughout the British Isles, and is commoner in the south. The name 'hairy' tare comes from its downy pods.

Britain's vetchlings Among the closest relatives of the vetches are members of the genus *Lathyrus*, commonly known as vetchlings or peas. They are very similar to the true vetches, the two genera sometimes being difficult to distinguish, but they can usually be told apart by looking at the leaves and stems. Plants in the genus *Lathyrus* have, in most cases, fewer leaflets to a leaf and their stems have small wings running along the edges.

One of the most common and widespread species in this group is the meadow vetchling, a scrambling, climbing plant of hedgerows whose rich yellow flowers often cast a golden hue over country lanes and pastures during the summer months. But perhaps the most distinctive species is the yellow vetchling. This plant lacks true leaves; instead it has very large stipules shaped roughly like a spearhead. Yellow vetchling is fairly rare in Britain, largely because a great proportion of the young plants are killed by frosts during the winter. Not surprisingly, the species is most common in southernmost England.

Other vetches Finally, there are a few species that have the common name 'vetch', but do not belong to either of the genera *Vicia* or *Lathyrus*. One of the best-known of these is the kidney vetch, in the genus *Anthyllis*. This plant is easily recognised by its dense head of deep lemon-yellow flowers protruding above a ring of conspicuous white and woolly calyces. Kidney vetch is found throughout the British Isles, but it is more common on shallow calcareous soils, especially those near the sea.

The horseshoe vetch, in the genus *Hippocrepis*, has golden-yellow flowers borne on long-stalked heads. The pods have a curiously sinuous appearance and look like streamers blowing in the wind. They sometimes break

Above: With its white petals marked with purple or blue veins, wood vetch (*Vicia sylvatica*) is one of the most attractive plants in the pea family.

1 Hairy tare (*Vicia hirsuta*). Hedgerow plant flowering May to August.
2 Smooth tare (*Vicia tetrasperma*). Hedgerow plant flowering May to August.
3 Yellow vetch (*Vicia lutea*). Coastal species flowering from June to September.
4 Purple milk-vetch (*Astragalus danicus*). Grassland and dune plant flowering May to July.
5 Common vetch (*Vicia sativa*). Hedgerow and scrub plant flowering May to September.

up into horseshoe-shaped segments.

The milk-vetches belong to the genus *Astragalus*. The purple milk-vetch is one of the most attractive of this group, bearing deep purple flowers from May to July. It is confined to the eastern counties of England and Scotland, and occurs in just one locality in Ireland, the islands of Aran off the west coast.

A smaller and less attractive species is the alpine milk-vetch. This plant is extremely rare, being found only on a few Scottish mountains. It flowers in July, producing pale blue blooms.

Vetches and their allies

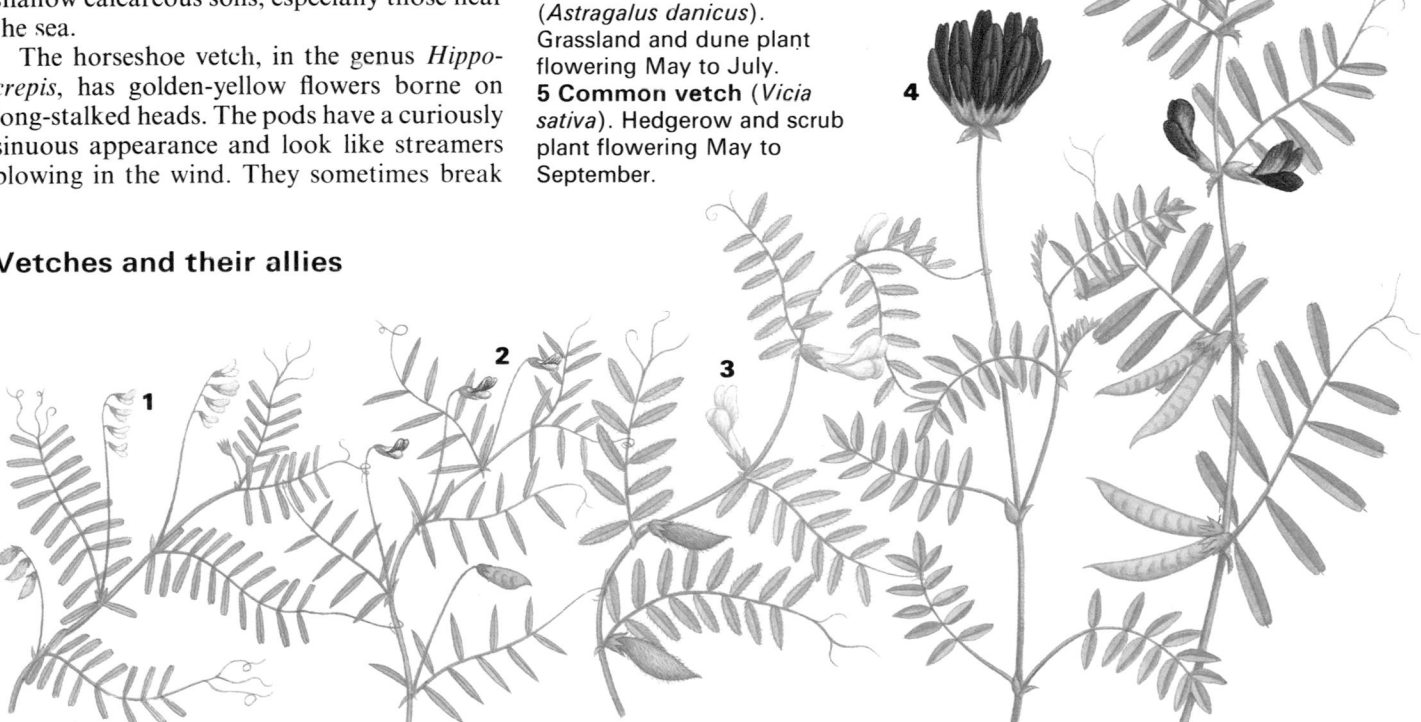

SUMMER ROSES OF HEDGES AND DUNES

Of our native wild roses, only the dog rose is at all well known to most people. Yet, there are three other species of rose to be seen in our hedgerows and another that has even become adapted to the seemingly hostile environment of sand dunes.

Opposite: A mixture of field roses (in the foreground) and sweet briars (behind) in flower on the Chiltern Hills. Both are common hedgerow plants in the south of England, though less so than the dog rose.

The dog rose is the most common of our native roses, being found in hedgerows and scrubland throughout England and Wales, but there are three other species of native rose that share a similar habitat. These are the field rose, the downy rose and the sweet briar. Of these, only the field rose is easily confused with the dog rose; the other two species are quite distinct.

The field rose Like the dog rose, the field rose is a climbing shrub covered with hooked thorns with which it anchors itself to supporting plants. Its leaves and flowers are also similar, each leaf consisting of five or seven oval toothed leaflets and each flower having five white petals with yellow stamens inside.

A close examination of a field rose, however, reveals several differences between it and a dog rose. First, its stems are purplish rather than the green colour typical of a dog rose stem. More important are the differences between the flowers. Field rose flowers are scentless and always white, whereas dog rose flowers are always scented and often pink. Field roses also come out later in the year than dog roses–in June instead of May–and they stay in flower longer into the summer.

Another difference between the two species may seem rather obscure but it provides an infallible guide. The difference is in the styles, to be found at the centre of the stamens. In a field rose they are united into a column

Left: **Field rose** (*Rosa arvensis*). Flowers in June.

Left: **Sweet briar** (*Rosa rubiginosa*). Flowers June-July.

that protrudes above the stamens, whereas in a mature dog rose (and on every other native rose) the styles are free.

The downy rose The most striking difference between the downy rose and the dog and field rose is that the former is a shrub, whereas the other two are both climbing roses. A closer look reveals another important difference, referred to in the name downy rose: its leaves are densely hairy on both sides. On the field and dog roses the upper leaf surfaces are smooth and shiny and the lower surfaces are hairy only on the veins. The leaves of the downy rose also have a more variable number of leaflets–between two and eight.

The thorns on the downy rose stick straight out from the sides of its erect green stems, which may grow up to 2m (6½ft) high. The pink or white flowers are scented and appear at the same time as those of the field rose. Otherwise, they are very similar to dog roses.

Botanists divide the downy rose into three subspecies. One has a similar distribution to the field rose, being common in hedgerows all over England and Wales, but rare in Scotland. The other two subspecies are the common wild roses of Scotland. They are found as far south as the Midlands and, locally, in Wales and Ireland.

The sweet briar Our third less common hedge rose is the sweet briar, sometimes called the eglantine. The name of this plant comes not from its flowers, which are scent-

Above: **Burnet rose**
(*Rosa pimpinellifolia*).
Flowers in May.

Above: **Downy
rose** (*Rosa
tomentosa*).
Flowers in June.

Left: The hip of a burnet
rose differs from other
rose hips in having long
sepals and being much
darker—reddish-purple when
young, becoming black at
maturity.

Below: The typical habitat
of a burnet rose is dry
open areas, such as this
limestone pavement in the
Burren, County Clare.

less, but from its sweet-smelling leaves. The lower surfaces of these are covered with glands that produce an aromatic oil. The fragrance is most noticeable immediately after rain has fallen, when it can be detected some distance away.

The sweet briar is the smallest of our hedgerow roses, with reddish arching stems covered with stiff thorns and stiff hairs. The leaves are hairless and divided into between two and eight leaflets. The pink flowers have the typical shape of a wild rose and appear in June and July.

Although the sweet briar can be seen in hedgerows it is more common in woodland, especially on chalk and limestone soils. It grows mostly in the south of England and Wales, is locally common in Ireland and rare in Scotland.

The burnet rose This is the odd one out among British roses, for it is found on sand dunes and similar dry open areas, rather than in hedgerows. It also has a very different growing habit from the other roses, forming extensive low-growing colonies, with stems branching from creeping shoots to reach no more than 1m (3ft) high.

The plant is named after the burnet saxifrage because of the similarity of the leaves. These consist of seven or nine hairless toothed leaflets. The stems are brown and bear a great many slender, sharply pointed thorns. In shape, the flowers of the burnet

Left: Field roses in full bloom. With its white petals and masses of yellow stamens, the field rose bears a close resemblance to the dog rose. Both are climbing hedgerow plants with hooked thorns, but the field rose is scentless, always white and flowers later in the year; the dog rose is sometimes pink and always scented.

Below: A cluster of ripe field rose hips. Hips are a characteristic feature of all rose species, but they are not true fruits. The fruits consist of small hard capsules called achenes that lie embedded in the fleshy pulp of the hip. Inside each achene is a single seed.

rose are similar to other wild roses but they are always borne singly, never in clusters, as sometimes happens on the other species. The flowers appear in May and are creamy-white or pinkish. The hips are unusual in being purplish-black, maturing to pure black.

Rose hips The multitudes of yellow stamens found in rose flowers of all species provide an abundance of pollen for insect visitors of all kinds. The flowers are followed by the fruits–the familiar rose hips. The hips are not, in fact, the true fruits; they are swollen fleshy receptacles. The true fruits lie clustered inside and consist of small dry capsules, each enclosing a single seed.

Rose hips are an important winter source of food for many birds and mammals, including blackbirds, thrushes, mice and voles. The seeds are distributed far and wide in bird droppings or partly eaten hips.

Roses in history Roses have long been important as emblems and in folklore, though most of this has been derived not from the native roses but from two foreign species introduced here by the Romans–the red rose and the damask rose. For example the red rose is the famous emblem of the House of Lancaster. The White Rose of York, however, is supposed to have been a hybrid between the dog rose, the field rose and the red rose. Again, it is the petals of the red rose and the damask rose, not our native species, that were used down the ages for making into potpourris and rose water, for the simple reason that they are much more fragrant.

None of our native roses is grown in gardens to any great extent, though the sweet briar is sometimes planted to make low-growing hedges. Yet, many of our modern hybrid roses owe part of their parentage to these species. The rose 'Frühlingsgold', for example, is a cross between one of the Hybrid Tea roses and the burnet rose.

Robin's pincushion

You may see a hedgerow rose with a moss-like ball of reddish-yellow strands on the stem. These balls are known as bedeguars or robin's pincushions and are galls formed around the larvae of a gall wasp, *Diplolepis rosae*. In spring the female wasp lays her eggs in the young leaf buds; when the grubs hatch, the gall begins to develop and becomes fully formed in July when the grubs have matured. Many other insects use these galls for shelter, among them parasites and another species of gall wasp. The galls were once ground into a powder and used to treat colic and kidney stones.

SPURRED SUMMER FLOWERS

The colourful and distinctive flowers of snapdragons and toadflaxes appear in summer in a variety of habitats, ranging from walls to sand dunes.

Snapdragons and toadflaxes belong to the figwort family where they form a group of genera, known as a tribe. They are distinguished from other figworts primarily by the way in which their seeds are released. Figworts have seed capsules which split downwards from the top to release their seeds, while the snapdragon tribe have capsules which open at the top with two or three circular pores.

There are about 300 species of the snapdragon tribe worldwide, most of them growing in the north temperate regions; the toadflaxes form the largest group within the tribe. Only a handful of species occur in the British Isles, and many of these have been introduced, either accidentally or deliberately as garden plants. They are, perhaps, most familiar from the characteristic way in which the flowers open when the sides of the flower tube are squeezed, snapping shut when released – hence the name snapdragon.

Seed statistics The seeds of snapdragons and toadflaxes are small, mostly less than 1mm in diameter, and they are released in a similar way to the 'pepper-pot' mechanism found in the poppy. When breezes buffet the plant, the seeds are shaken out a few at a time through the pores at the top of the capsule. They fall about a metre (39in) away although a strong wind, capable of picking up particles of dust and grit, can easily lift the seeds and disperse them over considerable distances.

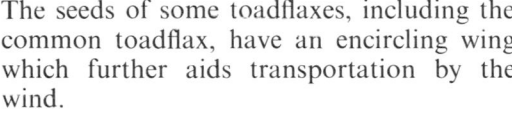

Above: The common snapdragon (*Antirrhinum majus*) often colonizes hot and dry places such as walls, derelict buildings, railway ballast and sand dunes.

Below: The deeply spurred flowers of the common toadflax (*Linaria vulgaris*) bloom from July to October.

The seeds of some toadflaxes, including the common toadflax, have an encircling wing which further aids transportation by the wind.

The seed production of many species is prodigious and it has been estimated that a single vigorous plant of the introduced purple toadflax can produce tens of thousands of seeds. Given these statistics it is not surprising that, once a toadflax finds a suitable habitat, colonization is rapid.

Garden escape The snapdragon must be one of the best known garden plants, cultivated for so long and naturalised in so many parts of the world that its origins are obscure. There are about 20 wild species of snapdragon or *Antirrhinum*, most of which grow in Spain or Portugal. In southern Europe, an old house bedecked with snapdragons is a common sight, for the walls of old buildings provide a similar habitat to the rock crevices where the wild plants are normally found. In Britain, it grows wild on walls and chalk cliffs in many parts of the country.

Bricks and stones The well-known ivy-leaved toadflax takes hold on walls in the same manner, particularly where the mortar is old

and crumbling. Although widespread, this species is not native, but was first recorded in Britain in 1640, having been introduced from further south in Europe.

As its name suggests, the leaves are lobed and stalked like those of ivy. The small purple or lilac flowers have a gold or yellow palate that presents a striking contrast. Each flower is borne at the base of a leaf, but when conditions are poor and the plant is starved, the flowers appear in clusters as in other toadflaxes. This species does not grow well when transferred to gardens – the attractive flowers are lost among straggling stems reaching up to 1m (39in) in length.

Dunes and sandy soils By way of contrast to the familiar snapdragon and ivy-leaved toadflax, some of the rarest species of the tribe are found on sand or sandy soils. One such species is the native Jersey toadflax, very much a rarity in the British Isles where it grows only on sandy soils in Jersey, although it is widespread in southern Europe and the Near East. An annual, it has small, violet flowers bearing a long, slender spur, and seeds that are unusual in that the wing is repeatedly divided to form an encircling fringe.

Two rare species are found on dunes and sandy soils in Devon and Cornwall. The sand toadflax is a small, sticky-leaved plant with tiny yellow flowers, and is probably an introduced species. Prostrate toadflax, larger, with hairless leaves and yellow flowers which

measure up to 15mm ($\frac{3}{5}$in), may be a native species.

Arable fields and waste ground On the light, often sandy, soils of waste ground and arable fields in southern England and Wales, our two very similar fluellen species can be found. These are sharp-leaved fluellen, which is slightly more common, and round-leaved fluellen. Both species have broad, stalked leaves, creeping stems and yellow flowers with a spur and a purple upper lip. Each of the two pores of the seed capsule opens by means of a circular lid, which drops off entirely as the capsule reaches maturity.

The small toadflax, an upright annual with tiny pale purple flowers, is also found in

Above: The ivy-leaved toadflax (*Cymbalaria muralis*) is well adapted to life on a wall. The flowers are held out from the foliage on long, slender stems so that they can be pollinated by insects. After pollination, the petals fall and the flower stalk curves away from the light, pushing the capsule into a dark crevice. The ripe seeds are shaken out of the top of the capsule. Their thick corky ridges wedge them firmly into crannies in the wall.

Toadflaxes and their seeds

1. Small toadflax (*Chaenorhinum minus*). Flowers May to October. Ht to 20cm (8in).

2. Weasel's snout (*Misopates orontium*). Flowers July to October. Ht to 30cm (11$\frac{3}{4}$in).

3. Prostrate toadflax (*Linaria supina*). Flowers June to September. Ht to 20cm (8in).

4. Sharp-leaved fluellen (*Kickxia elatine*). Flowers July to October. Length to 40cm (16in).

5. Sand toadflax (*Linaria arenaria*). Flowers May to September. Ht to 15cm (6in).

6. Jersey toadflax (*Linaria pelisseriana*). Flowers May to July. Ht to 30cm (11$\frac{3}{4}$in).

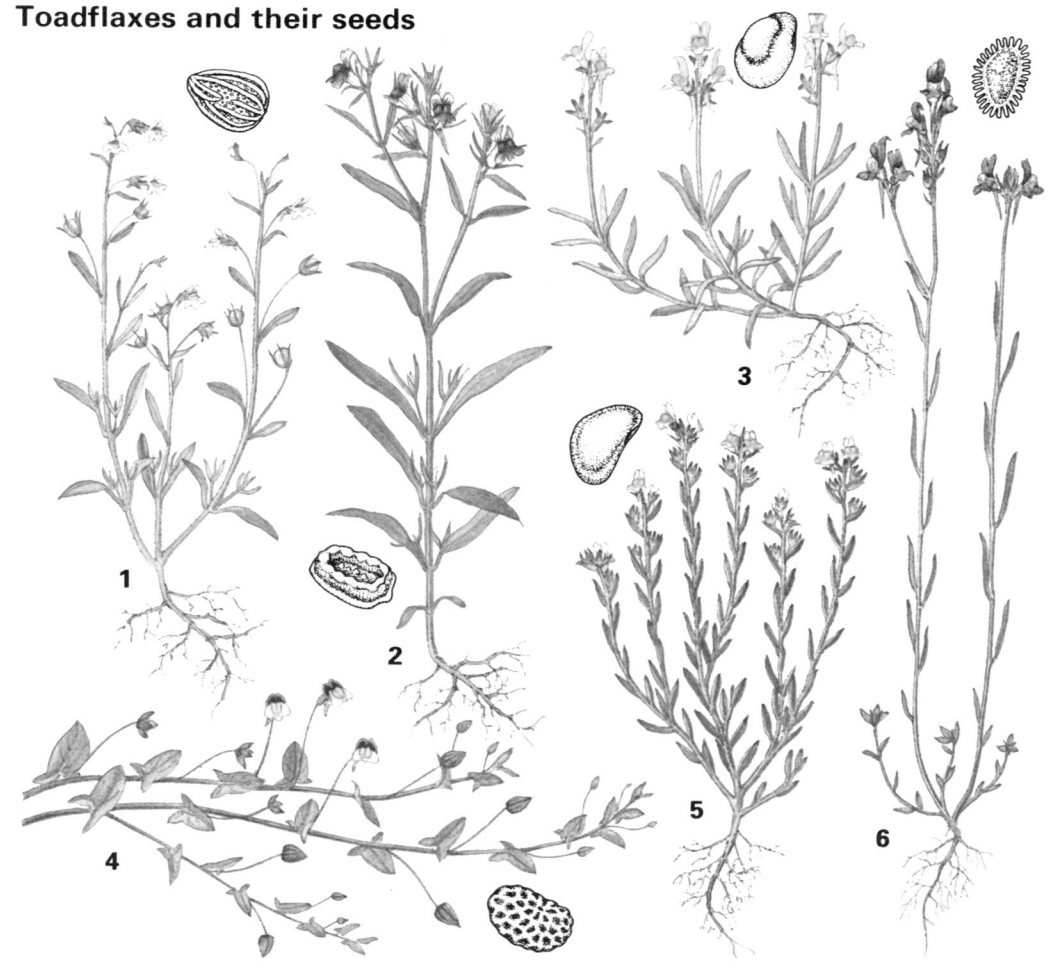

arable fields and on waste ground, although it is probably most characteristically seen growing in delicate masses on the ballast of railway embankments.

The weasel's snout, or calf's snout, is less common than the small toadflax. It is also a native species, and usually found on cultivated land. The flowers resemble those of the snapdragon, but are about half the size, dull pink, and partly concealed by the long lobes of the calyx.

Field margins and road verges Our two most familiar species of toadflax are often seen on field margins, where they occasionally grow together. Pale toadflax prefers lime-rich soils and is more or less restricted to the southern

Above: The more or less circular leaves of this round leaved fluellen (*Kickxia spuria*) distinguish it from the very similar sharp-leaved fluellen (*Kickxia elatine*) which has arrow-shaped or triangular leaves with pointed lobes at the base.

Below: The flowers of the pale toadflax (*Linaria repens*) are rather broad with a short, blunt spur. They are in bloom from June to September.

half of the British Isles. The rather small flowers, measuring up to 15mm ($\frac{3}{5}$in), are white or pale lilac with darker violet veins. The palate is sometimes yellow or orange and the spur is short and blunt.

As its name suggests, the common toadflax is by far the most widespread and abundant of the toadflaxes in Britain. It is found in moist, grassy places where, like the pale toadflax, it spreads by means of underground 'stems' called rhizomes. The yellow flowers measure up to 2.5cm (1in) long and have an orange palate with a long, broad, pointed spur. In common with most species of the tribe, the flowers of the common toadflax are pollinated by bees, and the complex flower structure ensures effective transfer of pollen from plant to plant.

In spite of this complex flower structure, and the normally discriminatory behaviour of bees, pollen of one species of toadflax is occasionally transferred to the flowers of another species. Under these circumstances, hybrids are produced, and it is not uncommon to find hybrids between the pale toadflax and the common toadflax. These have dull yellow flowers, veined with violet, and appear intermediate between the parent species in other respects. Since the hybrid is partly fertile, it can hybridise again with either parent to produce a considerable range of variable plants between the two species, with widely differing colours and forms.

Inside a toadflax flower

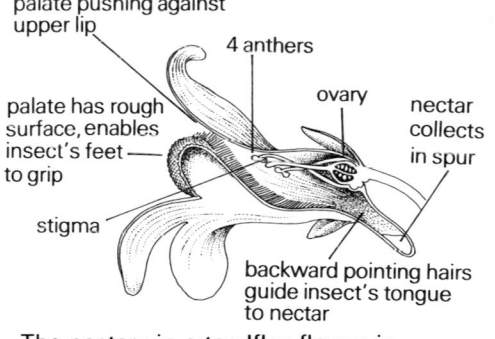

mouth of tube closed by palate pushing against upper lip

4 anthers

ovary

nectar collects in spur

palate has rough surface, enables insect's feet to grip

stigma

backward pointing hairs guide insect's tongue to nectar

The nectary in a toadflax flower is beneath the ovary, and secretes nectar into the spur. Bees are attracted to the brightly coloured flowers and are directed to the mouth of the tube by the contrastingly coloured palate, or coloured veins in the case of the pale toadflax. The bee lands on the palate, which forms an excellent landing platform, and the weight of the insect causes the palate to spring open, revealing the mouth of the tube. The bee forces its head into the tube and probes for nectar in the spur with its long tongue. The stigma brushes against the bee's head and thorax and any pollen from a previous visit to a toadflax is transferred, while the anthers dust the bee with fresh pollen.

COLOURFUL PLANTS OF LATE SUMMER

As summer draws to a close there are numerous species of flowering plants which still provide a marvellous array of colours. Some, like the autumnal crocus, are rare and you have to look hard for them in the grass; others, such as members of the daisy family, are tall and widespread.

Opposite: **Autumnal crocus** (*Crocus nudiflorus*) flowers Sept-Oct in damp meadows, woods. Rare in the wild. Ht 10cm (4in).

Several native or introduced species which were grown in cottage gardens for their supposed medicinal properties have escaped from cultivation and become naturalised. Others have become so invasive that they are classed as weeds, and are no longer welcomed in the garden. Many, like nipplewort and groundsel, have gained wide distribution, and they bloom over a long period.

The large bindweed or bellbine is a vigorous climber which is native in Europe and North America. It twines in an anticlockwise direction, and in warm sunny weather it can make a complete revolution of its support in as little as two hours. Where there is no support, the stems twine round one another to form a thick rope-like structure. The smooth stems are angled.

The dark green leaves, often with a bluish tinge, are large and roughly heart-shaped and borne on long stalks. The handsome white trumpet-like flowers are about 7cm (3in) wide, making them one of the largest of all British wild flowers. They sometimes have pale pink stripes.

Like native bindweed or cornbine, large bindweed does not set seed easily, but reproduces readily by vegetative means. Once it has become established, it is difficult to eradicate.

Feverfew is a tall perennial herb with yellowish-green pinnate leaves which have deeply cut segments. The white, daisy-like flowers have numerous yellow disc florets.

Feverfew is a medicinal plant. An infusion of the strongly scented leaves was believed to banish fevers and headaches— hence its common name. A native of Europe, it is also a herb garden escape. Both double and single forms are grown in gardens, and the dwarf golden form is used for edging flower beds. The seedlings are so prolific that it is also a difficult species to eradicate once

Above: **Large bindweed** (*Calystegia silvatica*) flowers July-Sept in hedges, thickets and on waste ground. Climbs several metres.

Right: Common ragwort is a troublesome species on agricultural land. An average-sized plant can produce 50,000 seeds, 80% of which will germinate.

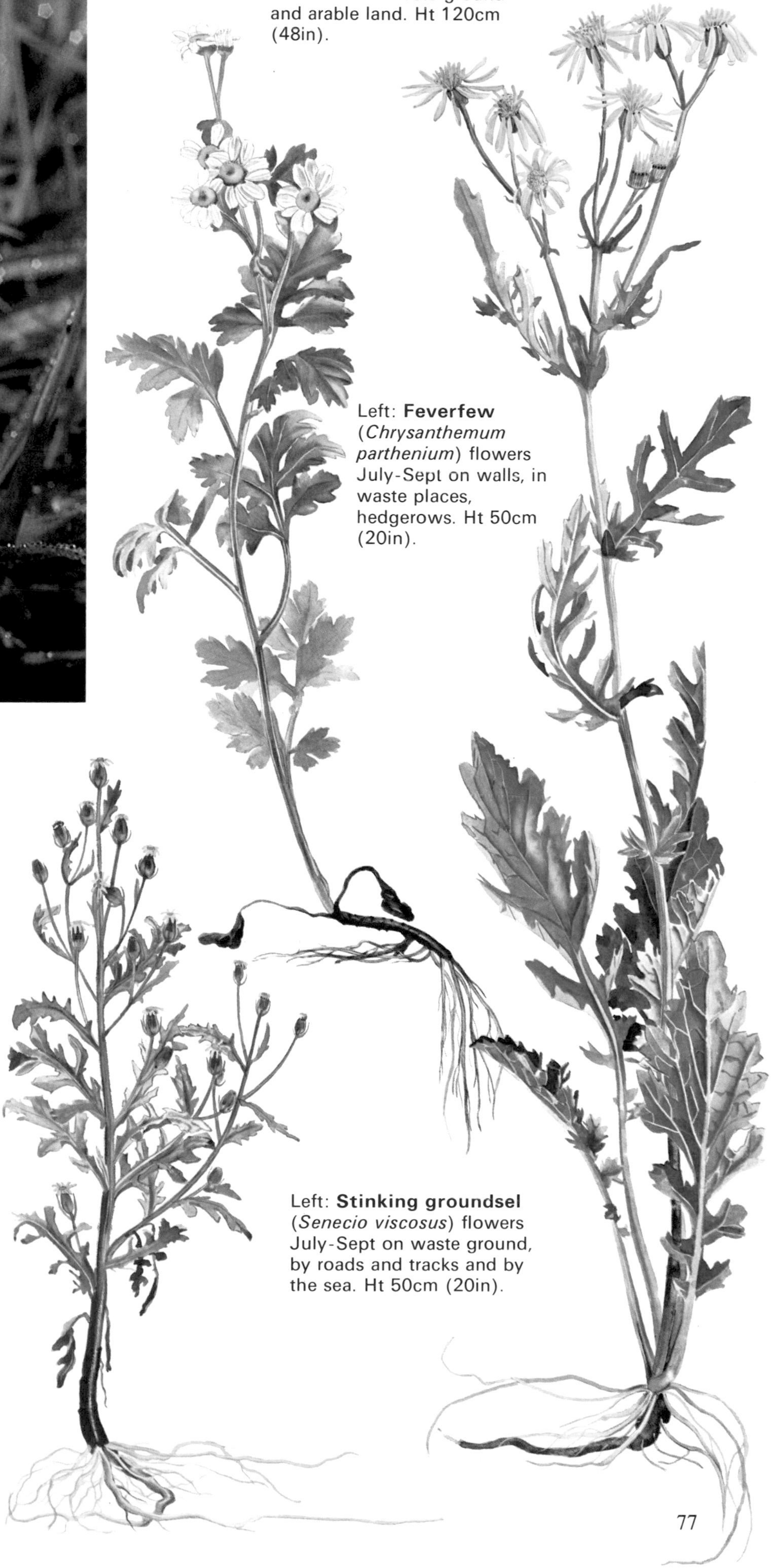

Right: **Common ragwort**
(*Senecio jacobaea*) flowers
June-Oct on waste ground
and arable land. Ht 120cm
(48in).

Left: **Feverfew**
(*Chrysanthemum
parthenium*) flowers
July-Sept on walls, in
waste places,
hedgerows. Ht 50cm
(20in).

Left: **Stinking groundsel**
(*Senecio viscosus*) flowers
July-Sept on waste ground,
by roads and tracks and by
the sea. Ht 50cm (20in).

it is established.

The autumnal crocus, or naked autumn crocus as it is sometimes known, is a native species of north-west France and Spain. It grows best in dampish areas of gardens but it is naturalised in a few local districts where it may be quite prolific. The three to five strap-like leaves appear in spring but die down by the time the beautiful flowers emerge in autumn. This species is often confused with the meadow saffron or autumn crocus (*Colchicum autumnale*), but you can distinguish the two by the number of their stamens. The autumnal crocus has three stamens and the meadow saffron six.

Stinking groundsel was first sighted in the Isle of Ely in the 17th century and is now a widespread species. Although it is similar to the common groundsel, this south European native does have distinguishing characteristics. The general stickiness of the plant comes from the many glandular hairs—hence another of its common names, sticky groundsel.

The yellow ray flowers usually have about 13 petals which bend back as the flower develops. It has been estimated that each flower head contains about 70 seeds, and so the average annual production by one plant over its long flowering period is potentially colossal. However, many of the seeds formed at the end of the season are often sterile.

Common ragwort, like Oxford ragwort, is a

weed of waste ground and over-grazed pastures. It is taller than the Oxford rag-wort, the bracts are brown-tipped rather than black-tipped, and the leaves are a greyer green and very divided. It is a particularly attractive species to bees because of its copious supply of nectar and pollen. The whole plant is bitter and contains a poison; if animals eat too much of it, they can eventually die. Yet it is a popular food of the cinnabar moth.

Nipplewort was once thought to have medicinal properties that cured sore nipples, but now it is simply regarded as a weed. A much-branched annual, its slightly hairy lower leaves are rounded with a few small lobes along the stems, whereas the upper leaves are much narrower and entire. The small yellow flowers look rather like dandelion blooms. They open early in the morning and close before noon; on very dull days, however, they do not open at all.

Fool's parsley is an annual species with dark green leaves that are very like those of parsley; when rubbed, the leaves and stems give off an acrid smell. All parts of the species are poisonous, and illness can be caused if it is eaten in mistake for parsley—hence its common name. The small white flowers are borne in an umbel. The bracts under the smaller umbels point downwards, so making them a distinctive feature. The smooth oval fruits are green.

Above and left: **Nipplewort** (*Lapsana communis*) flowers July-Sept in hedgerows, waste places, at the edges of woods and on walls. The tightly closed buds resemble nipples and their appearance led people to believe that the species could cure sore nipples. Ht 60cm (24in).

strongly ribbed fruits

bracts

infructescence of fool's parsley

Above right: **Fool's parsley** (*Aethusa cynapium*) flowers July-Aug on cultivated ground. Ht 50cm (20in).

Above: Feverfew flowers in profusion in the summer and is especially common on walls. It was thought to be a particularly effective cure for feminine ailments.

SUMMER FLYING HAIRSTREAKS

The hairstreaks, among the most attractive of our butterflies, are small and swift-flying but rather fragile in appearance. As many of them fly in woodland, sometimes around the tree tops, even the more common species can be hard to spot.

Above: Although the green hairstreak (*Callophrys rubi*) is the most common of the British hairstreaks it is perhaps the least typical of the group. It lacks the 'tails' of the hind wings and the 'hairstreak' itself is represented by a series of white dots, or may even be absent. The green coloration is limited to the underwings in both sexes, the upper wings being dark brown. The wings are fragile and become tattered after a few days of flying.

Hairstreak butterflies belong to the Lycaenidae, so are closely related to the blues and coppers, the other members of this large family. There are five British species – the black, the white-letter, brown, purple and green hairstreaks. They are usually characterised by their 'tailed' hind wings (which are highly developed in some of the exotic species), and by the hair-like streaking on the underside of their wings which gives them their common name. Their underwings are often more attractively coloured than the upper wings, especially in the case of the brown and green hairstreaks.

Restricted range The black hairstreak is locally common in only a very limited region of the English Midlands, an extreme localisation that has an interesting background. The species is widespread on the European mainland, but absent from north-west France and the Low Countries. Curiously, the transverse band of remnant forest inhabited by the black hairstreak – extending north-east from Oxford almost to the Wash – appears to be a continuation of a broader band of distribution running south-west to north-east through central Denmark and the extreme south of Sweden.

The black hairstreak is clearly on the edge of its European range in these countries and probably once occurred throughout the surrounding areas during a warmer climatic period, long ago. When the climate subsequently deteriorated, isolated populations of the black hairstreak presumably survived by adapting to the environmental conditions; it is possible that these populations were established during the latter stages of the last Ice Age.

Despite the very restricted range of the black hairstreak in Britain, its larval food plant – blackthorn – can be found growing almost everywhere. The caterpillars are usually found only in old blackthorn thickets along woodland borders and rides, and in clearings. The butterflies, which appear on the wing in June and July, feed on the flowers of dogwood and wild privet.

Elm-dwelling species The white-letter hair-

Brown hairstreak
(Thecla betulae)

Right: The male brown hairstreak is smaller than the female (above), and lacks the bold patches of orange she has on her forewings. Both sexes have tawny-orange undersides.

Above: The purple hairstreak (*Quercusia quercus*) is easily identified by its coloration but, as it generally swarms around the tops of oak trees, it is rarely seen. The blackish forewings are shot with a purple iridescence which is brighter in the female (shown here), but confined to large patches on her forewings. The amount of purple visible depends on the angle of the wings to the light, and the position of the observer.

nectar, and lime for its abundant honeydew, which is also a source of nourishment.

Secretive brown hairstreak The largest of our hairstreak species, the brown hairstreak is locally plentiful over most of southern England and Wales, but rarely seen. It also occurs in Ireland where it is very rare and confined to a few localities in the south-west.

The tawny-orange undersides of both sexes of the brown hairstreak readily distinguish them from other British hairstreaks, with the possible exception of the black hairstreak which is, however, a darker orange-brown with black-spotted bands on the hind wings.

Brown hairstreaks tend to hide among blackthorn thickets (their larval foodplant), only flying when the weather is bright, and then usually high up. They can occasionally be observed feeding at the flowers of brambles and other plants in August and September– particularly in the latter month when they fly along woodland borders and thick, old hedgerows.

Oak tree dweller Purple hairstreaks are locally common wherever oaks grow, except in northern Scotland and Northern Ireland. They fly in July and August, but as they often swarm around the tops of their larval food plant, the oak, or sometimes other trees, they can be difficult to spot. When they are seen, feeding on the honeydew that accumulates on the foliage of such trees, they are easy to identify because of the purple iridescence on the blackish forewings.

Unusual hairstreak The green hairstreak is generally common throughout the British Isles and is immediately identifiable by the green colouring of its underwings. This brilliant colour–unusual among butterflies– is not due to pigmentation, but to the special structure and arrangement of the scales. Green hairstreaks are also unusual in lacking the characteristic 'tailed' hind wings of the other hairstreak species.

They are on the wing in May and June– rather earlier than the other species–and frequent a greater range of habitats, from woodland edges and scrub to downland and heathland wherever some of their food plants are present. These are numerous and include

streak is common but localised throughout most of southern England and Wales. Since 1900 its range has contracted southwards from North Yorkshire to a present-day line from Cheshire to The Wash.

It is a drab butterfly, apart from the distinct white 'W' mark on each hind wing, and is generally found in woods and hedgerows where the larvae feed on species of elm–the wych elm in particular. There are fears that the ravages of Dutch elm disease will have adverse effects on its present distribution, but so far there is little clear evidence of this taking place. In June and July, the butterflies can be seen around elm trees, and visiting the blossoms of bramble, privet and buddleia for

Hairstreaks with false heads

Hairstreak butterflies have evolved an ingenious device to deflect the surprise attacks of predators from their head. When they are at rest with their wings closed, the characteristic 'tails' of the hind wings, combined with the adjacent eye-like spots or markings, look remarkably like a conspicuous head with antennae and are thus more likely to attract an attack than the real head, but with less harmful results.

Some of the more exotic species may also turn around on alighting. Therefore, if a predator notices one arrive and launches an attack, it is additionally confused by its victim flying off in an unexpected direction. All British hairstreaks, save the green hairstreak, possess false heads but they are convincing to our eyes only in the purple, (right), and black hairstreaks.

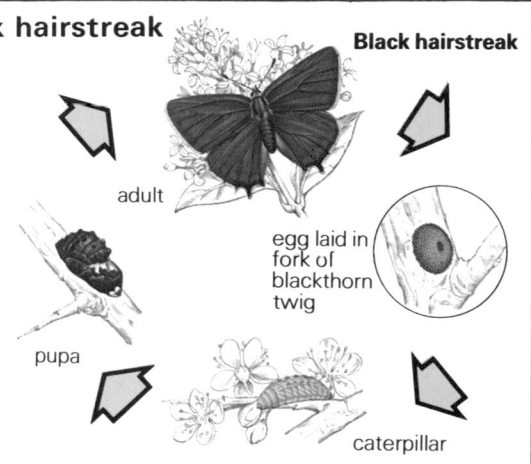
broom, gorse, dogwood, bramble, heather, bird's-foot trefoil and rock rose.

Cannibalistic caterpillars The green hairstreak is not only different in appearance from the other species, its life-cycle is also different. While the other hairstreaks hibernate in the egg-stage, the greenish eggs of the green hairstreak hatch about a week after being laid, in June or July. The resulting pale green caterpillars, striped with yellow, feed until ready to pupate in late July or early August. The entire autumn and winter is then passed in the pupal stage, lying amid the leaf litter on the surface of the ground.

After they have moulted their skins for the first time, the caterpillars of the green hairstreak are noted for their ferocious cannibalism—a characteristic they share with several other species of lycaenid butterfly. Black hairstreak caterpillars in captivity have also proved to be cannibalistic.

Hairstreak life-cycle The other four hairstreak species spend the winter as eggs, which are deposited singly on the twigs of food plants. The eggs vary in colour, from white in the brown and purple hairstreaks, to pale brown ones which turn grey later in the case of the black hairstreak.

The full grown caterpillars, hatching in spring, resemble woodlice; they are predominantly green apart from the purple hairstreak caterpillar which is chestnut-brown. They feed on or within the buds of their food plants, later switching to the flowers or leaves when these develop. The caterpillars of the green and white-letter hairstreaks possess honey glands, the sweet secretions of which are attractive to ants who, in consequence, guard them against potential predators.

With the exception of the green hairstreak, all the caterpillars may be found feeding from April to June, before they pupate. The pupae, which are shaped like tiny, trussed chickens, are brown with darker markings (apart from the black hairstreak pupae which are black and white and resemble bird-droppings). They are generally attached to the twigs or leaves of the food plants by silken pads and girdles, although the brown hairstreak is held by the half-discarded larval

skin, and the purple hairstreak often lies in oak bark crevices or on the ground among fallen leaves. Apart from the green hairstreak, which overwinters as a pupa, the butterflies usually emerge from the pupal case in three to four weeks. Late summer is the best time to look for most of the species as they fly among the woodland trees.

Above: The white-letter hairstreak (*Strymonidia w-album*) takes its name from the pronounced white 'W'-shaped streak on the underside of each hind wing. It bears a striking resemblance to the black hairstreak although this species has orange blotches on the margins of the upper wings, and a more indistinct 'W' mark. The black hairstreak is further distinguished by its lighter underwings, which may be almost orange in colour, and the row of white-edged, black spots on the inner side of the orange marginal band.

Above left: The eggs of the white-letter are laid singly on twigs of the food plant. They are green with a white rim, the green turning brown after a few days.

BUTTERFLY MIGRANTS

Some butterflies seen regularly in Britain cannot survive our winter, so their appearance here is dependent upon migration from their main breeding areas in the Mediterranean region.

The most regular of the migrant butterflies to reach Britain are the red admiral, painted lady, clouded yellow, pale clouded yellow and Berger's clouded yellow, but a number of other species, including the Continental race of the swallowtail, the Bath white, Queen of Spain fritillary, long-tailed blue and short-tailed blue, reach our shores from time to time. Moreover, some of our resident species, such as the large, small and green-veined whites, peacock and small tortoiseshell, are supplemented by considerable influxes from the European mainland.

A familiar threesome The most commonly seen of the migrants are the red admiral, painted lady and clouded yellow. All three arrive in southern England in the spring and early summer. They lay eggs which give rise to a British-bred summer generation of butterflies; these fly until the onset of prolonged cold weather in the autumn causes them to disappear.

Until comparatively recently it was believed that the vast majority eventually died, only a few red admirals managing to hibernate. Now, however, there is some evidence that many of them fly south in the same way as do those birds which are summer visitors to Britain. The essential difference is that these butterflies which return south are not the same individuals which reached Britain in spring, but their offspring. With our summer migrant birds, of course, the surviving parents as well as their progeny make the return migration. By migrating south, these British-

Above: A red admiral butterfly on ivy. Some seem to be able to hibernate through a British winter in the adult state. Fully proven records are few, but an analysis published in 1972 by Dr Robin Baker showed that there is sufficient evidence to conclude that hibernating red admirals could be overlooked because the sites they choose – high up in trees, either exposed on the trunks or hidden among dead leaves and ivy – are not well known. Dr Baker has even argued that red admirals are probably mainly resident in the British Isles; but most entomologists still believe it most unlikely that this butterfly could perpetuate itself here indefinitely by this means and without immigration.

Above: A painted lady butterfly feeding on a knapweed. The sexes are similar except that the males are slightly smaller and have more pointed wings than the females.

Right: When the painted lady emerges from its chrysalis, it is suffused with a lovely pink tinge which, unfortunately, it soon loses.

bred butterflies would be able to continue breeding successfully, thus making the migratory habit thoroughly worthwhile for guaranteeing the survival of the species.

It is well worthwhile looking for these return migrations in favourable locations, such as the southern coasts or islands of Britain, or from the shores of inland lakes or broad rivers where the butterflies are not deflected from their migratory path by trees, hills, buildings or the need to refuel with nectar from flowers. But even in less favourable places inland, such movements can be looked for. North-south aligned valleys in hill and mountain ranges are other possible places where migrations, not unlike those seen on a huge scale through the high passes of the Alps and Pyrenees, may be seen.

The existence of a partial return autumn flight in migrant butterflies and other insects proves that the regular movements of these species are true migrations of biological value to the individuals that perform them, and not simply overflows due to overcrowding and food shortage in their normal breeding area. Otherwise the offspring that hatch in Britain would fail to breed and therefore be wasted. It also explains the persistence of the migratory habit in the absence of such overcrowding.

Fluctuating numbers The number of red admirals, painted ladies and clouded yellows arriving here each spring varies a great deal, especially those of the last two; in some years they may be abundant, in others quite rare. In a bad year those that do arrive may not penetrate much beyond the southernmost counties of England; but, in a good year, they and their offspring may be seen all over the British Isles, even in the far north. This was true of the exceptionally good year of 1947, the like of which has not occurred since. In that year some 12,000 painted ladies, 13,000 red admirals and 36,000 clouded yellows were counted by entomologists alone – and they must have missed many more! One day that October an observer on a ship in the English Channel estimated more than 100,000 clouded yellows flying south-south-west on a 50-mile front. Another observer

Below: **Clouded yellow** (*Colias crocea*) butterfly, caterpillar and egg. The wingspan of the adult is 4.5-5.5cm (1¾-2in).

Above: **Red admiral** (*Vanessa atalanta*) butterfly, egg and caterpillar. The adult has a wingspan of about 5.5-6.5cm (2-2½in).

Above: **Painted lady** (*Cynthia cardui*) butterfly, caterpillar and egg. Adult 5.5-6cm (2-2⅓in).

Migration route

Above: The main breeding area of migrant butterflies is in the Mediterranean region. The adults fly up through Europe across a broad front, and arrive in Britain by May or June.
Below: A clouded yellow butterfly. A white or pale yellow form of the female, known as *helice*, is quite common and can be mistaken for the pale clouded yellow or Berger's clouded yellow—both rarities—which are far less heavily marked with black on the hindwings.

remembers seeing fields in Kent almost yellow with butterflies that passed in a constant procession under his classroom windows throughout the summer.

In these good years, exceptional population explosions seem to occur in the butterflies' chief breeding grounds around the Mediterranean, where all three species produce a series of broods throughout the year. As a result, many more migrate than usual to find suitable breeding places elsewhere. The search for nectar by these highly active butterflies may be one of the chief stimuli for them to migrate: hot, dry weather in particular may so parch the flowers on their home ground that nectar is in short supply, especially when their numbers are high, and so they are obliged to seek it further afield. They are more likely to find abundant flowers to the north than to the south where deserts prevail.

Sometimes conditions in the Mediterranean region cause these butterflies to appear in northern Europe, including Britain, at unseasonal times of the year. This most often happens with the painted lady which, incidentally, is one of the most widely distributed butterflies in the world. For example, in 1952 painted ladies arrived as early as the beginning of February and on through March in considerable quantity. Similarly, some painted ladies appeared in England early in March 1977, along with some moths from the western end of the Mediterranean. On this

occasion, their arrival was correlated with a very warm southerly airstream over northwest Africa and western Iberia which reached southern England on March 2nd.

Some individuals of all three species migrate every year. How they normally find their way is not yet fully understood, but there is some evidence that they can orientate by the position of the sun and make adjustments for the wind's direction and speed. But like birds, they can be temporarily swept off their normal path by abnormal weather situations and their associated wind systems. This can lead to some butterflies turning up in unexpected places, and can account for the appearance of a rare species.

Life cycles However they get here, the migrant butterflies fly actively in search of nectar and the right foodplants on which to lay their eggs. They are not restricted to any particular habitats, so can be found feeding at flowers almost anywhere from a city park or garden to open moorland. If you want to observe these butterflies on your garden, the best plant to attract them is the sweet-scented buddleia—justly known as the 'butterfly bush'.

However, the places where they can breed are more limited: female painted ladies deposit their eggs on thistles and sometimes on stinging nettles, burdock and a few other plants; red admirals on stinging nettles; and clouded yellows on various leguminous plants, especially clovers and lucerne.

On emerging from their green eggs, which are laid singly, each spiny, greyish-coloured painted lady caterpillar draws together a leaf with silk and feeds concealed within its shelter. When full-grown, the caterpillars form 'tents' by spinning the surrounding leaves together and, suspended upside down from a silk pad, change into greyish chrysalids spangled with silver or gold. They emerge about two weeks later.

Red admiral females also lay green eggs singly on the leaves of the foodplant and their caterpillars feed and pupate in silk shelters spun among the leaves, like those of the painted lady. Similarly, their reddish-brown chrysalids are spangled or studded with metallic gold spots and the butterflies emerge from them in about a fortnight. Although the females tend to be slightly larger, the sexes look alike.

When first laid, the eggs of the clouded yellow butterfly are pale yellow, but they soon turn to orange. They are also laid singly or in small batches on the upper leaf surface of the foodplant. The well-camouflaged, velvety-looking green caterpillars feed quite openly on the foodplant on which they also pupate. The yellowish-green chrysalis is attached to a stem by a silk girdle and resembles a withered leaf. Late caterpillars and chrysalids perish during the winter; otherwise the butterflies usually emerge from the earlier chrysalids in August.

COLONIAL MOTHS

Burnet and forester moths, day-flying colony dwellers, spend the winter as young caterpillars. They hatch in summer and feed until the approaching winter impels them to hibernate.

Burnets and foresters belong to a primitive family of day-flying moths, the Zygaenidae, and are notable for their sluggish and colonial habits. Being so sluggish, they are sedentary, rarely flying far from their haunts. The glossy, iridescent green or blue-black burnet moths, brightly spotted with crimson, are easily distinguished from the generally smaller, fragile-looking foresters which have uniform, brilliant metallic green forewings and smoky grey hind wings.

The burnets can be seen in their hundreds, swarming on the red or purple blossoms of knapweeds, scabiouses and thistles, usually in open, grassy countryside, but fairly often in woodland clearings and rides as well. You

Below: The six-spot burnet (*Zygaena filipendulae*), with a wingspan of 5cm (2in), is the commonest and most widespread of the seven burnet moths that occur in the British Isles. It can be found flying on sunny days from June to August. Like all burnets, it flies rather heavily but deceptively fast, appearing in a whirr of crimson as its hind wings come into play. It loves flower-filled, grassy places, where it lives in very large colonies.

may sometimes come across four or five crowded together on a single large flowerhead, all busily imbibing the nectar.

Brilliantly spotted burnets The six-spot burnet is the commonest of the seven species occurring in the British Isles. It lives in large colonies in flower-filled, grassy areas and can be identified by the six conspicuous crimson spots on each forewing.

The number of spots on its wings clearly distinguish the six-spot from the five-spot burnets, the two commonest of which are the very similar broad-bordered and the narrow-bordered. The narrow-bordered five-spot burnet can generally be distinguished from the broad-bordered by the two central spots on its forewings. If these are joined together, it is the broad-bordered; if they are clearly separated, it is the narrow-bordered. Unfortunately, the frequency of variation in these species, especially the broad-bordered, often complicates identification. Sometimes specimens can be found in which some, or all, of the spots are united, and others where the red colour is replaced by yellow or orange.

The broad-bordered five-spot burnet is not as widespread as the six-spot, but is locally common over much of England and Wales and also in the Isle of Man. Two distinct subspecies are found in Britain: *palustrella* flies in May and June on downland, whereas the larger *decreta* appears on the wing in late July and August and frequents marshland. *Decreta* caterpillars feed on greater bird's-foot trefoil, and construct cocoons high up on grass stems (presumably as a protection against flooding); those of *palustrella*, on the other hand, feed on common bird's-foot trefoil and pupate low down.

The narrow-bordered five-spot burnet, which usually spins its cocoon fairly high up on grass stems, is also locally common in England and Wales, as well as in the western parts of Scotland and the northern half of Ireland. The transparent burnet, which flies in June, is locally common in Ireland, Wales and Scotland; it has streaked rather than spotted wings. The other burnet species in the British Isles—the mountain, slender Scotch

and New Forest—are all rather rare.

Forest-green moths All three of our forester moths—the common, scarce and cistus—are on the wing in June and July, and some occasionally appear before the end of May. They can be found feeding in the sunshine on scabiouses and thistles, though the common forester seems to prefer ragged robin to all other plants. The scarce forester is particularly partial to the blossoms of salad burnet, one of the characteristic plants of its very localised haunts on the chalk downs of Kent, Sussex, Gloucestershire and Wiltshire.

The cistus forester is also very local, being confined to calcareous soils, mostly on hillsides in England and Wales as far

Above: Newly emerged six-spot burnet moths mating. When the moth is ready to emerge from its pupa, it forces its way up through the weak upper end of the cocoon and breaks out of the protruding pupa case, finally climbing higher up the stem to expand and dry its wings. Here you can see the black pupa case projecting from the papery white cocoon.

Left: A pair of short, plump six-spot burnet caterpillars.

Narrow-bordered five-spot burnet (*Zygaena lonicerae*).

Broad-bordered five-spot burnet (*Zygaena trifolii*); wingspan 3cm (1¼in).

Poisonous protection

If a predator, such as a bird, attacks a burnet, the moth exudes both a strong-smelling colourless fluid and a greenish-yellow one from its thoracic glands; the latter fluid contains histamine and the extremely poisonous hydrocyanic acid. As soon as it tastes these highly unpalatable substances, the predator rejects the moth at once and does not readily forget the distinctive red and black pattern of the insect that contained them. In future the predator will avoid all burnet moths and probably other red and black insects too.

Curiously, although moth collectors had long known that burnet moths were remarkably resistant to the fumes of their cyanide killing bottles, it was only fairly recently that they found the moths' poison was hydrogen cyanide. All stages of the moth contain the poison, from the egg to the perfect insect. Fortunately, not enough poison is released to harm a bird seriously, much less a human being. Forester moths are also protected in this way.

Cistus forester moth (*Adscita geryon*) and its caterpillar, which feeds only on common rockrose.

Left: Common forester moth (*Adscita statices*); the female of this species is slightly smaller than the male, which has a wingspan of 2.8cm (1⅛in).
It is not easy to separate the three British foresters. The common species is much larger than the cistus (*Adscita geryon*), which has a wingspan of 2·5cm (1in). The male scarce forester (*Adscita globulariae*) is as large as the common, but its antennae are pointed at the tip, not thickened. Female scarce foresters, with a wingspan of 2·2cm (⅞in), are considerably smaller than female common foresters, though slightly larger than the diminutive females of the cistus.

Below: Transparent burnet (*Zygaena purpuralis*). The caterpillars of this species, unlike those of most other burnets, feed chiefly on burnet saxifrage and wild thyme.

north as Durham, Lancashire and Yorkshire. In such places the moths fly on sunny, south-facing slopes where the smaller females seek out patches of common rockrose on which to deposit their eggs.

The common forester, although also local, is much more widely distributed in the British Isles. It can be found in many districts, especially in the south where it frequents meadows, downland, heaths and woodland clearings.

Overwintering caterpillars Burnets and foresters overwinter as caterpillars. They hatch from yellow eggs laid in the summer and feed until the approach of winter, then hibernate low down at the bases of their food plants and in nearby vegetation. The warm days of spring cause them to awaken and resume feeding on the fresh leaves of their food plants until they are fully grown and ready to pupate.

They are all fairly similar in appearance, being rather short and plump, and marked with rows of black spots and blotches. Those of the burnets, and the scarce forester, are green or greenish-yellow, while the caterpillars of the other two forester species are whitish. All species are fairly hairy, short hairs arising from the black or dark spots.

The caterpillars of five of our seven species of burnets normally feed on various leguminous plants, especially bird's-foot trefoil. The transparent burnet, however, feeds mainly on burnet saxifrage and wild thyme, and the mountain burnet almost exclusively on crowberry. The foresters, as a group, are rather more choosy. The caterpillars of the common forester feed on both common and sheep's sorrel, the cistus only on common rockrose and the scarce forester on greater and lesser knapweeds. When very young, the forester caterpillars feed between the upper and lower epidermal cell layers of the leaves. Later they consume only the lower cell layers, so that the attacked leaves take on a transparent appearance. When nearly full grown, the caterpillars dispense with the shelter provided by the upper layer and devour the whole leaf.

Spring-time pupation When fully fed and ready to pupate, usually in May in most species, the caterpillars spin somewhat boat-shaped cocoons. The foresters weave their strong, silken cocoons on their food plants and, when they are complete, change within them to shiny, olive-coloured pupae. The caterpillars of most burnet species attach their tough papery cocoons, which are whitish, shiny and sometimes tinged with yellow, to grass stems.

It is not difficult to find burnet cocoons. Since the moths live in colonies, often of a large size, the discovery of the first one or two should lead you to locate dozens more. Birds find it awkward to obtain a foothold on grass stems, so that most of the cocoons in such situations escape their depredations.

BEETLES THAT FLY IN THE NIGHT

Both stag-beetles and cockchafers fly readily at dusk and the stag-beetle is a common sight around London, whirring along its way on a warm summer's evening. The cockchafer is attracted to lights and sometimes blunders into lighted rooms.

Above: The mandibles of the male stag-beetle are said to resemble a stag's horns, hence its common name. If molested, the male adopts a threatening attitude, holding its mandibles wide apart. However, the jaw muscles are weak, with insufficient leverage to bite properly, and so they are mostly used for wrestling with other males in the presence of a female. Despite these large jaws, the adult beetles do not eat solid food, but may take some fluids.

Stag-beetles and cockchafers are two of our largest beetles; the male stag-beetle is certainly the longest, although it lacks the bulk of the great silver waterbeetle. Together with the dung beetles they form the superfamily Scarabaeoidea, which takes its name from the Latin for the ancient Egyptian scarab beetle.

Family characteristics Not all the beetles in this group are as large as the stag-beetles, but they all have several features in common. These are: the fat, sluggish larvae, shaped like a letter 'C'; the spiny, digging front legs of the adults; and their antennae, which have a loose, one-sided club at the end. In addition, their eggs are large and oval and are not produced in great numbers—a maximum of about 70 are laid by the cockchafer. They may take over three years to complete their life-cycles. The adults are strong and powerful, but are not agile and move rather clumsily and slowly.

Another beetle feature that can be seen clearly in these large species is the structure of the mouthparts. Beetles have straightforward chewing mouthparts with a pair of strong biting mandibles and two pairs of accessory jaws equipped with feelers or palps, the second pair joined together and forming a lower lip. In the male stag-beetle, the mandibles are greatly enlarged, and are used in aggressive displays.

Stag-beetles can only be found today in the south-east, particularly Kent and Surrey, although they used to occur as far north as Cumbria. Cockchafers are more widespread, being found all over Britain, with a related species appearing in the north, although they, again, are much more common in the south.

Sizeable stag-beetles These large blackish or reddish-brown beetles are a familiar sight from June to August, flying in the evenings or crawling slowly along the pavements of the London suburbs in the morning. Their appearance frightens many people, but they are quite harmless, even though the female can nip if handled.

Male stag beetles vary from 4-5cm ($1\frac{1}{2}$-2in) in length to the tip of their mandibles; females have a similar-sized body but lack the elongated jaws. They therefore only reach up to 3.6cm ($1\frac{1}{2}$in); even so, this is large for a British beetle.

After mating in the summer, the female stag-beetle digs down in rotten, moist tree stumps and roots with her spiny front legs and lays her small batches of large, yellowish brown eggs, each measuring up to 4mm long. She chooses oak for preference, but will lay in other hardwoods such as beech. In gardens, rotten apple tree stumps are often attacked.

Large larvae The eggs hatch into the characteristic white C-shaped larvae with brown heads and large jaws. There are three larval stages before pupation takes place, and the full-grown larvae are bigger than the adults, reaching 8cm (3in) in length and 15mm ($\frac{1}{2}$in) in diameter.

The larvae lie on their sides while feeding on the rotten wood. This is not easily digested but it contains cellulose-fermenting bacteria which are taken in by the larvae and retained in their hind intestines in large 'fermentation chambers'. In these chambers, easily visible through the white skin, the bacteria break the wood down into a form which the larvae can absorb.

If you find a larva and pick it up between your finger and thumb it will produce a squeaking noise by working a row of pegs on its hind legs across a toothed ridge on its middle pair of legs. The function of this noise is obscure as the larvae do not have obvious hearing organs. However, the larvae of some related foreign beetles squeak when a strange larva invades their territory, and it may help to deter intruders from encroaching on their food supply.

After three or four years the larvae are fully grown and leave the wood to make cells in the earth close by, where they change to pupae. The large mandibles of the male are tucked under during pupation, which lasts until the autumn when the pupae change to adults. The adult beetles stay in their cells until the following late spring or summer.

Flight mechanisms Both the stag-beetle and the cockchafer have hard, horny front wings, called elytra, which meet in a straight line down the beetle's back when it is not flying, protecting both the long hind wings and the soft upper surface of the abdomen. The membranous hind wings, which are folded at rest, are the ones used for flying.

When the beetle wishes to fly, it raises its elytra and contracts the direct flight muscles, causing the hind wings to swing forwards. The stiffness and springiness of the membrane

Above: A male cockchafer. The short grey hairs covering the wing cases give the beetles a rather dusty appearance.

Right: The C-shaped larva of the cockchafer is white with a brown head. The large fermentation chamber visible in the hind intestine helps in the digestion of cellulose.

Below: An encounter between male and female stag-beetles. If two males meet, they adopt a threatening attitude which is actually all bluff. In fact, the female can give a stronger nip than the male if handled.

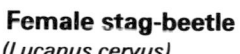

Female stag-beetle
(Lucanus cervus)

Female cockchafer
(Melolontha melolontha)

Different types of larvae

Although all insects have a basic three or four stage life-cycle, the young stages or nymphs of the 'lower' insects, such as cockroaches and plant bugs, and the larvae of the 'higher' insects, such as butterflies, flies and beetles, are very different.

In the 'lower' insects, the eggs hatch into nymphs, usually with a similar life-style and feeding habits to the adults, differing only in their lack of wings. They do not pupate and the wings develop gradually.

In the 'higher' insects, the eggs hatch into larvae often known as caterpillars or grubs. These usually have a completely different life-style and diet from those of the adults. They do pupate, their wings appearing as pads during this stage.

There are four obvious types of larvae, as shown right:

Polypod This means many-legged. The larva is also known as eruciform, from the Latin for caterpillar. It has three pairs of true legs on the thorax and several pairs of false legs on the abdomen.

Campodeiform This active and predatory larva takes its name from its resemblance to *Campodea*, the two-pronged bristletail. It has only three pairs of thoracic legs and usually a pair of tail appendages.

Scarabeiform This also has legs only on the thorax, but is thick and C-shaped. It is typical of members of the dung beetle superfamily but is also found in beetles where the larva has plenty of food close by.

Apodous This is a legless larva with no body appendages. It often feeds inside its food source, where it has no need for legs.

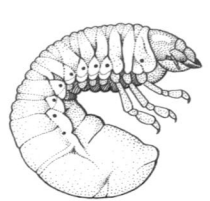

Below: The larvae of moths, butterflies and sawflies are known as **polypods**.

Right: **Campodeiform** larvae are found in some beetles, and lacewings.

Left: Cockchafers and stag-beetles produce **scarabeiform** larvae.

Right: **Apodous** larvae are found in leaf-miners, fly maggots and wood-borers.

Right: The elaborate divided antennae of the cockchafer are a guide to the beetle's sex. A male (shown here) has seven divisions, while the female has six. When the beetle is active, these spread out like a fan.

Below: A male cockchafer taking off from its favourite foodplant, an oak tree. The membranous hind wings used in flight are folded back for protection under the wing cases when the beetle is at rest.

ensures that the hind wings open out fully from their folded position. These beetles tend to fly in straight lines and they are not very manoeuvrable insects.

Cockchafer life-style Cockchafers are active and feeding during May, hence they are sometimes called 'May bugs'. They fly strongly at dusk and sometimes appear in swarms around trees and bushes, producing a loud humming or buzzing sound. They feed on the leaves of trees, especially oak, and can cause considerable damage.

They measure up to 2.5cm (1in) long and are blackish, with brown, ridged elytra. The beetles are also covered with short, grey hair, so that they look as though they have been dusted with flour. On the sides, the hair is much denser, forming a series of white triangles. Another easily identifiable feature is the characteristic triangular spiked tip of the abdomen. Male and female can be distinguished by their antennal clubs, which have segments drawn out into 'leaves'–there are seven in the male and six in the female.

After mating, the female digs down about 20cm (8in) into the soil, where she lays batches of 12-20 eggs. These hatch after three weeks into the characteristic C-shaped larvae which, like those of the stag-beetle, lie on their sides. They tunnel in the soil and can be very destructive, feeding on the roots of grasses, cereals and young trees, although the larvae in turn are eaten in large numbers by moles, rooks, starlings and gulls.

The larvae are fully grown by the end of the summer two years after the eggs were laid, that is, in their third summer. They are then 3.6cm (1½in) long and make oval cells in the earth at a depth of 60cm (2ft) or more for pupation. The adult beetles emerge in October but remain dormant throughout the winter; they do not leave the ground until next May.

TOADS IN SUMMER: A LIFE ON THE LAND

Toads spend most of their adult life on land, returning to water only in the spring to mate and to spawn. Life for toads during the summer can be precarious because of their many enemies, but the toads can produce a few surprises themselves when they are faced with a predator.

Above: A common toad basks in summer sunshine on a toadstool. Although common toads are usually brownish, their skin colour varies from one locality to another. This toad is a rich brick-red, matching the colour of the local soil.

Below: A mass of common toads gathering for mating in a pond. Soon they will disperse to live on dry land for the summer.

As soon as spawning is completed in spring, toads leave their aquatic habitat to spend the summer on land. The common toad's breeding season ends in late May, while that of the natterjack continues until early June. From then until the end of hibernation, early the following year, toads are terrestrial animals.

Skin care All through the summer toads tend to be more active at night than during the day. Being cold-blooded, however, they also sit out in the bright sunshine of a summer's day, in order to obtain extra bodily warmth. They can do this for short periods, say a few minutes at a time, but if they bask for any longer their bodies begin to overheat: if this continues for too long, the animals die. To prevent overheating, toads have moist skins, and the constant evaporation of water from their skins cools them down. Toads control their body temperature by keeping a balance

91

between the cooling effect of evaporation and the warmth that comes directly or indirectly from the sun.

Toads have various methods of keeping their skins moist. Although land-based, they remain near water so that they can take a short dip, as well as drink, from time to time. They have numerous glands beneath the skin which secrete a mucus that keeps the skin moist in between dips. Toads also shed their skins several times during the summer, and one effect of this is to maintain the skin in good condition. Although only a thin, transparent layer is shed, you can sometimes see parts of the cast skin glistening among the dew on the grass on a cool summer's morning.

If the summer is particularly dry and hot, toads sometimes bury themselves in loose, sandy soil in an attempt to avoid excess water loss. Common toads are remarkably good at burrowing, and can bury themselves very fast: their strong, long legs are highly useful for this task. The toads lie buried and sheltered from the sun, conserving moisture until conditions become a little cooler—for example, when night falls.

Daily routines For certain periods during the summer, the activity of toads during both day and night is very predictable. For some weeks at a time, an individual toad feeds in the same place each night (unless prevented by extreme weather conditions) and hides in the same place by day. After maintaining this pattern of activity for a few weeks, the toad then selects a new feeding place. Toads seem to have no difficulty in locating favourite

Above: These natterjacks were photographed in the south-west of Ireland. The stone under which they were hiding has been lifted, suddenly exposing the toads, but their skin colour still serves to camouflage them. Not only is the colour well matched, but the warty, granular texture of the skin also resembles that of the soil.

feeding places each night, then returning to the safety of their daytime refuges.

Natterjack toads are somewhat unusual among toads and frogs in general in that rather than hopping or crawling they tend to run. They are capable of running in short bursts, thus covering a large area while at the same time looking about for food. Natterjacks feed on a variety of small creatures including spiders, insects (especially beetles) and worms. Common toads are reputed to eat almost any small animal as long as it moves. They have been known to eat earthworms, insects, spiders and also nestling mice; sometimes they even take the young of slow-worms and snakes.

Defence systems Toads fall victim to many kinds of predators throughout the summer. Small mammals such as hedgehogs and stoats prey on toads, as do many species of birds, including gulls and blackbirds. Snakes also feed on toads. Although they appear defenceless, toads protect themselves by means of their poison glands and also by some interesting and unusual forms of behaviour.

Situated on either side of the toad's body, just behind the eyes, are the paratoid glands. These can be seen clearly as pale oblong bulges, and they produce a secretion which is mildly poisonous to the toad's enemies. Usually it does little harm other than causing an inflammation of the skin, but this is sufficient to deter predators.

If you are handling a toad, therefore, do so with care, for if roughly treated the animal may secrete its poison, and this may give you a skin inflammation.

When toads are alarmed, if approached by a predator for example, they sometimes inflate themselves so as to appear as large as possible. A very rounded and fat toad with legs stiffly outstretched and head lowered can be a strange and intimidating sight for the attacking animal, causing it to withdraw.

Where toads are found The common toad

How toads catch their prey

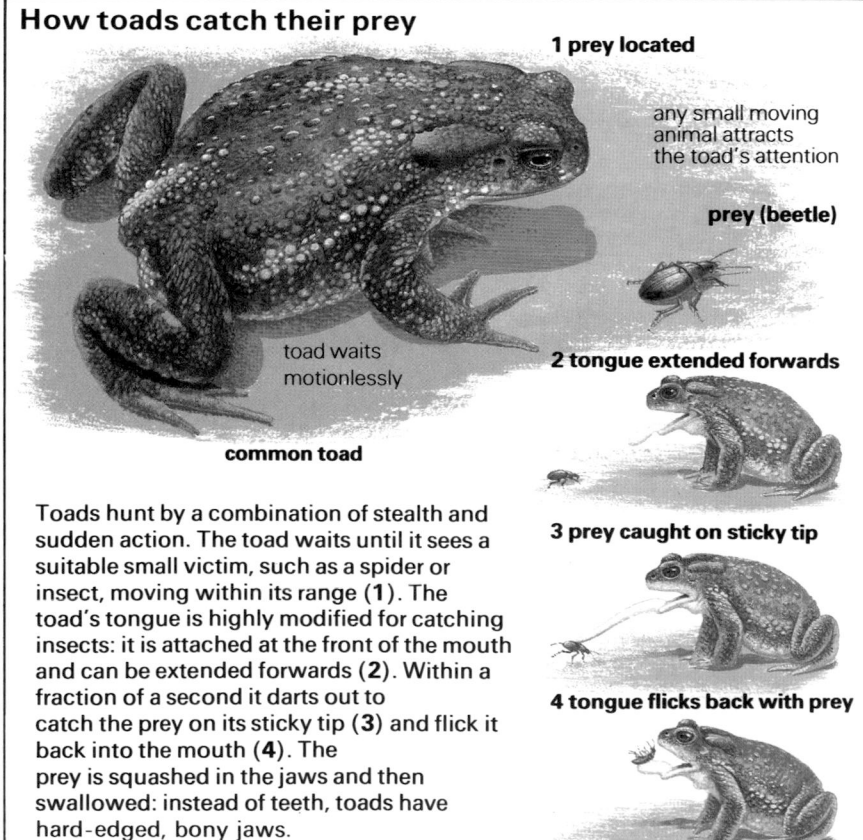

1 prey located

any small moving animal attracts the toad's attention

prey (beetle)

toad waits motionlessly

common toad

2 tongue extended forwards

3 prey caught on sticky tip

4 tongue flicks back with prey

Toads hunt by a combination of stealth and sudden action. The toad waits until it sees a suitable small victim, such as a spider or insect, moving within its range (**1**). The toad's tongue is highly modified for catching insects: it is attached at the front of the mouth and can be extended forwards (**2**). Within a fraction of a second it darts out to catch the prey on its sticky tip (**3**) and flick it back into the mouth (**4**). The prey is squashed in the jaws and then swallowed: instead of teeth, toads have hard-edged, bony jaws.

has a very widespread distribution, being found throughout most of Europe. It occurs in England, Scotland and Wales, but strangely not in Ireland. At the end of summer, when common toads seek overwintering sites, they sometimes hide in rather unusual places, including cellars and greenhouses; and they have even been found in bags of potatoes.

The distribution of the natterjack toad includes western, central and northern Europe, where in most cases its habitat consists of sand dunes and other areas close to the seashore. Some populations seem tolerant of salt water, or at least brackish water. The natterjack's present distribution in Britain has been the cause of considerable concern, and it is now believed that this toad is in danger of extinction. It has been recorded in south-west Ireland, north Wales, on the west coast of southern Scotland, and in Dorset, Hampshire, East Anglia, Merseyside and

Above: A natterjack crouches on the trunk of a fallen birch tree. In this raised position it is relatively safe from predators. This natterjack derives additional safety from the perfect match of its skin colouring with that of the birch bark.

Below: A natterjack calling in the breeding season: the display posture resembles the 'threatening' posture seen in summer.

The 'threatening' posture

Sometimes when a toad perceives an approaching predator, it fills itself with air and maintains a very rounded, inflated posture. Its head is held close to the ground and the back legs are stretched out stiffly. This strange appearance often has the effect of saving the toad from attack: either the predator (in this case a grass snake) fails to recognise the motionless animal as prey, or it may be discouraged by the size and unfamiliar appearance of the toad.

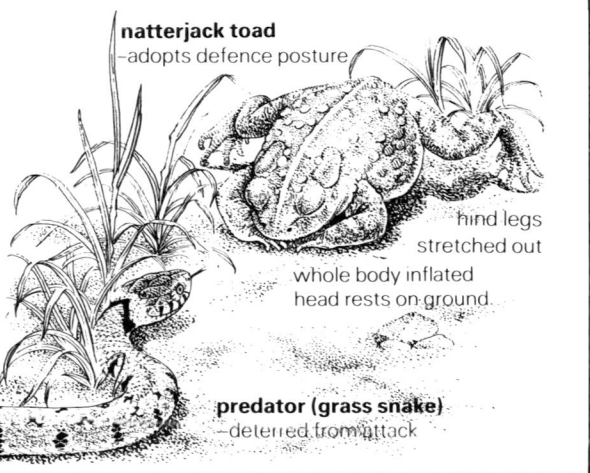

natterjack toad
–adopts defence posture

hind legs stretched out
whole body inflated
head rests on ground

predator (grass snake)
–deterred from attack

Cumbria in England.

Populations of the natterjack have undergone dramatic decline in recent decades, particularly in southern and eastern England. In contrast, the south-west Scottish population seems to be thriving. There is no doubt, however, that the natterjack toad is now very rare; because of this, and because the few remaining populations are geographically isolated, the species is fully protected by the law. It is an offence to collect, injure, kill or sell natterjack toads.

The natterjack's decline seems to result from a combination of factors. Fewer and fewer suitable breeding sites are available to the species. Like the common toad, it is best suited to breeding in old and undisturbed ponds, but many of these have now been destroyed, particularly in coastal areas where there has been considerable drainage and alteration of land use. It also appears that the common toad competes with the natterjack both for food and habitats. The common toad generally starts breeding before the natterjack, and where the two species share the same habitat it is not unknown for the tadpoles of the common toad to eat natterjack tadpoles thus eliminating their competitors.

BIRDS IN SUMMER: TIMING IT RIGHT

The onset of summer quickens the pace of bird life: foraging becomes a race as young chicks grow, and all bird species suffer heavy mortality. Each species has its own characteristic schedule of breeding activities, to be completed before autumn.

Above: Spend some time near water if you go birdwatching in summer. Besides water birds, you are bound to see land birds coming to drink and bathe, like this blue tit.

Opposite page: The redstart is a summer visitor to Britain's woodlands.

Left: This young wheatear is not yet fully fledged. By late summer it must be fully independent because its migration to Africa could begin as early as August.

Birds do not waste summer: the season of plenty is short, and throughout it most adult pairs are engaged in a constant struggle to produce young birds for recruitment to their species. The number of recruits that eventually survive to breed is always a small fraction of the number of eggs laid, for birds live hazardous lives, perhaps especially in summer. But whatever the day-to-day risks may be, the overall limiting factor is time, and so the breeding season follows a tight schedule. Autumn will soon bring extra urgency to bird life.

Plants in leaf Summer foliage is exploited as cover for hiding nests by dozens of species that seek to raise their young within trees, bushes or on the ground among grass and other low plants. As May progresses, hedges and thickets become impenetrable, and jays and magpies experience greater and greater difficulty in finding unguarded nests to plunder.

One of the factors that permits this quick growth of new leaves is the increased day length of summer. Throughout May, June and July the sun is above the horizon in Britain and Ireland for over 15 hours a day. Such long days also give plenty of time for birds to forage, both for themselves and for large, growing families.

Arrival of the migrants Plants are the primary producers of food, and the small animals that thrive on their sudden growth produce a rapid peak of protein-rich food at the secondary level–the herbivorous animals. A large amount of this flies in the air in the form of an enormous feast of insects, and it is for these that many species of insectivorous migrant birds visit Britain and Ireland each summer. Warblers, chats, flycatchers, swifts, swallows, martins, nightjars, wagtails and others arrive annually, so by the end of May the total of breeding birds in Britain and Ireland swells to an estimated 120 million. By the end of August, these may have raised enough young to produce a total of over 500 million birds.

Summer mortality It seems at first surprising, but records kept by the British Trust for Ornithology show that for a wide range of species more dead birds are found in summer than in winter. Young birds are obviously vulnerable, but even adults display a peak of mortality spanning the breeding season. Those reporting the discovery of their remains often find evidence of the causes of death: cats, traffic and collision with windows are frequently mentioned. It is intriguing to speculate how much of this loss of life is due to lack of wariness resulting, perhaps, from the distractions of a hectic breeding season.

Having made a nest, parent birds are constrained to return to it at regular intervals, easily attracting the attention of cats and certainly, if a road lies *en route*, increasing the risk of being hit by traffic. Many summer visiting birds die in this country, though we know little of the severity of dangers that face

such birds on migration or in their winter quarters.

As for the fledglings, many die within a month. Their instinct for danger is not yet reinforced by practical experience, their flight is often weak, and they must call to their parents to demand food at regular intervals: surely an invitation to disaster if cats or other predators are common.

When to see birds breeding For the bird-watcher who takes an interest in breeding behaviour, it is fascinating to observe the great variety in the schedules followed by the different species.

Among the earliest breeders are the ground-feeding birds, such as the song thrush and the blackbird. Taken as a group, the ground-feeders are not particularly selective in the foods they eat, though animals are generally predominant in summer rather than seeds, nuts or fruits. They take worms, slugs,

millipedes and any other similar animal they find in the soil. This kind of food is less seasonal than most; good quantities are available in milder phases of winter, and certainly as soon as March begins there is sufficient for some blackbirds to start laying eggs.

Apart from the problems large ground-feeders such as rooks experience if dry weather in July hardens the earth into an impenetrable crust, the soil and its surface continue to provide nourishing small animals all through the summer. Both blackbirds and song thrushes are able to continue their breeding over a long season, and may raise three or even four broods, the last becoming independent in September.

Insect-eaters do not start their season quite as early as the song thrush and blackbird, waiting at least until late April. May is generally the time when the winter moth

Above: The hobby is an insect-eating predator, but it also takes swallows and swifts, particularly as food for its young. The best time for it to raise chicks is July and August, when young victims are plentiful.

Below: A guide to the breeding activities you can expect to see in ten sample species as summer progresses. A dotted line shows where an activity may be taking place in only part of the British and Irish population of the species. It reflects north-south variation and other differences. Because of the problems of observation, the time spent in parental care is an estimate.

Timing the clutch

Different birds breed according to different schedules. The first six birds here represent small species: ground-feeders breed earliest, followed by insectivores (except migrants like the swallow) and then seed-eaters. Among birds of prey, two contrasting strategies are shown: the flexible timing of the barn owl and the fixed timing of the sparrowhawk. To complete the picture, two seabirds are shown.

		JAN	FEB	MAR	APR	MAY	JUNE	JULY	AUG	SEPT	OCT	NOV	DEC
GROUND FEEDERS	Song thrush												
	Blackbird												
INSECT EATERS	Long-tailed tit												
	Swallow												
SEED EATERS	Yellowhammer												
	Goldfinch												
BIRDS OF PREY	Barn owl												
	Sparrowhawk												
SEABIRDS	Oystercatcher												
	Black-headed gull												

_____ eggs present _____ nestlings present _____ fledglings in care of parent birds

caterpillars hatch in their millions, and blue tits and other members of the tit family choose to mate at the precise time when their ensuing single brood of young will develop in time to thrive on these caterpillars.

The breeding season of swallows, swifts and martins is determined both by the time these migrants arrive in this country and by their dependence on flying insects. Their first eggs are laid from mid or late May onwards.

Of resident birds, the seed-eaters are generally the latest breeders, for seeds do not become abundant until late May. The first broods of finches and buntings can be expected to be on the wing from this time onwards, feeding from each plant species in turn as the seeds ripen.

Birds of prey Among the larger birds are those that feed by swooping down upon other birds or on terrestrial animals: the predators. Within this diverse group, timing strategies of breeding vary. Barn owls feed on many different kinds of prey, from mice and birds to earthworms and large insects. They can take whatever is available at the time, and this enables them to be flexible in the timing of their breeding. Though pairs raise only one brood, they can choose to lay their clutch of eggs in almost any month of the year. Most are incubating in April and May, the young taking wing some ten weeks later.

This does not apply to all predatory birds, however. The sparrowhawk feeds almost entirely on birds, often specialising on particular species. Thus males (the smaller sex) frequently catch finches, sparrows, buntings or tits, while the female hunts thrushes and starlings. Like barn owls, the sparrowhawks are single-brooded, but their breeding season must synchronise with the peak availability of young, easily caught victims. Their young are in the nest from mid May to July or August.

Precocious young The chicks of most waders and gulls are relatively mature when they hatch—able to see and run about when only hours old. This does not shorten their breeding season: incubation and fledging times of three to four weeks and five to six weeks respectively are typical.

Above: The superb summer camouflage colouring of the ptarmigan ensures that it has a chance of survival against the predators of its moorland and mountain home.

Below: This puffin chick has been lifted out of its burrow for photographing (if done with proper care, this will not harm it). The chick is fed by both parents throughout June and into July, when it emerges to fend for itself.

SUMMER VISITING TREE PIPITS

Pipits are small, insect-eating birds related to wagtails but which look more like larks. Of all eleven species occurring in Britain, the tree pipit is the only summer migrant. Some 75,000 pairs breed in Britain, though hardly any are seen in Ireland.

Eleven species of pipits can be seen in Britain and Ireland. Eight of these – the olive-backed, Pechora, red-throated, tawny, Richard's, water, Blyth's and American pipits – occur mainly in autumn, and only as vagrants or rarities. Three – the meadow, rock and tree pipits – are all common breeding birds, but the tree pipit is the only true migrant.

What is a pipit? The name 'pipit' derives from the high-pitched squeaky calls that almost all pipits possess. Pipits are all small birds with slim bodies, finely pointed bills and jerky, flitting flight. Virtually all pipits are brown above with darker markings, and creamy below. They have dark brown streaks on the breast, flanks and around the throat,

Right: The tree pipit's resemblance to a lark has earned it such local names as titlark, field lark, dusky lark and blood lark.

Tree pipit (*Anthus trivialis*). Summer visitor to open country with trees. Sexes alike. 15cm (6in).

Below: A tree pipit nest on the ground. The bird never nests in trees, but derives its name from its habit of singing in trees. The song flight, too, begins from a tree or bush.

forming distinct moustachial stripes. Usually there is a creamy stripe above the eye, and the outer tail feathers are white.

Pipits live in open country, and when on the ground they walk or run, but never hop. They live almost entirely on insects and larvae, caught on or just above the ground.

The great similarity among the species of pipits causes real problems of identification for birdwatchers; not only the eleven species recorded in Britain, but all of the worldwide total of 36 pipit species are very similar in appearance.

A brighter colour The tree pipit is typical of the genus *Anthus*, but is rather more colourful than its British relatives, having yellower, less olivaceous plumage than the meadow pipit and being much lighter in colour than the rock pipit. It also has fewer but more prominent breast markings, and its legs are pinkish, whereas those of the meadow pipit are light brown and the rock pipit has grey legs.

Song posts and habitats The tree pipit is the only pipit which regularly perches in trees. Indeed, trees are almost essential to these birds, not for food or nesting cover (though they do fly into trees when disturbed), but to add a vertical component to their otherwise low-lying habitat. Trees provide high perches, from which they can launch into their characteristic and musical song-flight.

As well as song posts, tree pipits require open ground for feeding. Thus a variety of habitats may be suitable: heaths, clearings in woods, woodland edges, parkland, even mature woodland if it is sufficiently open. Mature forestry plantations are of little use, but if some old trees are left when the others are felled, subsequent plantations provide ideal conditions for a short while.

Singing males The tree pipit's breeding season starts in mid-April when the first birds (usually males, but quickly followed by the females) return from their wintering grounds south of the Sahara. Up until the end of July is the best time to listen for the male's musical,

Song-flights

Song-flights are usually as distinctive as the songs themselves—not surprisingly, since they serve much the same purpose: to advertise the owner's mastery of his territory. Open-country birds, with their unrestricted view of neighbouring territories, adopt this visual display more frequently than woodland or garden birds. The **skylark's** continuous twittering, at extraordinary heights and in winter and summer alike, is perhaps the best known song-flight. Britain's other, rarer lark, the **woodlark**, has a high, circling song-flight, usually from one tree to another. The **tree pipit** also takes off from a tree, returning in a parachuting descent. The **meadow pipit** starts and ends its flight on or near the ground, also with a parachuting descent. The **wheatear's** flight is a short, dancing ascent before returning to the ground.

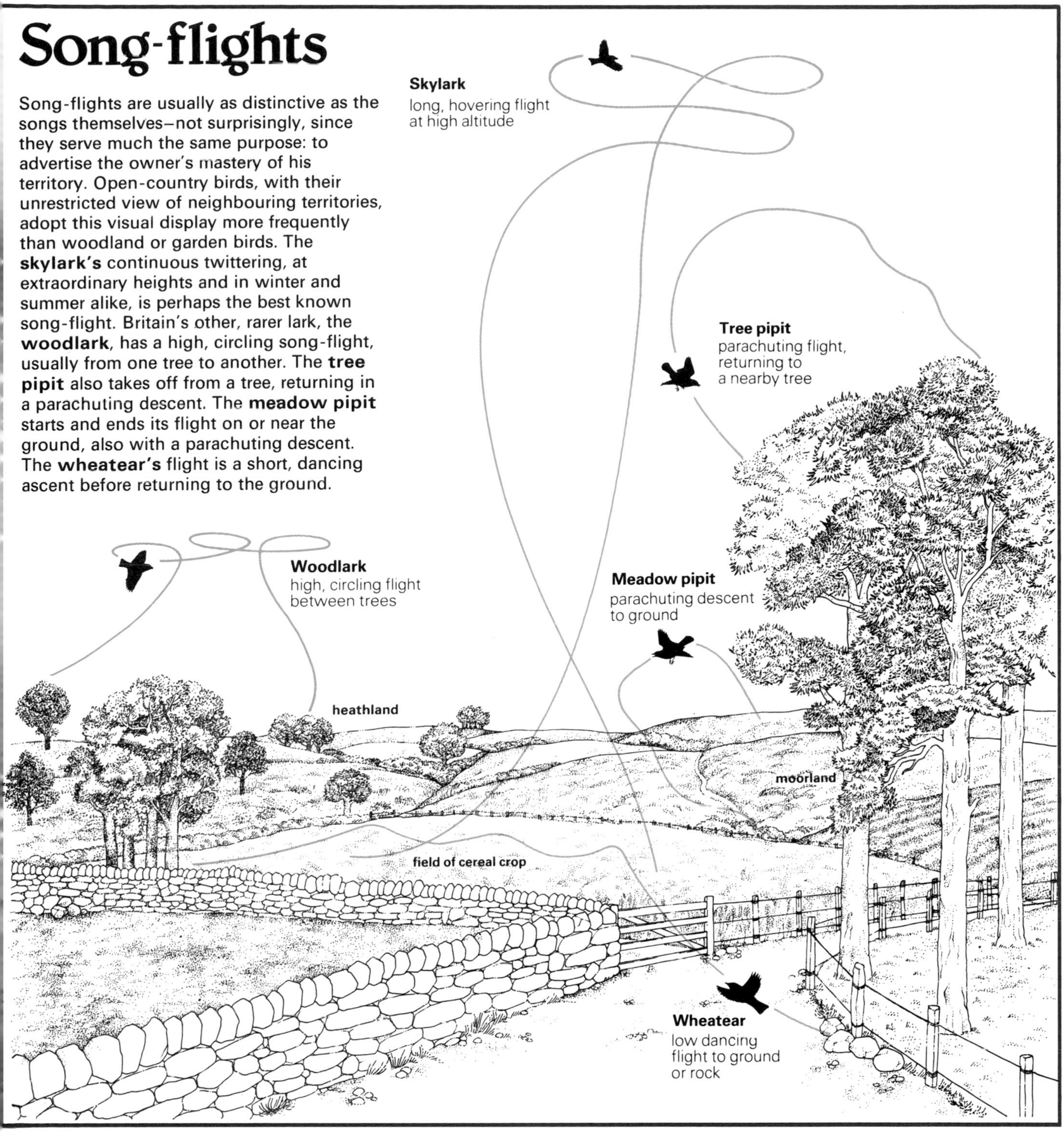

Skylark
long, hovering flight at high altitude

Tree pipit
parachuting flight, returning to a nearby tree

Woodlark
high, circling flight between trees

Meadow pipit
parachuting descent to ground

heathland

moorland

field of cereal crop

Wheatear
low dancing flight to ground or rock

far-carrying and distinctive song—the final shrill 'seea-seea-seea' notes being the most memorable. This song, designed to warn other tree pipits that 'this territory is mine', is delivered in a shortened form from a perch, or in its full splendour in a song-flight.

Nests on the ground In its nesting details the tree pipit is typical of most pipits. Moss and dry grass comprise the main bulk of the nest, which is built by the female on the ground in a hollow sheltered by grass or other vegetation. Having lined the nest with finer grasses and hair, the female lays 4-6 eggs, noted for their variable colour: grey, brown or reddish with blotches and streaks or with more uniform speckles, often concentrated at one end.

Tree pipits are among over a dozen British birds known to be capable of rearing young cuckoos, both species being insectivores, but only about one per cent of nests are parasitised in this way.

Tree pipits in autumn In August and September song and habitat lose their usefulness as aids to identifying tree pipits, for at this time they become much quieter and leave their breeding territories in preparation for their migration flight south. However, they do have a call which, with practice and a good memory, you can learn to recognise. It is a short, high-pitched; rasping 'teez', much less squeaky than the meadow pipit's 'tsipp', and usually uttered in flight.

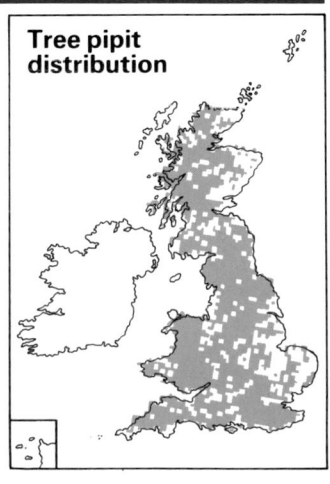

Tree pipit distribution

THE NIGHTJAR: A SUMMER VISITOR

The nightjar, a summer visitor to Britain, breeds on heaths and in young woodland, and feeds at twilight by flying with its mouth open to catch moths. When perched it utters a long call surprisingly like the sound of a distant motorcycle.

Above: A fine example of a nightjar's breeding site. The birch-invaded heath offers plenty of open ground or small clearings in which the scrape nest can be located. This incubating female is so well matched in colour and markings with the layer of birch leaves on the ground that if it were not for the egg in this picture, you might not notice her at all.

Nightjars of various species form a world-wide family, but there is only one member that regularly visits Britain and Ireland, and that is the European nightjar, which most people know simply as the nightjar. It is a summer visitor, wintering in Africa, and when in Britain it is generally found on scrubby heaths or in areas of newly planted (or newly felled) forest.

Superb adaptation The nightjar is unique among British birds for its method of feeding: it hawks for moths and other flying insects in the darkness just before dawn and just after dusk. Many of its special features are adaptations to this feeding method.

The nightjar has large, black eyes that are highly suitable for seeing its aerial prey in poor lighting. Its mouth opens very wide, literally from ear to ear, with a wide fringe of bristles spreading out on each side, effectively increasing the size of its 'trawl'. For this is how it feeds: the nightjar catches all its food in its mouth as it flies along, just as if it were an aerial trawler.

One problem arising from this way of feeding is that the nightjar's plumage is showered with the tiny scales that fly from the wings of the moths at the moment of impact when they are caught. The birds must remove these or they will impair the flight efficiency and general functioning of the feathers. Therefore most species of nightjars –including the European nightjar–have developed a special comb on the central toe of each foot. The nightjar uses this comb, in addition to the bill, as an instrument for preening the feathers.

Most birds have preen glands which secrete oil that is used for cleaning and conditioning the plumage, but no nightjar has a well-developed preen gland; it is thought that they use powder-down instead. This substance, which is also used by many species of heron, derives from the tips of constantly growing feathers, mostly on the underparts.

Having fed by daybreak, the nightjar rests during the daylight hours; for this it shows an effective adaptation for safety from predators: its plumage is a superb mixture of

nightjars twist and turn in flight, with short glides

male

female

stiff bristles around mouth

white on three outer feathers

white outer tail feathers

brown, cream and grey tones, so patterned as to cause its outline to be lost against the background.

Sound of a nightjar The sight of nightjars hawking over the heath on swift, silent wings is not usually the first moment at which the birdwatcher realises that these birds are about, for they have a highly characteristic call: a long, almost continuous 'churring' noise. This is generally delivered from a perch, rising and falling in a rhythmic sequence. The calls of nightjars have been timed, and it is found that the churring frequently lasts for more than five minutes on end. It has been likened to the noise of a distant two-stroke engine, and many enthusiasts have been deceived in the past by a motorcycle travelling on some far-off road, causing them to think that it was a nightjar.

Nightjars in spring The first migrants return to Britain in April, and by early May most of the breeding areas are occupied. Although few have been seen on migration at bird observatories, it is estimated that they fly on a set migration route with great accuracy.

The males generally arrive first.

Both sexes perform the churring call, possibly from different song-posts. The birds use the sound to advertise their claim to a chosen territory. To establish and maintain the territory, they patrol its boundaries. If they meet their neighbours, they may utter an alarm note, a 'koo-ick' sound, which is also uttered during normal activity, particularly as the bird takes off. Softer versions of this call are sometimes used to give the alarm, and these may be meant only for the breeding partner—or, later in the season, for the young.

Displays between the male and female involve a variety of calls and chases, and a rapid, loud clapping of the wings, which is

Nightjar (*Caprimulgus europaeus*); summer visitor to heaths and young woodland; semi-nocturnal. Length 27cm (10½in).

Below: The middle toe of the nightjar is shaped like a comb and is used in preening the feathers.

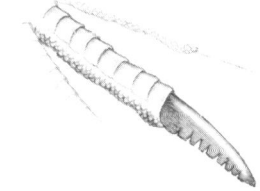

Right: Young nightjars hatch about 18 days after the start of incubation. Both the male and the female feed them and they become independent after about five weeks. They make their first flight about half-way through this period, and by the end of it the male will normally have taken on all responsibilities for the first brood—for by then the female usually has a second clutch of eggs which she incubates without any help from him. The second brood is usually hatched in late June, and the young are then ready for the migratory flight by the end of August.

Left: When perching in a tree nightjars, unlike most other birds, sit along the branch instead of across it. In the evening, when they start to fly, the difference between males and females becomes apparent. The males have brilliant white patches on three of the outer wing feathers and on the tail. One of the wing patches is visible in this picture, proclaiming the bird to be a male. These white patches show up very well in flight, and allow the bird-watcher to identify the sex of any nightjar seen in the spring or early summer—but not later, for by then adult-sized juveniles will be about, and both sexes of these lack the white.

mainly done by the male. Up to 25 wing claps are given in a single, sharp fusillade. The male draws attention to his white wing and tail patches by gliding through the air with raised wings. Before mating, both birds stand swaying their tails from side to side, and shortly before mounting the female, the male bounces up and down with spread tail and raised wings. Within a day or two after mating, the clutch of two pale eggs, blotched and marbled with brown, grey or sepia markings, are laid in a simple scrape, usually on open ground.

Breeding sites may include bracken-covered hillsides, but are most often sited near trees. Once again, dead leaves – whether from trees or bracken – form the ideal background for the female's camouflage to have effect while she is incubating. The male's stints at incubation seem generally to be short relief periods at dusk and dawn, to allow the female to leave the nest to feed.

Nightjars normally raise two broods, even where they are at the limits of their breeding range in northern England and Scotland. They then leave the breeding sites and migrate south; some pairs leave as early as mid-August, but some young birds, still unfledged, are found in September. These are often the result of replacement broods, raised late in the season after the loss of the original brood.

Nearing rarity Unfortunately the nightjar is a declining species in Britain and Ireland, in spite of the fact that it is able to occupy many kinds of habitat, and has even been known to nest in industrial tips in suburban areas. A century ago, it was considered a common species, but writers even 50 years ago commented that it was declining. It is, perhaps, the great increase in the ploughing of heathland in World War II, and the continuing destruction of heathland since that

Below: A nightjar utters a call while sitting on the ground. Its wide mouth is far larger than the beak alone. The size of the mouth may have inspired some of the many folk tales concerning nightjars, for it is often said that the birds suck milk from goats and other farm animals. Indeed, a frequent country name is 'goatsucker', and even the scientific name *Caprimulgus* means the same. It is quite certain, though, that no nightjar could ever feed in this way.

time, that have dealt the hardest blows to the species. Even in areas where new planting of trees provides a seemingly ideal habitat nightjars are scarce. Their numbers have, however, become more stable during the 1980s, with 2000 pairs now breeding in Britain and Ireland.

This situation must be seen as part of the general decline of many species associated with heathland, one of the habitats that has been most seriously affected by urban spread and modern methods of farming. To conserve the nightjar, the same efforts need to be pursued that will save the other threatened heathland species – namely all steps that can be taken to save the remaining heathlands from further encroachment. Otherwise this bird's unique sound will no longer be heard in any part of our countryside.

RED-BACKED SHRIKES: A THREATENED FUTURE

The fate of the red-backed shrike in Britain hangs in the balance. There is hope that some birds will return to their traditional breeding areas in south-eastern England, and there is always a chance that a pair arriving from Scandinavia to breed here may build up a sparse but regular population.

Above: A male red-backed shrike is easy to identify by his dark, piratical eye stripe. Although the male may perch conspicuously on a post, pole or bush, his song is not very loud or distinctive, generally consisting of nothing more than a diffuse jumble of warbles.

Red-backed shrike (*Lanius collurio*). Passage migrant and summer visitor. 17cm (6¾in) long.

The male red-backed shrike is an exceptionally striking bird, with chestnut back, blue-grey head and nape, and a broad dark stripe through the eye. The female is brown above and buff below, while the youngsters are liberally barred above and below. In size these shrikes are rather bigger than a greenfinch, but with a longer and broader tail which they often weave from side to side.

In Britain these birds are summer visitors or passage migrants and have seldom been recorded here earlier than the end of April or later than the start of October.

Fall and rise? Fifty years ago the red-backed shrike was a familiar member of the bird community over much of southern Britain. Un-fortunately, over the last few decades the species has become more scarce. Ornithologists appear to have correctly predicted that the red-backed shrike would become extinct in Britain before the end of the century.

As the decline set in, the population seemed to remain fairly high in the Brecklands and coastal heathland areas of East Anglia, and in parts of Kent and the New Forest. (The birds prefer scrubland and heathland, although, when they were common, they would nest in hedges in farmland and even in gardens.) During the 1960s even these last strongholds started to lose their birds, and a disastrous decline in the New Forest reduced that population from more than 60 pairs to less than 10.

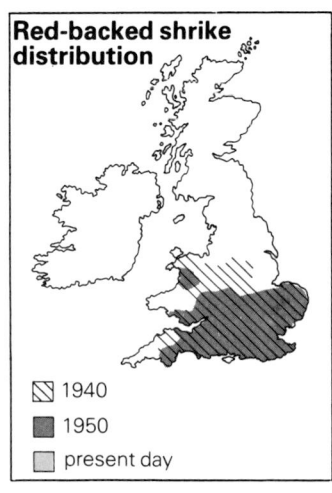

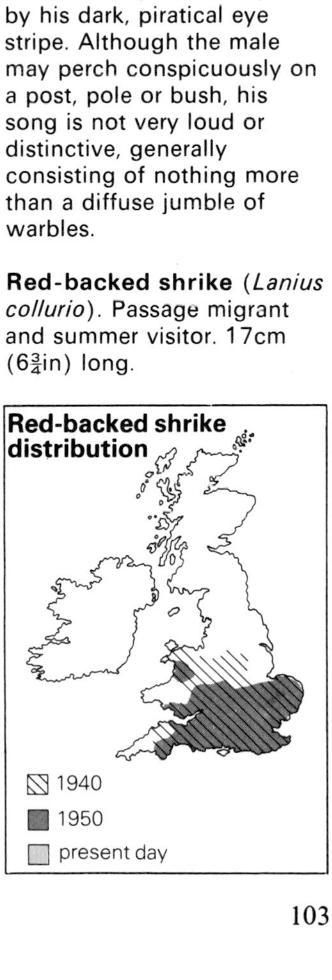

Red-backed shrike distribution

◿ 1940
■ 1950
▢ present day

Above: Among the shrikes only the red-backed shows marked differences in plumage between the male and the female. The male's chestnut, blue-grey and black colouring is rather conspicuous, while the female's brown and buff is much more discreet.

For a short time there was some cause for optimism – odd pairs were found in several counties where none had bred for 20 years or more, and there were breeding season records in Wales and Scotland where there had previously been very few attempts at nesting. Now, apart from occasional breeding pairs recorded in isolated sites, the red-backed shrike no longer has a regular breeding population.

The occasional scattered breeding in previous

years was due to an expansion in the range and numbers of Scandinavian breeding red-backed shrikes, rather than an increase in the traditional population which had inhabited Britain for centuries.

Reasons for the decline The reasons behind the long-standing decline of the red-backed shrike are not well understood. The bird is a predatory species, feeding mainly on large insects – particularly beetles, butterflies, crickets and grasshoppers – all creatures whose populations have undoubtedly declined considerably. This is almost certainly due principally to gradual and subtle changes in climate, but the introduction of new and more poisonous insecticides cannot have helped.

The gradual loss of scrub habitat has also been blamed, but this does not seem very likely: many suitable sites have lost their shrikes although their ecology seems to have changed but little. Another factor is that the red-backed shrike does lay extremely attractive eggs which show a great deal of colour variation; this has made them a particular favourite among egg-collectors. It seems likely that local populations were wiped out completely through the activities of collectors – who are known to have been busy in recent years even though the species has been given special protection since the revision of the Bird Protection Act in 1967.

Nesting and rearing young The red-backed shrike arrives in Britain to breed (or on passage) during the month of May. The male may be very conspicuous, perching high in a bush, on wires or on a post or pole. Even at a distance, his characteristic bouncing flight, with an abrupt upwards sweep to land on the next perch, can give his presence away.

It is, however, quite possible for breeding birds to conceal themselves from view throughout the whole of the first part of the breeding season. The nest is a fairly large structure, often built in the midst of thick cover and generally a metre or so from the ground. The eggs show a wide variety of ground colour, with reddish markings often concentrated at the blunt end. The full clutch is generally of five or six eggs; they are incubated, mainly by the female, for about 15 days. The chicks fledge after a further two weeks.

The butcher bird's larder One of the most interesting aspects of red-backed shrike behaviour is the formation of larders – an aspect which has earned it the name of 'butcher bird'. The larders are stores of food apparently made mainly by the male at the start of the breeding season. Not all males do this and it used to be thought that the food was being stored for the incubating female to eat or to give to the chicks. It now seems more likely that the male is demonstrating his ability to catch food, as shown by a well-stocked larder, to attract a female.

As well as the large insects already mentioned, the shrike also catches mice, shrews,

The shrike's 'larder'

The 'larder' of the male red-backed shrike is a gruesome sight; it can consist of lizards, bees, wasps, beetles and other insects, and even of a mouse or small vole. It is thought that the male makes these stores of food as much to attract a female and induce her to mate with him as to feed her and the hungry chicks. Females rarely make such larders.

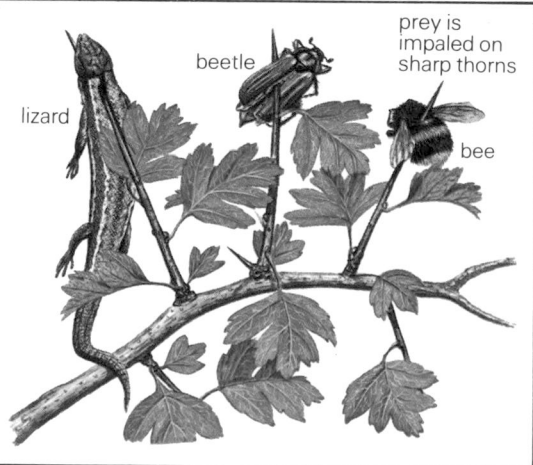

beetle

prey is impaled on sharp thorns

lizard

bee

Red-backed shrike — grey head and nape, chestnut back, white underparts

Woodchat-shrike — chestnut head and nape, white shoulder patch

Great grey shrike — grey head and nape, stubby primaries

Lesser grey shrike — grey head and nape, black forehead, pinkish breast, long primaries

lizards and even birds. A wide variety of prey species has been recorded, often at the larders where the food is impaled on thorns or barbed wire. The bird's hooked beak, just like that of a miniature hawk, is well-adapted for catching such food, although the shrike has not developed similar talons for gripping prey.

Shrike or warbler? Once the young shrikes have fledged, there is no chance of concealment. The whole area within a few dozen metres of the nest reverberates to the incessant harsh 'tchack' calls of the young as they beg for food from their parents.

The youngsters bear an extraordinary resemblance to the adult barred warbler – a large relative of the whitethroat, found in eastern Europe and parts of Asia. Both birds may be found in Britain on the east coast after south-easterly winds in September; they sometimes provide an interesting problem in identification. What is even more surprising – since they are not at all closely related – is that the two species seem to have a nesting association, at least in parts of Poland and the Balkans where their distributions overlap. Out of 21 shrike and 20 warbler nests studied, 11 were close together, sometimes with complete overlap of territories. The shrikes often chased other birds from their territory, but tolerated the barred warbler. It is thought that the two birds benefit from mutual warning on danger from predators.

The shrike is a particularly good indicator of the presence of other birds of prey. The professional hawk catchers of the medieval times in the Netherlands, Belgium and other countries used to tether a shrike by their nets to tell them when a hawk was in the area. The shrike would see the hawk when it was a very long way off and start to flutter and call. This would be the signal for the catcher to manipulate his decoys and try to catch the approaching hawk or falcon.

Autumn migrations In the autumn British red-backed shrikes migrate south-east to winter in Africa, crossing the eastern end of the Mediterranean on their way. In east Africa, in Kenya for instance, they find large tracts of suitable land for wintering, with bushes and

isolated trees and good supplies of large insects. Here they are joined by other shrikes from Europe and western Asia.

There is considerable variation in plumage between different populations of red-backed shrikes: all the way across the mid-southern area of Asia a slightly separate species is known as the Isabelline shrike, while in the west it is called the brown shrike. However, in south and south-east Europe the red-backed shrike and the woodchat-shrike can be found living alongside one another.

The future? In Britain the fate of the red-backed shrike is uncertain. Ornithologists hope that some birds will return to their traditional breeding areas in south-eastern England, provided that the reclamation of heathland for farming does not consume all the suitable sites. Elsewhere, the occasional pair from Scandinavia may arrive to breed somewhere along the east coast of Britain.

Above: Shrikes are birds with striking colouring, hook-tipped bills and the habit of impaling prey on thorns, forming 'larders'. The red-backed is a summer visitor and passage migrant here, while the woodchat-shrike and the lesser grey shrikes are rare vagrants. The great grey shrike is an autumn and winter visitor.

Below: A female red-backed shrike feeding her young at the nest. Both male and female birds feed the chicks as they become older, but at first the cock bird brings food for the hen to give to the young.

THE EDIBLE DORMOUSE

The edible or fat dormouse is an alien species from the Continent which has managed to establish a foothold in Britain. It is out and about in summer only – it hibernates for seven months each year.

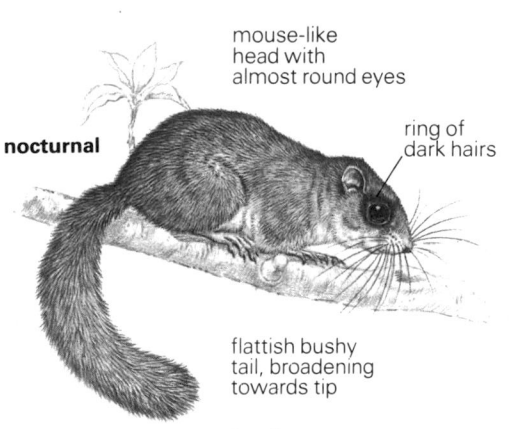

mouse-like head with almost round eyes

nocturnal

ring of dark hairs

flattish bushy tail, broadening towards tip

Adult fat dormouse

almond-shaped eyes

diurnal

round bushy tail becoming pointed at tip

Young grey squirrel

The fat dormouse, also known as the grey, edible or squirrel-tailed dormouse, is one of the two members of the Gliridae family found in the British Isles. The common dormouse is a native, but the fat dormouse, which looks similar to a small grey squirrel, is an alien from Continental Europe and has become naturalised in an area of about 160 square kilometres (100 square miles) in the Chilterns, within a triangle formed by Aylesbury, Beaconsfield and Luton.

Arboreal habitat When the fat dormouse wakes from hibernation in April or May its priority is to regain the weight it has slowly lost in its long sleep, and the first few weeks are spent searching for food. It is mainly a vegetarian, feeding on a diet of nuts, seeds, fruit and tree bark, although insects, birds' eggs and nestlings are sometimes eaten. In Britain it eats a high proportion of stored fruit, especially apples, and causes damage to willow, plum and conifer trees by gnawing the bark.

Fat dormice are the most arboreal of the dormouse family, spending most of their lives in bushes and trees. They are easily mistaken for grey squirrels, and indeed they are squirrel-like in many respects. They are well adapted for life above ground, and are accomplished acrobats. They are able to jump up to 7m (23ft) between branches, and can fall safely from great heights. They are skilled climbers, using their sharp pointed claws to grip the bark, and they can climb even very thin branches, using their long bushy tails as a balance.

Nocturnal habits Fat dormice usually emerge from their nests at dusk to begin the night's activity, although they are occasionally seen by day. They are very vocal, especially during the breeding season.

As well as having good nocturnal eyesight, the fat dormouse has other senses that help it to explore its surroundings at night. It has very sensitive touch pads on the face, chin and lower arms, and stiff facial hairs (vibrissae) up to 6cm (2.4in) long. These pads and hairs inform the dormouse of its surroundings as it brushes them against twigs, leaves and other obstacles. The ears are broad and prominent, and the dormouse flaps the outer section

backwards and forwards twice each second when it is listening.

During summer the fat dormouse makes a nest of soft vegetation, either in a tree hole or in a fork close to the trunk. The nest is usually built in deciduous woodland, or in mixed woodland. In the British Isles fat dormice often make their nests in buildings – barns, stables, and the lofts or wall cavities of houses–using materials such as cloth or paper as bedding.

Single litter The breeding season begins in midsummer. Males court females by following them around in the trees, uttering a soft twittering sound until allowed to mate. Pregnant females isolate themselves and build a breeding nest, either by bringing fresh nesting material into the usual home, or by constructing a new nest in the crown of a tree. The young are born naked and do not open their eyes until 30 days old. They are nursed until their eyes open, the mother straddling them with her legs to form a 'box' in which the young lie on their backs to suckle. This position becomes increasingly uncomfortable

Left: The German name for the fat dormouse is 'der Siebenschläfer', the seven sleeper. It may spend its seven months of hibernation in a burrow, a hollow tree, a woodpecker's hole, a rock or root cavity, the loft of a house, or even a beehive.

Opposite page: Edible dormice are particularly fond of fruit.

FAT DORMOUSE (*Glis glis*), (also known as the grey, edible or squirrel-tailed dormouse).
Size head and body 15-18cm (5.9-7in); tail 13-16cm (5.1-6.3in); weight 150-200g (5.3-7oz).
Colour Silver-grey above, light grey to white below. Ring of black hair around each eye. The silver-grey tail has a parting on the underside which is lighter in colour.
Breeding season June-August. Usually one litter with 5-9 young.
Gestation 30 days.
No of young 5-9.
Food Fruit (mainly stored apples and cherries), nuts, insects, bark of some trees.
Predators Dogs, cats, rats, stoats, weasels, owls. Man–trapping.
Distribution Roughly 100 square miles between Luton, Aylesbury and Beaconsfield.

for the mother as they grow.

Within a few days of birth the mother begins licking the mouths of her offspring, possibly stimulating them to suckle. As they grow they in turn lick their mother, (but never each other). In the nest the young dormice may pick up a parasite, an American squirrel flea *Orchopeas wickhami*, introduced by the grey squirrel.

The young dormice reach adult size in about three months, but do not breed until they are about two years old. They soon become accomplished acrobats, making great leaps between branches, sometimes hanging on by their hind feet. If they lose their footing, they spread their tail and legs to form a 'parachute' and land safely. They may remain with their mother for several months, even through hibernation.

Heavy sleepers In autumn fat dormice prepare for hibernation by steadily increasing their food intake and becoming very fat. If warm material is not already present in the hibernation quarters, the dormice make nests of grass, leaves and moss. Hibernation starts between late September and mid-November, individuals nesting either alone or in communal nests of up to eight animals.

Males hibernate first, followed by females and young animals. During hibernation the dormouse's metabolism is severely reduced and the body shows little sign of life as its stored energy reserves are used. By the end of the seven month hibernation between 35% and 50% of the animal's body weight will have burned up.

Dormice domesticity Under most circumstances fat dormice are not aggressively inclined, and when searching for food several may congregate in a single tree. They may even live in small colonies. Individual home

Above: Young fat dormice with their mother. It takes them about three months to reach adult size, and they may eventually travel up to 1.2km (¾ mile) to set up a new territory of their own.

Below: To help conserve energy the dormouse sleeps with its tail drawn over its head and abdomen, and with its outer ears folded inwards, considerably reducing the surfaces from which heat might be lost.

ranges, about 100m (330ft) in diameter, are scent marked with gland secretions.

Fat dormice can live for up to six years in the wild, but the majority fall victim to predation before then, especially during hibernation when they are at their most vulnerable. The most common predators are nocturnal hunters such as owls, stoats, weasels, rats and domestic cats and dogs. They have an escape mechanism that sometimes helps them to give predators the slip: the vertebrae in the tail are very brittle, and if the tail is seized by a predator, the tip breaks off.

Roman delicacy It is probable that during the Roman occupation fat dormice were imported to Britain from Italy. The method of rearing them for the table is well documented. They were fed on acorns, chestnuts and fruit, and for a final fattening they were put into barrel-like earthenware pots (*dolia*) and kept in darkness. They were killed, stuffed with minced pork and dormouse meat, roasted and served with a sweet sauce. Hosts competed to have the fattest dormice, and even today the almond-tasting flesh is regarded as a gourmet's delight in parts of Europe.

Fat dormice are a protected species under the European convention. Although the British population is small and restricted, it has the rather unique distinction of being classed as both a notifiable pest (since it damages trees), and also a protected species listed in the Wildlife and Countryside Act of 1981.

As they are largely nocturnal, they are not easy to observe in the wild, though you may hear them among stored fruit as they roll and bounce apples around. Other signs of their presence are nuts with a large jagged hole in them; nibbled fruit and chewed fruit peel around human habitation; and scuff marks on the ground made by the dragged tail.

THE UBIQUITOUS BANK VOLE

This small, mouse-like rodent leads a short but active life in woodlands throughout the summer. Quite recently it has made its first appearance in south-west Ireland. Like the closely related field vole, it is an important source of food for many predators.

Above: Bank voles have chestnut red upperparts, grey flanks and silvery grey to creamy buff underparts. They vary considerably in weight and size. Animals born late in the summer overwinter measuring about 9cm (3½in) in length. At the start of the breeding season in spring this increases to 11cm (4¾in). Weight also varies from 16g (½oz) in winter to 30g (1oz) in summer.

The bank vole, also known as the red backed vole, is small and mouse-like. In fact in some country districts it is called, rather mis-leadingly, the bank mouse or red mouse. However, several distinctive vole features distinguish it from a mouse. It has a shaggy coat of bright chestnut-coloured fur, quite unlike the sleeker, finer coat of a mouse. It has a blunt nose, small eyes, small ears which are almost hidden in fur, short legs and a short tail.

The bank vole is distinguished from its close relatives the field vole and the much larger water vole by its smaller size and the rich red of its upperparts. Its tail is long for a vole, being about half the length of its head and body, and its ears are slightly more prominent than those of other voles.

Woodland whereabouts The bank vole is found in deciduous woodland and scrubland, and along banks in hedgerows. Each bank vole occupies a home range of at least 45m (148ft) in diameter. It usually makes its home where there is thick cover, especially brambles and bracken, but it occasionally ventures on to open ground if the vegetation is sufficiently tall to give it cover, or if a bank or wall is present. It also lives along river banks and is an excellent swimmer. It could possibly be confused with a young water vole–however, a small, immature water vole would almost certainly be accompanied by a parent.

A busy forager The bank vole is a lively creature, busy by day and by night, but with an increase in nocturnal activity in the summer months. These short bursts of foraging are interspersed with periods of rest or sleep. It is an agile climber, but spends most of its time rushing about on the ground.

It is mainly vegetarian in diet, feeding on a great variety of plant material, such as leaves, fruits, seeds, nuts, berries, roots, fungi and the grain of wheat and barley. It also eats a small quantity of snails, worms, insects and larvae. In winter when green food is scarce the bank vole sometimes gnaws the bark of trees. The thick outer corky layer is of no interest and is often scattered on the ground below the gnawed branch. The inner living

How to tell voles and mice apart

Look for the typical vole features—shaggy coat, roundish head, short tail and limbs and small eyes.

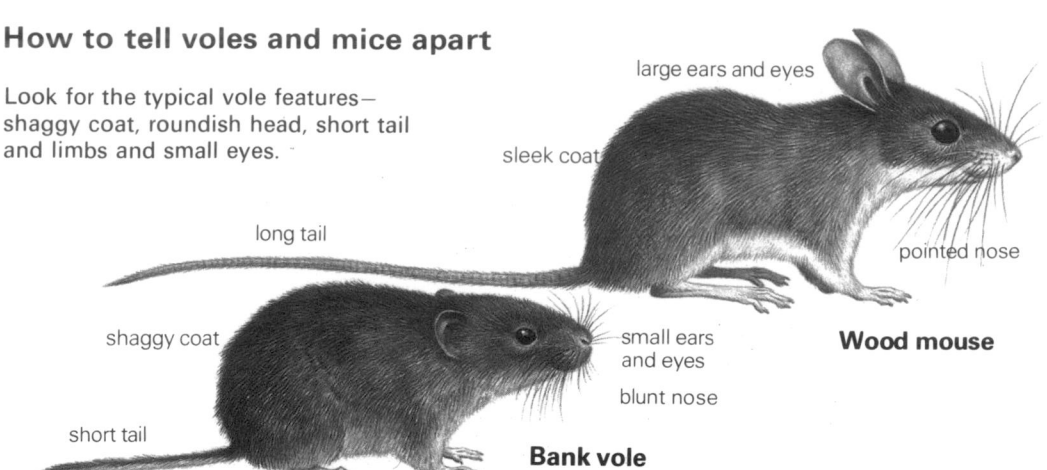

large ears and eyes

sleek coat

long tail

pointed nose

Wood mouse

shaggy coat

small ears and eyes

blunt nose

short tail

Bank vole

BANK VOLE (*Clethrionomys glareolus*).
Size Max length (excluding tail) 11cm (4¾in). Max weight 30g (1oz).
Colour Reddish above, grey on flanks, pale beneath.
Breeding season Usually April-October but may last through winter.
Gestation Usually 17-18 days, but up to 30 days.
No of young Average 4.
Lifespan 2-18 months.
Food Mainly vegetarian, but also eats insects and worms.
Predators Most predators.

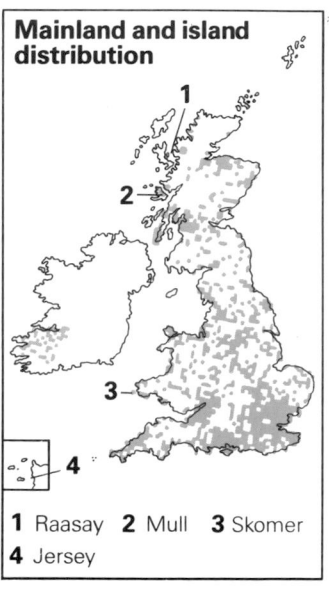

Mainland and island distribution

1 Raasay **2** Mull **3** Skomer
4 Jersey

Above: *Clethrionomys glareolus* is separated into five sub-species. The mainland sub-species is *C.g. glareolus*, *C.g. caesarius* is found on Jersey, *C.g. skomerensis* on Skomer, *C.g. alstoni* on Mull and *C.g. erica* on Raasay.

Opposite: A predator's eye view of a bank vole.

Below: Young bank voles in the nest.

part of bark attracts the vole, but because it is a small, weak animal its teeth do not penetrate very deep. It prefers trees with soft bark and climbs agilely up a tree to sit in the angle of a branch where it can gnaw in comfort.

The bank vole chatters and squeaks as it goes about its business, but its sense of smell, rather than these vocalisations, is probably a more important form of communication. Drops of urine are released at regular intervals, probably to mark the extent of its home range. The odour of faeces, and body smells, can convey an enormous amount of information and bank voles can even distinguish between their own odour and that of other sub-species.

The bank vole's home range is criss-crossed by a network of overground runways, and also underground tunnels, that centre on a nest constructed at a depth of 2-10cm (1-4in). Surplus food is sometimes stored in these underground tunnels.

A brief but busy life The breeding season is a long one, starting in April and continuing until late into October. If food, such as acorns, is in plentiful supply, breeding may continue through winter. On average there are four young to a litter and the female may produce up to five litters in a season. The female is ready to mate again immediately after the birth of her young.

The young are born blind and naked and spend the first days of their lives, when they

are completely helpless, in the breeding nest. This may be below ground but usually it is above ground level, wedged in a crevice in a tree trunk or in an old tree stump. The female uses locally available materials to construct the nest, so in a woodland habitat leaves, moss and feathers are used, while in grassland grasses and moss are utilised.

At birth the young weigh only 2g. The grey-brown juvenile coat appears after four to ten days, and the first moult to longer denser fur occurs between four and six weeks later. Their eyes open at around twelve days old, they are weaned at two and a half weeks, and are sexually mature after four to five weeks.

Animals born early in the breeding season

Above: All four island sub-species of bank voles are larger than the mainland one. This Skomer vole is at least 30% heavier than the mainland vole. Its upperparts are a brighter red and its underparts are cream.

Left: The droppings are cylindrical, usually with rounded ends. The colour varies with diet: in summer they are usually greenish but in winter they are brown to black.

The bank vole's predators The bank vole forms part of the diet of most birds of prey and carnivores, especially those animals, such as the barn owl, tawny owl, kestrel and weasel, that hunt in woodland. A build up in the bank vole population is often accompanied by an increase in the numbers of those animals that prey upon it. These predators stay and breed in the area for a couple of years and then move on to new hunting grounds once the voles have declined in number.

Occasionally, when the food that forms its usual diet is in short supply, or when there is pressure upon that food supply due to an increase in numbers, the bank vole may become a forestry pest. Under these conditions it relies increasingly on tree bark as a source of nourishment, and can cause considerable damage, especially when it attacks young trees.

Distribution The bank vole is found throughout mainland Britain. As recently as 1964 a population was also found living in a limited area in the south west of Ireland. The Irish population is probably a recent introduction, although no one is sure how it arose. In addition to the mainland population the bank vole also inhabits certain widely distributed offshore islands. Four sub-species have been recognised on islands off Britain. They are Raasay, Mull, Skomer and Jersey – named after the islands on which they were found.

nature quickly and breed in the same year. These are likely to be sufficiently large and strong to survive the rigours of winter and will breed again the next season. However, those animals born late in the season grow slowly and do not reproduce until after their first winter, if they manage to survive at all. It is unlikely that any bank vole survives more than one winter, so two breeding seasons is probably the maximum. The lifespan varies considerably, from two or three months up to eighteen months, although they can live for 40 months in captivity.

Population fluctuations The bank vole population varies considerably throughout the year, usually reaching a peak in June and falling off towards the end of the breeding season when fewer females are reproducing and the average litter size is smaller.

The bank vole population may also vary considerably from year to year. The most common pattern is for the size of the population to increase gradually over several successive years and then quite suddenly, for no obvious reason, there is a dramatic drop in numbers. These cycles last on average three to four years, although British woodlands are not subjected to the enormous fluctuations that occur on the Continent. The reasons for these cyclical population changes have not yet been satisfactorily explained, although the sudden decline at the end of the cycle may be due to overcrowding.

How rodents open hazel nuts

Like other rodents, the bank vole has its own special method of opening the thick, hard shell of the hazel nut to get at the kernel inside. It holds the nut underneath its body, using its forefeet to brace the nut against the ground. The base is wedged under its chest and the tip slopes away from the animal. Once the vole has made the initial hole in the shell it puts its snout inside and gnaws the side nearest to it, from the inside. This leaves a very clearly marked gnawed inside edge which contrasts with the undamaged outer edge. The wood mouse handles hazel nuts in much the same way as the bank vole, but it holds the nut with the base pointed outwards and the nut inclined towards its body. It makes a hole in the tip, occasionally in the side, and then inserts its lower incisors. It turns the nut as it gnaws, the upper incisors leaving a series of marks on the outside of the shell around the hole. The squirrel holds the nut in its forefeet, gnaws a hole in the top and inserts its lower incisors, using them like a crowbar to split the nut.

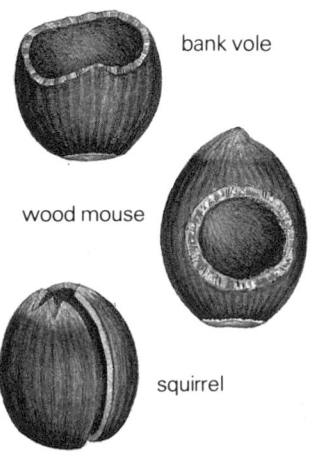

bank vole

wood mouse

squirrel

Autumn ~
season of mists and harvests

The first shades of autumn fall in the gentle changeling month of September. Sunny days, but longer, cooler nights, then increasing wind and rain, cause plant and animal communities to undergo profound changes in their lifestyles. The fields stand bare, the annual harvest already gathered and stored for the long cold winter ahead.

In early autumn the sun, though in retreat, is still strong by day, drawing moist air upwards from the land surface. The lengthening nights, however, accompany a sharp drop in temperature, bathing the countryside in mist, heavy dew and, on still clear nights, frost. High pressure and its attendant warm sunny days often hold sway, so that summer seems to steal a march on autumn, giving farmers some leeway with late harvesting. Towards October, however, deepening depressions far to the north of the British Isles can put a swift end to this Indian summer. The winds they generate are typically vigorous northwesters which bring chill blasts and squally rain. This turn for the worse has long been associated with the autumn equinox, when the latitude of the sun decrees a day and night of equal length. It is often a foretaste of future storms, the more so in Scotland where October sees the first flurries of snow on the hills.

Throughout summer the life support system of deciduous trees has been the green pigment chlorophyll, which interacts with sunlight to provide the power source to manufacture all the trees' nutrients. With shorter days, and a weakening sun, trees can no longer sustain chlorophyll production and the system begins to shut down. The decaying green pigment is replaced by yellow and red which are more resistant to sunlight than chlorophyll.

A sudden bout of chill weather after an Indian summer triggers hurried adjustments in pigment when sap pressure is still high, often gilding leaves with especially flamboyant colours. The colours of autumn leaves are, however, mere staging posts in a more radical withdrawal. As ground temperatures drop, the root systems of trees find it harder to extract water, and the leaves are shed so that the tree may husband its resources. Each leaf stem is sealed off by a special layer of cells, and the autumn winds do the rest.

The woodland floor is now awash with the colours of discarded leaves, uniquely enhanced in autumn by fungi. They emerge overnight, drawing sustenance from the decaying litter around them. The type of litter or soil may explain an otherwise unpredictable and erratic distribution of fungi. The scarlet fly agaric, flecked with creamy scales, flourishes in conifer woods along with many

Left: The brightly coloured leaves of autumn carpet a woodland floor.

Below: Autumn sunlight highlights the golden colour of these bracken fronds.

of the other more exotic growth forms. The strange earthstars often pop up in beechwoods, while the giant puff-ball may lurk in field, hedgerow, or even garden. In general, a hot summer followed by a moist autumn seems to produce the best turn-out of this bizarre community of lowly plants.

A blanket of leaf litter helps to protect not only the roots of trees, but also a host of cold-blooded animals which, like deciduous trees, can no longer maintain the metabolic turn-over needed for all-out activity. In October many creep into crevices in fence posts, under stones or bark or, indeed, into any refuge where they can hibernate safely in a state of torpor. The hollow withered stems of hog-weed make a perfect over-wintering chamber for earwigs, for instance, and a cosy cushion of moss an inviting haven for ladybirds.

Cold as these insects are, there often appears to be a slight advantage in the added insulation given by bedfellows. Scores of ladybirds may huddle together, and several garden snails can cluster underground, cemented in a mucous embrace. Each snail also protects itself by sealing off the aperture of its shell with a mucous plug.

Amphibians and reptiles may also hibernate together, especially in northern areas. Sometimes they are united in their common attraction to a traditionally good overwinter-ing site, but possibly they also benefit from what little collective body warmth they muster when entwined. Communal living among snakes in winter also guarantees readier access to mates in spring. Toads may over-winter with lizards, and both in turn with snakes. Snakes often begin to hibernate about the end of September, but many remain active for up to a month after that if it is warm enough for them to do so.

Faced with up to five months to eke out their summer savings of body fat, reptiles remain active in the warmth of autumn for as long as possible. The tenacity of animals – and plants – in capital-ising on the vagaries of the weather is one of the hallmarks of autumn. In some years it is short and sharp, in others it crawls sedately into winter. If the weather is mild, many plants, such as daisies, herb robert, and even poppies, continue to flower late into November. The coastline supports some particularly handsome late flowers in sea rocket, and the sea holly whose colours seem to echo to perfection the soft blue-green mist of the autumn seascape.

Some plants which flowered profusely in spring, such as the sweet violet and wood sorrel, are now quietly engaged in a second wave of self-propagation. Darwin was the first to unravel this largely unseen process and suggest an explanation for it. Only close inspection of the plant's foliage will reveal these curious autumn flowers which, having no petals, no nectar, and almost no pollen, exude no scent and have evidently not evolved to attract insects.

Instead, these flowers are closed and self-fertilising as an insurance against the chance that the main blooms open to a cold wet spring when there are no insects about to fertilise them. Darwin's meticulous experi-ments demonstrated that these autumn flow-ers, which include the dead-nettles, vetches and peas, seed just as heavily as their spring counterparts, so providing an ingenious ad-dition to the plant's strategies for survival.

Although bees are now deprived of sum-mer's rich bank of nectar and pollen, ivy offers a late bonanza. In October and Novem-ber its drumheads of seemingly modest flow-ers produce a heavy nectar flow, while its pollen is highly accessible to insects with short tongues, such as the numerous flies and wasps. On a sunny day ivy attracts legions of flying insects, including such butterflies as the red admiral, comma and painted lady. They have an invaluable opportunity to stock up on their energy reserves before laying a batch of overwintering eggs, or before hibernation. The fruits of bramble, now pulpy and easily breached as they rot in the autumn frosts, likewise serve as a last-ditch fuelling station, and are gratefully tapped for their sugary secretions.

For many insects, however, in the end there is no escape from the autumn cold. We can readily witness the death throes of flies on our window-sills, like clockwork toys running down. Indoors, spiders such as *Tegenaria* grow to startling proportions on their feast of easily trapped prey, while normally discreet beetles such as the devil's coach-horse boldly break cover in search of victims.

Out in the open, decaying foliage shimmers with a riot of spiders' webs. Especially prolific are the hammock webs of the money spider *Linyphia*. Their elfin 'seine nets', cast wholesale over bramble, gorse and grassy fields, are deadly efficient, and have been shown to trap over 150 sorts of insects. On warm mornings masses of these webs float aloft on rising air, often alighting miles away. The spiders frequently pilot their own webs, apparently using this power of levitation as a convenient means of dispersal.

With the decline of insect life, birds and small mammals switch to autumn's grand profusion of fruits, berries and seeds. A rain of acorns, hazel nuts, sweet chestnuts and other nutritious seeds descends to the woodland floor, to be hoarded by mice, voles and squirrels for winter consumption. Though most mammals specialise in particular sorts of seeds, some enjoy a remarkably catholic diet in autumn. Least choosy of all is the badger, which supplements its basic diet with nuts, berries, windfall apples and plums, and even edible fungi. The fox, too, takes all it can find.

For trees, armies of attentive birds and mammals are valued agents of seed dispersal and accordingly they freely advertise their wares. Many, such as spindle, holly and yew proclaim their ripe seeds by lurid red colours, and offer a sweet, palatable, fleshy coat as a reward. Mistletoe berries glisten an eye-catching white against their evergreen foliage, and are especially relished by thrushes. Jays, which skulk shyly in the depths of the woods in summer, may now be seen flying high over oakwoods, their crops gorged with acorns which they cache in the ground against leaner pickings in winter. Inevitably some of these hoards are forgotten or are scattered by plundering animals, to the benefit of the parent oak. Jays play a specially intriguing role in the spread of oak-woods uphill, since the tree has no other means of sending its bulky seed in this direction. (The seeds always fall downhill.)

At first, autumn appears to offer a limitless bounty for wildlife. Much is short-lived, however, and as the season wears on the food supply becomes patchy. Some birds, such as the robin and kingfisher, now annexe a feeding territory for themselves and defend it fiercely against rivals. Most birds, however, choose strength in numbers, forming large nomadic flocks, perhaps the better to discover the whereabouts of dwindling resources. Starlings fall on elderberries in squabbling hordes, while tits and finches comb the woods for beechmast, spindle and other manageable seeds.

In a good beechmast year they are often joined by bramblings, which migrate to escape the grip of their native Scandinavian winter. Many other birds adopt the same strategy, resulting in a huge influx of autumn migrants. Typical of foggy October nights is the thin plaintive 'seep' of redwings which, along with fieldfares, navigate across the North Sea to join our thrushes in exploiting the berry harvest. Tens of thousands of pink-footed geese make the journey from Iceland, flighting noisily into Scottish stubbles and pastures.

These, at least, we can distinguish as foreign visitors, but for others it becomes impossible to establish nationality. Our estuaries, for instance, now throng with redshank and other waders from polar regions, mingling freely with British representatives of the same species. Many British blackbirds and song thrushes leave in autumn for the relative luxury of southern Europe, while others of their kind arrive from abroad.

By mid-November our plant and animal communities have therefore made often far-reaching adjustments for their well-being and survival, and now brace themselves for winter.

AUTUMN COLOURS
IN OUR COUNTRYSIDE

As the heat of the summer slowly gives way to the oncoming winter with its frosts and snow, the colours of the countryside shift from the predominant greens of summer foliage and unripe fruits to the yellows, reds and browns of dying leaves, juicy berries and ripe nuts.

Above: No other type of wood takes on such glorious autumn colours as a beechwood—this is Bratley Wood in the New Forest. Throughout this time of year the colour of the leaves gradually deepens from yellow to a rich shade of orange or yellow-brown before the leaves fall. Young beech trees, however, retain their leaves through the winter to protect the new buds from frost.

Just as leaves give summer its overall impression of greenness, so do they contribute most to autumn's hues–and none more so than tree leaves. Leaves are the power houses of a tree, producing simple sugars directly from water and carbon dioxide. At the end of the growing season these small power houses close down and, on most British trees, are cast off. This loss of leaves at a certain time of year (known to us as autumn, but more picturesquely described by the American word 'fall') is due mainly to the fact that leaves encourage the passage of water through the tree. In winter, with water hard to come by from frozen ground and trees generally being less active metabolically, the less they need the better.

The leaves are discarded by the formation of a watertight boundary (the abscission layer) between the branch and the leaf stem. This brittle boundary effectively isolates the leaf from the tree and the break that removes the leaf occurs here. Before this layer has been built up, however, the most obvious sign of the leaf's impending fall, that of colour change, has already taken place. This is the breakdown of chlorophyll, the green compound essential to the leaf's production of sugars. The useful constituent parts of the chlorophyll are ferried away into the main body of the tree, where they are stored until the following spring. As this process goes on, other compounds in the leaf, which were previously masked by the intensity of the chlorophyll's green, become noticeable. The most abundant of these are compounds known as flavenoids, which are yellow, and carotenoids, which are red or orange. It is the presence of these compounds in autumn leaves that is responsible for the colours we associate with this time of the year.

The purpose of the flavenoids and carotenoids is to protect the chlorophyll against too much sunlight, which can cause this complex molecule to break down. The greater the amount of sunlight, the greater the production of flavenoids and carotenoids, and so the finer the autumn colours. This is why northern North America has such spectacular autumn colours: its summers are short but the light intensity is always very high.

Trees in autumn Perhaps the trees with the most brilliant autumn colours are the maples. In Britain our own native field maple has small leaves that turn a delicate shade of reddish-brown or yellow. The introduced Norway maple turns a bright yellow in the autumn, while the sycamore–the most common maple in this country–also ends the season yellow. None of our maples, however, can match the brilliant yellows and reds of two North American species, the red maple and the silver maple. Even in Britain, both these trees can often be seen with leaves that are quite literally scarlet, which makes them popular as ornamental plants in public parks and large gardens.

Outside the maple genus, many cherry trees brighten up the autumn with their leaf colours just as they do the spring with their blossom. Even our own native wild cherry–a common hedgerow species–turns red or pink in the autumn.

Among our native trees, however, by far the most common autumn colours are yellows and browns. On birches and the wych elm the leaves turn yellow before falling. The English elm–a species sadly much reduced after the ravages of Dutch elm disease–has yellow-brown leaves and the endearing habit of shedding them in a short space of time, often only a single day. Our native poplars all have yellow leaves in the autumn, as does the horse chestnut, a tree that adds another dimension to autumn with its rich brown 'conkers'. Beech leaves undergo a gradual change from yellow into a rich shade of orange or yellow-brown before they fall, while oak has golden-brown autumn leaves, which stay on the tree a long time before falling.

Smaller plants In contrast to trees, which by

Above: One of the most vividly coloured shrubs in the autumn is the spindle tree. Throughout the summer it remains an inconspicuous plant with narrow lance-shaped leaves and tiny yellowish-green flowers. Come late summer, however, the fruits begin to develop into coral-pink, four-lobed capsules which split open to reveal bright orange seeds. As the autumn progresses the plant becomes even more colourful as the leaves take on a pinkish hue.

Below: The brilliant yellow autumn colour of a sycamore in the Lake District. Maples (of which the sycamore is one) provide us with some of our most spectacular autumn leaf colours.

virtue of their size remain noticeable whatever the season, many smaller plants–both herbaceous and woody–may catch the eye only in the autumn. Plants that may not have been particularly visible around the middle of summer suddenly reveal their presence a month or so later by the colours of their fruits and seeds. In hedgerow bottoms the cuckoo pint reveals its bright red berries, while the wild dog rose loses its pale pink flowers, which are replaced by the more eye-catching shiny red hips.

Woodlands and hedges on chalk soils are particularly well endowed with autumn decoration, with three climbing plants taking pride of place. The first of these is old man's beard, whose fluffy white seed heads, bereft of any spectacular colour, are still a characteristic sight in autumn hedgerows. The other two species both have red berries and both share the same common name–bryony. White bryony, however, is a member of the cucumber family while black bryony belongs (rather surprisingly) to the yam family. Both plants are far more conspicuous in fruit than they are in flower–despite their names, both bear small white flowers. Black bryony is especially noticeable because it loses its leaves in the autumn, leaving the bare stems hung with bright red berries. Winding through the undergrowth like this, it resembles a string of beads.

Chalkland fruits Several bushes and small

Above: These bright red berries of the wayfaring tree are not yet ripe. They will slowly darken to become black at maturity, while the leaves simultaneously take on their reddish autumn hue.

Below: Horse chestnut leaves showing the complete range of colours from green through yellow to red and brown as green chlorophyll in the leaf cells is broken down, allowing the yellow and red flavenoids and carotenoids to show through.

trees of chalk scrubland have distinctive fruits. The common buckthorn, for example, which is a thorny shrub growing to a height of 2.5-5m (8-16ft) tall, has clusters of black berries, which contrast very effectively with its yellow or yellow-brown oval leaves. These berries have a very strong purging effect; hence its alternative common name of purging buckthorn.

The small wayfaring tree, which despite its name is often a bush, is a distinctive plant in both spring and autumn, its early heads of white flowers being replaced by red berries later in the year. Another very handsome small tree, the whitebeam, looks attractive from spring through to autumn with the silvery-white undersides to its leaves (hence its common name) and the lovely heads of white flowers that appear in May and June. Like the wayfaring tree it, too, produces heads of red berries in the autumn, though whitebeam berries tend to be round whereas those of the wayfaring tree are more oval and they also turn black later in the season.

Elder is another tree or large shrub that shows well in the autumn, its heads of blue-black berries attracting both birds and winemakers alike.

Spindle and dogwood The two most colourful shrubs of chalkland in the autumn are undoubtedly the spindle tree and dogwood. The spindle tree remains an insignificant plant for much of the year until the late summer when its fruits begin to form. These are coral-pink, four-lobed capsules and contain orange seeds.

Dogwood is slightly more conspicuous than the spindle tree. It is a small shrub with oval leaves that produces small creamy-white flowers in early summer. These develop into black berries by September, and towards the end of autumn the leaves turn crimson and the shoots blood-red. The shoots stay this colour after the leaves drop, and remain so until they are hidden by new growth next spring.

As the colour balance shifts from the greens of summer and its brightly coloured flowers to the more subtle yellows and browns of dying leaves, there are still splashes of eye-catching colour to be seen in the abundance of fruits.

Autumn colours

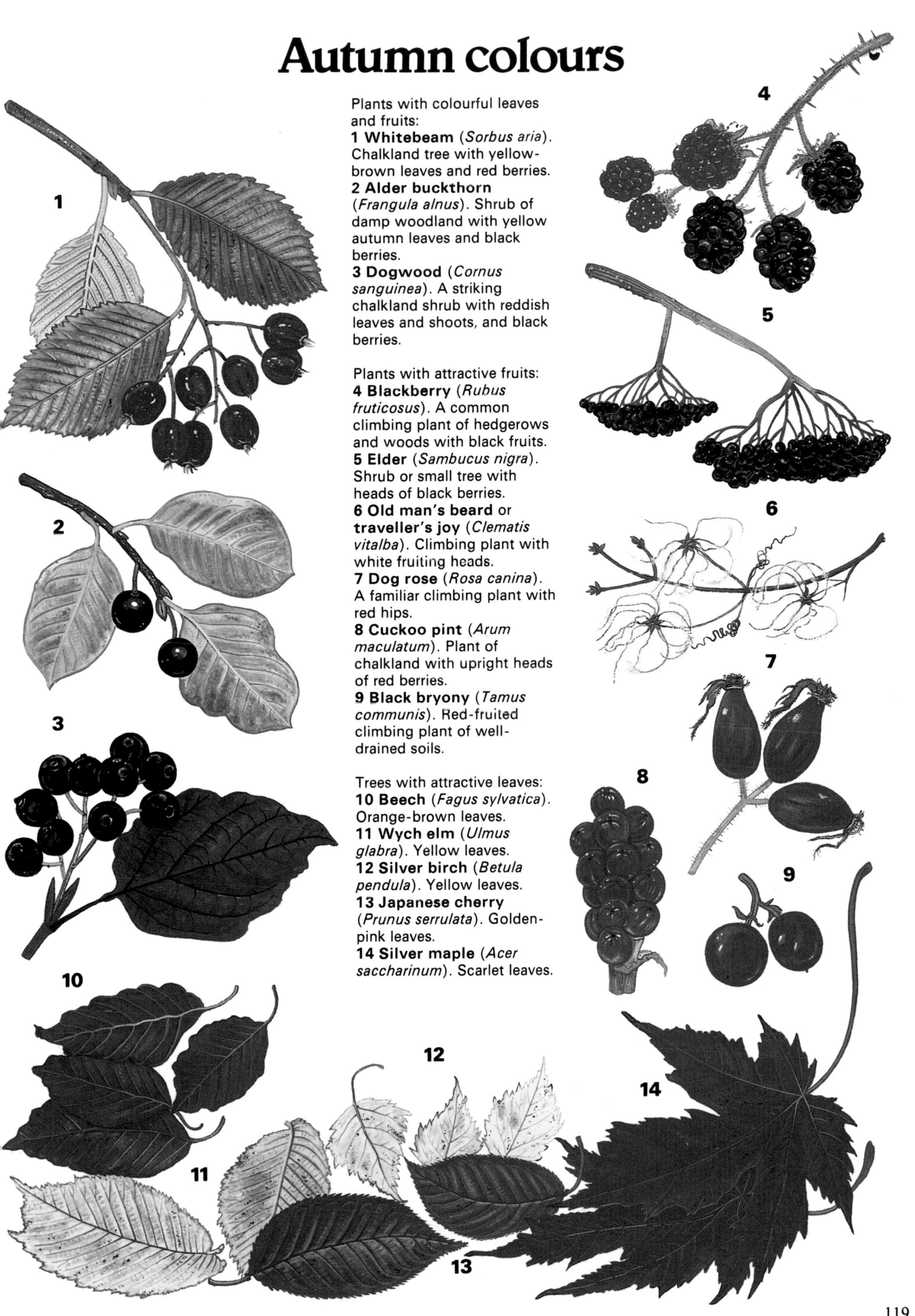

Plants with colourful leaves and fruits:

1 Whitebeam (*Sorbus aria*). Chalkland tree with yellow-brown leaves and red berries.

2 Alder buckthorn (*Frangula alnus*). Shrub of damp woodland with yellow autumn leaves and black berries.

3 Dogwood (*Cornus sanguinea*). A striking chalkland shrub with reddish leaves and shoots, and black berries.

Plants with attractive fruits:

4 Blackberry (*Rubus fruticosus*). A common climbing plant of hedgerows and woods with black fruits.

5 Elder (*Sambucus nigra*). Shrub or small tree with heads of black berries.

6 Old man's beard or **traveller's joy** (*Clematis vitalba*). Climbing plant with white fruiting heads.

7 Dog rose (*Rosa canina*). A familiar climbing plant with red hips.

8 Cuckoo pint (*Arum maculatum*). Plant of chalkland with upright heads of red berries.

9 Black bryony (*Tamus communis*). Red-fruited climbing plant of well-drained soils.

Trees with attractive leaves:

10 Beech (*Fagus sylvatica*). Orange-brown leaves.

11 Wych elm (*Ulmus glabra*). Yellow leaves.

12 Silver birch (*Betula pendula*). Yellow leaves.

13 Japanese cherry (*Prunus serrulata*). Golden-pink leaves.

14 Silver maple (*Acer saccharinum*). Scarlet leaves.

FLESHY FRUITS: THEIR FORM AND FUNCTION

All flowering plants bear fruits but those that come to mind most readily are the ones we eat, such as apples, plums and blackberries. These fleshy fruits are a special adaptation by plants to tempt both man and animals alike into eating them and so dispersing the seeds inside.

Above: The honeysuckle bears fleshy berries while some of its flowers still remain on the stalk.

Right: This dormouse, by eating the blackberry fruits, acts as a major agent in the dispersal of seeds.

Below: Cranberry fruits are true fruits because they consist of seeds embedded in a fleshy structure developed from the ovary wall.

To most people the word 'fruit' conjures up the image of a succulent fruit–an apple or a peach, or perhaps something more exotic like a mango or a pineapple. But to a botanist the word has a rather different and more precise meaning. Many of the 'fruits' of the layman are not fruits at all–for example the fleshy leaf stalks of rhubarb are not, strictly speaking, a fruit.

Fertilisation and fruits In the narrow botanical definition, a fruit is a structure formed from the wall of the ovary and containing the matured, usually fertilised ovules–the seeds. All flowering plants have fruits. When a flower is pollinated, pollen grains land on the flower's stigma and each

Above: The attractive red fruits (actually berries) of the misnamed strawberry tree, a member of the same family as cranberry.

Below: The true strawberry bears its fruits in the form of pips embedded on the surface of a fleshy red mass—the receptacle.

produces a tube which tunnels through the style and ovary wall. The ovary contains one or more ovules, each containing a female sex cell. When the pollen-tube reaches the ovule a nucleus from the pollen grain, acting as a male sex cell, fertilises the female sex cell.

Once fertilisation has taken place the ovules mature to form seeds, while the ovary wall develops into the fruit. In some plants the ovary wall swells up to become succulent,

forming what is often called a fleshy fruit.

Why fleshy? Most fleshy fruits represent a particular adaptation to ensure that their seeds are dispersed. A fleshy fruit is there to be eaten by an animal—including man. Even fruits that are poisonous to us are usually edible to some species. For example, deadly nightshade is eagerly eaten by pheasants with no apparent harmful effects.

Once eaten, the fleshy part of the fruit is digested but the seeds have a resistant coat that protects them against digestive juices until they are voided. Because of the time lapse, this is likely to happen some distance from the parent plant, so the seeds will have been successfully dispersed and, moreover, with a ready supply of fertiliser.

Some species of plant have become so well adapted to this mechanism of seed dispersal that the seeds will not germinate under normal conditions until they have been acted upon by enzymes in the digestive tract.

Fleshy fruits come in all sorts of different shapes, sizes and colours, and they can be divided into groups according to which parts of the original flower form the various parts of the fruit.

Berries These are fruits in which the entire wall of the ovary becomes more or less fleshy. Within this flesh are embedded one or more seeds. Among the most familiar berries are those belonging to species of the nightshade family, such as deadly nightshade and black nightshade—both of which have black berries —and the red-fruited woody nightshade. The tomato also belongs to the same family; in this case what we usually regard as vegetables are actually fruits—berries.

Among the more exotic fruits eaten in Britain, oranges, bananas and marrows are all berries, though they seem very different. Our own native member of the marrow family, white bryony, has globular red berries which look quite unlike the small, gherkin-like fruits of the squirting cucumber, an introduced member of the same family. This species is naturalised in southern England, spreading itself vigorously by means of its explosive fruits. When ripe, the slightest knock sends a stream of watery, seed-laden juice several metres.

The white-berried mistletoe has sticky seeds that adhere to the beak of a bird as it feeds on the fruits. In the bird's attempts to remove the irritating seeds, it rubs its beak on the branch of a tree, thus depositing the source of its annoyance in crevices—the ideal spot for the seeds of this parasitic plant to germinate and grow.

Stony drupes In the second group of fleshy fruits the inner part of the fruit wall becomes hard and stone-like, encasing a single seed, and the outer part of the wall becomes fleshy. The whole structure is known as a drupe. The most familiar examples of drupes are provided by members of the genus *Prunus,* such as plums and cherries. Wild British species

include the gean, bird cherry and sloe, or blackthorn. The bullace is a naturalised member of this genus with fruits similar to sloes, though larger; the damson is probably a cultivated form of the bullace. Also in this group are greengages, which belong to the same species as plums.

If you look at the stone of a fruit in the plum group you can sometimes tell which species it came from. The stone of an almond is smooth except for numerous small pits. (What most people know as an almond nut is really the stone or the seed inside this stone.) The globular stone of a bird cherry, on the other hand, is covered with short curved ridges, while a sloe stone is covered with irregular bumps. A plum stone is elongated and slightly rough, with grooves along one edge.

Most people think of the elder's black fruits as being berries, but they are in fact drupes. The raspberry is also not a true berry. It is a compound fruit, consisting of a number of small round segments, each of which is a drupe containing a stone (the pip) just like that in a cherry. The thick stalk around which the drupes are arranged is derived from the receptacle of the flower. In the same genus, *Rubus*, is the blackberry, which may have more than 60 drupes to each berry.

False fruits One of the most unusual fruits in the British flora is that of the wild strawberry, which is not technically a fruit at all. The fleshy succulent part is the enlarged receptacle at the base of the flower, so the whole structure is known as a false fruit. The actual fruits are the small yellowish pips scattered over the surface. They correspond to the individual drupes of a blackberry, both plants belonging to the same family, the rose family. A plant very closely related to the wild strawberry is the barren strawberry, in the genus *Potentilla*. However, this plant lacks the fleshy receptacle and has just a head of tiny dry fruits.

Crab apples also belong to the rose family but in this case the inner part of the apple (the core) corresponds to the true fruit while the outer part is formed from the receptacle. The fruits of other members of the rose family are constructed in the same way, including the fruits of roses, known as hips, hawthorn fruits, which are known as haws, and rowan 'berries', which are not true berries.

Other false fruits may develop from different parts of the flower. In the mulberry the female flowers are borne in clusters resembling catkins. After fertilisation the sepals of each flower enlarge to form a small berry-like false fruit. These are borne in clusters in the same arrangement as the flowers, so the effect is of a compound fruit looking rather like a blackberry. A very familiar false fruit is the pineapple, which develops from the stalk and bracts of the flower head.

Fruit impersonators A few plants bear structures that seem to be fruits but are not. The fleshy red arils of a yew tree, for example,

are not fruits because they do not develop from flowers. Yew trees are conifers, not flowering plants, and the arils are equivalent to the individual scales found on the cone of a pine or fir tree.

Some fleshy, brightly coloured structures that resemble fruits are actually seeds, for example, the red seeds of the gladdon, or stinking iris. The fruit of this plant is the whole capsule containing the seeds.

Above: An unusual relative of the familiar black-fruited elder is the alpine elder, which bears red fruits. Native to the Continent, this shrub is widely naturalised in southern Scotland.

Below: Ripening berries of the deadly nightshade.

AUTUMN SEED AND NUT DISPERSAL

The word 'fruit' usually conjures up an image of something edible and succulent – a fleshy fruit. Yet much more common are the dry fruits, such as acorns or the parachute-like fruits of dandelion, all adaptations to ensure dispersal of the seeds.

Fruits fall quite naturally into two general categories: fleshy fruits and dry fruits. The fleshy fruits have become specially adapted to be eaten by animals as a means of ensuring that the seeds inside are dispersed. They can be divided into different types according to their structure. There are the berries, such as mistletoe and nightshade berries, drupes, which includes plums, cherries and sloes, and false fruits, such as strawberries and apples.

The dry fruits, on the other hand, form a much larger group than the fleshy fruits and are much more versatile in terms of seed-dispersal strategies.

Edible nuts One group of dry fruits has evolved a similar strategy to the one used by

Above: A stand of bulrush in the autumn when its flower heads have ripened into masses of fruits, each of which is equipped with tufts of hairs that will allow the fruit to be carried away on the wind.

Right: This close-up view of the fruits of wood avens shows how they are equipped with long, hooked spines with which they latch on to a passing animal and 'hitch a ride' until they fall off some distance away.

fleshy fruits. These are the nuts, a group that includes acorns and hazel nuts. However, instead of relying on the seeds passing through the animal undigested and being excreted, nuts rely on the fact that, although most are eaten and thus destroyed, some always survive. For example the squirrel, making stores of nuts for the winter, frequently forgets the locations of some of them: those nuts have been successfully dispersed.

This may seem a wasteful strategy yet only one out of the hundreds of thousands of acorns produced in the life of an oak tree needs to grow and reach maturity for the population of the species to be maintained.

Many species have fruits that are very similar to a nut, but much smaller. They are often called nutlets and they function in much the same way as a nut. Some of these smaller fruits may be eaten and pass through an animal undigested, like the seed of a fleshy fruit.

Some so-called nuts are technically quite different structures. The almond, for example, is the centre of a drupe and is equivalent to a plum stone. A horse chestnut is not a nut but a large, hard-coated seed, though the sweet chestnut is a nut. The spiny structure enclosing the sweet chestnut on the tree is formed from modified bracts surrounding the flowers, as are acorn cups and the cases containing beech nuts.

Clingers-on Many plants use animals to disperse the fruit – not by the fruit being eaten but by its hitching a ride clinging to fur or feathers.

With no potential food to attract an animal, such plants have to rely on chance encounters which are relatively scarce and brief, so an effective method of attachment is required. Species such as cleavers, enchanter's nightshade, hedge parsley and spotted medick all have fruits bearing numerous hooks, which function in the same manner as the hooks on a man-made 'Velcro' fastener.

Hound's-tongue has spiny fruits, each spine having microscopically small, curved hooks at the tip which are so sharp that, when magnified, they make the tip of a needle look blunt by comparison. Lesser burdock adopts

a slightly different strategy as the entire head of hooked fruits becomes detached from the parent plant, later to break up and spread the seeds.

Catching the wind A great number of plants have dry fruits that are specially adapted to be dispersed by the wind. Small size alone may be enough for the fruit to catch a free ride but, if the individual seed rather than the whole fruit is being dispersed, then the structure can be smaller still.

Plants such as orchids have adopted this strategy, their fruits opening to release the seeds. The method of opening differs from one species to another. A common method is to have small pores in the fruit so the wind shakes out a few seeds at a time.

Wings and parachutes More obvious adaptations for wind dispersal are the wings and parachutes employed by many species. Maples, silver birch, ash and Scots pine all have winged fruits. Parachutes are very common among members of the daisy family. One species, Oxford ragwort, which was introduced to Britain from its native Sicily, escaped from cultivation at the Oxford Botanic Garden and, aided by its parachute fruits, has now spread to much of the British Isles.

Among native members of the daisy family, perhaps the most spectacular fruits are those of goat's-beard, named after the tufts of silky hairs that make up the parachute. The thistles belong to the same family. Many of their fruits seem to have lost their original function: on an autumn day clouds of thistledown can be seen drifting across a meadow yet, frequently, none of the parachutes bears seeds. In the case of the Scots thistle, the fruits are probably dispersed by birds such as goldfinches, which avidly feed on them.

Floating fruits Water provides an efficient means of dispersing fruits, and many plants have been quick to take advantage of it. The large green fruits of the yellow water-lily –known as brandy bottles because of both their shape and their alcoholic aroma–are equipped with air spaces to make them buoyant. They are capable of floating for some distance. Pondweeds also have floating

Above: Like many members of the daisy family, the spear thistle produces parachute-like fruits that are light enough to be carried great distances on the wind. The seed itself is the small, pale brown structure at the centre of the long silver plumes.

Right: The four major categories of fleshy fruit differ according to their structure.

Below: Nuts, such as these hazel nuts, represent a particular adaptation. They all have large food reserves which are needed to supply the developing seedlings with nutrients, enabling them to grow tall enough to overshadow the competition. Yet the presence of such large food stores makes the nuts much heavier than any other type of dry fruit; certainly far too heavy for them to be distributed by wind, water or any other way. Without the assistance of animals, nuts would have little chance of being dispersed.

Fleshy fruit types

Berry

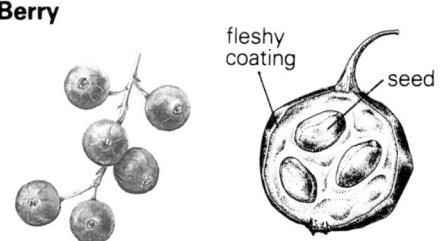

Berries consist of one or more seeds embedded in a fleshy coating. Example: redcurrant.

Drupe

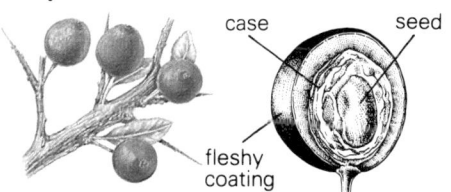

Drupes consist of a seed encased in a hard shell, itself surrounded by a fleshy coating. Example: sloe.

Compound fruit

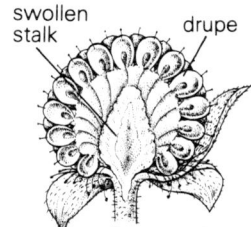

Compound fruits consist of many tiny drupes arranged around a swollen stalk. Example: raspberry.

False fruit

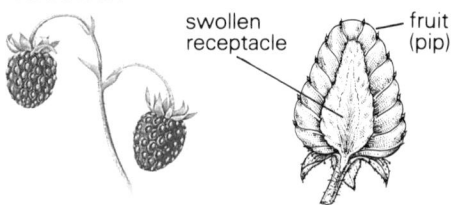

False fruits consist of fruits embedded in a structure such as the flower's receptacle. Example: strawberry.

Left: The winged fruits borne by many trees are one of the most familiar adaptations for dispersal by wind. The fruit of the introduced sycamore (shown here) and our native field maple both consist of pairs of seeds each enclosed within a wing. The two wings have slightly different shapes causing the fruit to spin as it falls from the tree. This slows its fall and allows the wind to carry it some distance from the parent plant.

Above: The fruit of a pansy is a capsule which opens before the seeds are ripe and then closes again to squirt out the mature seeds.

Below: A poppy's capsule contains small openings near the top, through which its thousands of tiny seeds are released—a few at a time—by the action of the wind.

fruits which disperse in freshwater ponds and streams.

A great many plants growing near the sea are dispersed by water, including sea radish and sea kale, both plants with corky fruits that can survive for days or even weeks and still remain buoyant. It is interesting to note that the first flowering plants to colonize the new volcanic island of Surtsey off Iceland included sea sandwort and a close relative of the sea rocket. In both cases the seeds would have arrived by sea.

Self-dispersal Rather than rely upon the vagaries of wind and water to disperse their seeds, some plants do the job themselves. A notable example is the pea family, many of whose members have explosive pods. The tree lupin, for instance, which was introduced to this country from California, rapidly spreads over shingle banks by firing its seeds on to uncolonized ground.

Two fairly common weeds of gardens can be a source of great annoyance to the gardener. Both hairy bitter-cress and yellow sorrel have explosive dispersal mechanisms, and any attempt to remove either plant results in a shower of tiny seeds being sprayed over the garden.

Buried alive A number of adaptations of fruits are concerned not just with dispersal but also with the subsequent establishment of the seedling by ensuring that it starts life in a favourable environment. A particularly in-

teresting example is provided by stork's-bills. This is a group of plants very closely related to crane's-bills and both have similar-looking fruits shaped like a long narrow beak—hence their common names. But the two fruits have quite different strategies. The crane's-bill fruit splits from its base to its tip, in doing so flinging out the seeds and dispersing them.

The stork's-bill has a quite different technique. The beak splits in the same way but the seed is not flung out. Instead, the seed, which is attached to a corkscrew-shaped tail formed from part of the 'beak', falls to the ground (or it may be carried away on an animal and then fall to the ground). Once on the ground any changes in the humidity of the air causes the tail attached to the seed to twist. But the presence of hairs on the seed means that the seed can be twisted in only one direction, not the other. The result is that the seed and its corkscrew-tail progress along the ground until they encounter a crevice. The same twisting motion causes the seed to become buried in the crevice, where it germinates.

A few species seem to have an apparently pointless adaptation in which the fruits are immediately buried in the ground or a crevice, so preventing their dispersal. However, from the point of view of providing the seedling with the right environment the strategy makes sense. Take, for example, the case of the ivy-leaved toadflax. This plant inhabits the crevices of rocks and walls. After fertilisation it pushes its fruits into a crevice where some of the seeds remain to germinate. This provides them with a much better environment in which to grow than they would have if they were left on the rock or allowed to fall to the ground to compete with other plants.

A similar adaptation is shown by the subterranean clover, a rather rare plant of sandy and gravelly soils in southern Britain. After fertilisation the whole flower head is pushed into the ground, where its modified sepals act as anchors, preventing the fruit from being pulled back out.

Dispersal mechanisms

Ingestion

Right: Most fleshy fruits, and several dry fruits such as nuts, are adaptations for being eaten by animals. In fleshy fruits the seeds are voided, while nuts rely on the animal gathering (and thus dispersing) them but subsequently forgetting their location.

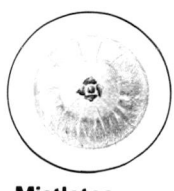

Mistletoe
(Viscum album)

Beech
(Fagus sylvatica)

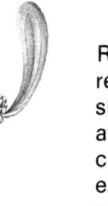

Water dispersal

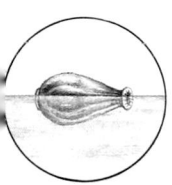

Yellow water-lily
(Nuphar lutea)

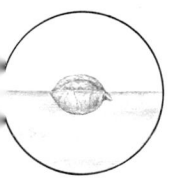

Sea kale
(Crambe maritima)

Right: Several plants, including most members of the pea family, rely on an explosive mechanism to fling their seeds sometimes several metres from the parent plant, thus avoiding the vagaries of wind, water and animals.

Left: Many plants growing close to water—whether fresh or salt—take advantage of this means of seed dispersal. Such seeds, however, have to be buoyant and are often equipped with air pockets for the purpose. Others have a specially light, corky texture.

Self-dispersal

Indian balsam
(Impatiens glandulifera)

Self-burial

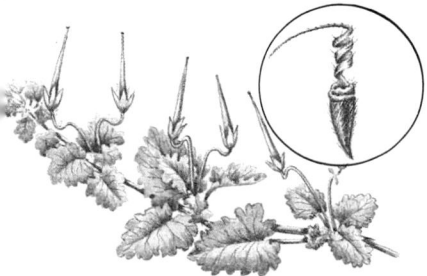

Sea stork's-bill
(Erodium maritimum)

Left: Burial of the seeds is a technique favoured by some plants, especially those that grow in crevices. The plant thus sacrifices long-distance dispersal for the security of at least some of its seeds germinating.

Wind dispersal

Right: Some plants rely on the wind shaking a few seeds at a time out of a capsule. Being extremely tiny, the seeds are then borne away, the distance and direction depending on the wind.

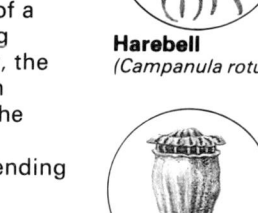

Harebell
(Campanula rotundifolia)

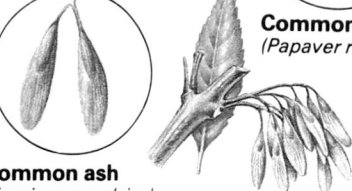

Common poppy
(Papaver rhoeas)

Common ash
(Fraxinus excelsior)

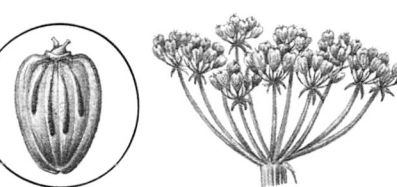

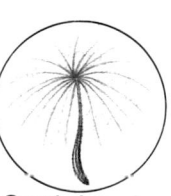

Hogweed
(Heracleum sphondylium)

Right: The other common strategy for harnessing the wind is to equip the seed with a 'parachute' that can catch the wind and carry the seed for perhaps several miles before settling down. Other plants have developed long feathery plumes that perform a similar function.

Left: Another method of utilising the wind is to produce fruits that consist solely of a lightweight seed and a wing to carry it away from the parent plant. This method of dispersal is fairly common among trees.

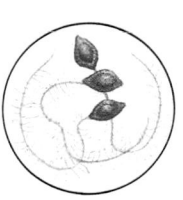

Goat's-beard
(Tragopogon pratensis)

Traveller's joy
(Clematis vitalba)

Animal dispersal

Herb Bennet
(Geum urbanum)

Nodding bur-marigold
(Bidens tripartita)

Left: As well as dispersing seeds by feeding or storing, animals can also perform the same function unwittingly by carrying them on their fur or feathers. Fruits that are dispersed in this manner have developed hooks or barbs as a quick, effective method of attachment to the animal.

WEIRD AND WONDERFUL FUNGI

Some of our most intriguing fungi appear in late summer and early autumn – from the delicate fairy ring champignons to the ill-smelling stinkhorn fungus that appears as if from nowhere and grows at the astonishing rate of 8cm (3in) per hour.

Below: **Sulphur tuft** (*Hypholoma fasciculare*) is found all year on and around old tree stumps. Not poisonous, it tastes very unpleasant.

In British woodlands the main fruiting season of fungi starts in autumn when the forest floor becomes covered with an assortment of mushrooms and toadstools that display seemingly endless variations in colour, shape and lifestyle. But some species fruit in summer, and a few may be found throughout the year.

Many summer fungi grow in grassland, and their fruiting is triggered by the first summer rain soaking into the sun-warmed soil. Fungi depend on water for the growth of their spore-bearing fruiting bodies. The fungus infiltrates its food supply – be it the compost of dead leaves on the woodland floor, rotten or living wood, or even cow-pats – by means of thin threads (hyphae). As their fruiting season arrives, the ends of some hyphae, swollen with rainwater, rapidly expand and push out their familiar stalks (stipes) and spore-bearing fruiting bodies.

Sulphur tuft is one of our commonest toadstools and is a glorious sight growing in large clusters on and around old tree stumps. Slender ochre stems support the masses of caps which are pale yellow at the edges but darken to a rich orange towards the centre. The gills are yellow at first but change to olive-green as the spores ripen.

The verdigris toadstool is one of the first species to appear in woods in summer, and it also grows in grassland. The pale stem is topped with a glistening blue-green cap dotted with fluffy white scales around its edge. The

striking slimy green coating may eventually be washed away by rain, leaving a yellowish cap. The cap is rounded when it first emerges from the soil, but it later flattens to expose the grey-brown gills. This rather evil-looking toadstool is not in fact poisonous but its unpleasant taste makes it inedible.

Shaggy ink cap is one of the most familiar summer toadstools that you often see growing in clusters in pastures, lawns, disturbed ground and along roadsides. When it first appears the cap is egg-shaped and clothed with curly white scales–hence its other name, lawyer's wig. After a few days the cap opens out to a bell shape and its interesting spore mechanism comes into play.

Above: **Verdigris toadstool** *(Stropharia aeruginosa)*, common from May-Nov in woods and pastures. Not poisonous, but not good to eat.

Left: **Shaggy ink cap** *(Coprinus comatus)* common in late summer-early autumn on rubbish tips, and anywhere where organic rubbish has been buried. Good to eat when young if they are peeled and the stems discarded.

Right and below: **Stinkhorn fungi** *(Phallus impudicus)* in deciduous woodlands, especially in Aug-Sept when the fungi can often be detected by the highly offensive smell they give off as they shed their spores.

Starting at the edges, the cap begins to dissolve in its own juices, a process called auto-digestion, and the spores contained in an inky black liquid simply dribble back into the soil. The whole process takes a couple of days, leaving the white stalk, streaked with black, standing alone for a while until it eventually rots into the ground. Shaggy ink caps are good to eat when young, and they can be eaten raw in salads or cooked in stews. Their 'ink' may be used for writing.

The stinkhorn, one of our strangest fungi, grows in deciduous woods throughout the summer. The young fruiting body is a white rubbery 'egg', 2.5-5cm (1-2in) across, which just breaks the surface of the soil. If you were to slice through the 'egg' you would find that the skin covers a thick jelly layer in which the compressed stem and cap are embedded. When the spores are ripe the 'eggs' 'hatch'–the spongy stem swells with water and breaks through the top of the 'egg', carrying the spore-covered cap with it. The growth of the stem is amazingly rapid–up to 8cm (3in) per hour.

The cap is coated with dark slime which contains the spores and emits a stench rather like rotting meat. This smell attracts swarms of flies that feed on the slime and carry away the spores which they later excrete elsewhere. Within just a few hours all the slime is consumed, leaving a white cap with its honey-comb surface.

In the past this weird toadstool was used as an ingredient in love potions and aphrodisiacs. And even today in some parts of the world it is fed to cattle to try to improve their fertility.

Spindle shank Unlike the sulphur tuft, which sprouts from and feeds on dead wood, the spindle shank emerges from the soil. But if you were to excavate around the stem you would find that it was attached underground to tree roots. It grows, often in tufts, in deciduous woods and attacks the roots of oak and beech trees, causing white rot. The brown stem is hollow and often spirally twisted. The surface of the chestnut-brown cap is rather uneven and wrinkled. The caps make a useful flavouring to soups and stews.

After a heavy summer downpour a ring of mushrooms springs up around the outer edge of the circle. The slender yellowish stems are each topped by a small cap which is bell-shaped at first, but later flattens out to form a tiny parasol. The caps are reddish-brown when wet, but they dry out to a yellowish-brown colour.

The rings grow at a rate of 10-20cm (4-8in) per year. The biggest rings have a diameter of 50m (164ft) which means that the fungus responsible is up to 250 years old. People used to think that these strange circles were magical spots around which fairies and elves danced, using the caps as convenient little stools upon which to rest.

The fairy ring champignon causes the appearance of green circles on lawns and playing fields – the 'fairy rings' that give trouble to gardeners and groundsmen alike.

The hyphal threads below the ground form an intricate matted web (a mycelium) which clogs the air spaces in the soil and so prevents the free drainage of water. The grass roots suffer from waterlogging which eventually stunts the growth of the grasses within the circle. But at the edge, where the mycelium is still actively spreading outwards, the grass growth becomes particularly luxuriant as the fungus digests dead plant matter and releases essential nutrients which fertilise the soil.

Above: **Spindle shank** *(Collybia fusipes)* is common in late summer, particularly at the base of beech and oak trees where it attaches itself to the tree roots.

Right: **Fairy ring champignon** *(Marasmius oreades)* is common in grassland in summer and autumn after rain. Edible, and can be dried and used as a flavouring.

How fungi reproduce

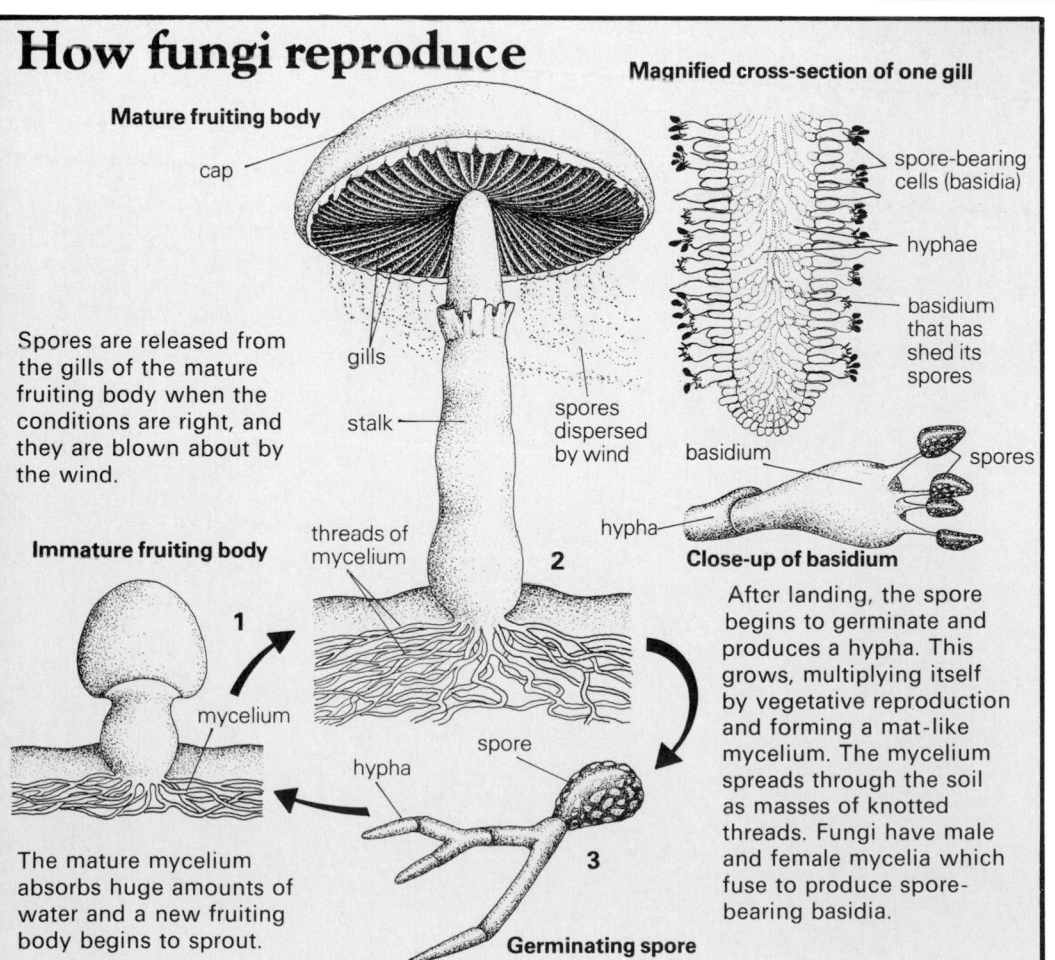

Mature fruiting body

cap

Magnified cross-section of one gill

spore-bearing cells (basidia)

hyphae

basidium that has shed its spores

Spores are released from the gills of the mature fruiting body when the conditions are right, and they are blown about by the wind.

gills

stalk

spores dispersed by wind

basidium

spores

hypha

Close-up of basidium

Immature fruiting body

threads of mycelium

1

2

mycelium

hypha

spore

3

Germinating spore

The mature mycelium absorbs huge amounts of water and a new fruiting body begins to sprout.

After landing, the spore begins to germinate and produces a hypha. This grows, multiplying itself by vegetative reproduction and forming a mat-like mycelium. The mycelium spreads through the soil as masses of knotted threads. Fungi have male and female mycelia which fuse to produce spore-bearing basidia.

Opposite page: Two types of fungus growing in close proximity. At the foot of the tree is the yellow sulphur tuft fungus, while clinging to the trunk is a bracket fungus, the birch polypore *(Piptoporus betulinus)*. Notice how different the sulphur tuft here looks from that on page 128 – for this reason, identification of a fungus is always difficult. Never eat a fungus if you are unsure of its identity.

Left: The different ways that spores are produced distinguish many different groups of fungi. The Basidiomycetes, shown here, are so-called because they reproduce sexually by means of spores which are produced on enlarged flask-shaped cells known as basidia. The gill fungi, such as toadstools and many types of mushroom, are all Basidiomycetes. Another prominent group are the Ascomycetes, including the flask fungi. Their spores are produced from a different type of cell.

ORB WEB SPIDERS: DEADLY SPINNERS

As summer begins to shade into autumn, hedges and banks become festooned with vertical, spirally-patterned webs made by orb web spiders. Each intricately woven web may display its fat-bodied occupant, clinging motionless and head down, waiting for prey to blunder into the trap.

Above: The dew-spangled web of an orb web spider, *Araneus quadratus*, in the morning. These webs can stretch to 60cm (2ft), or more across. The webs built by the young spiders are just as intricate as those of the adults, but it is generally only when they are seen at maximum size that their precision and regularity can be fully appreciated. The spider waits in the centre of the web for small insects to blunder in and get caught by the sticky threads.

In autumn orb web spiders reach full size and maturity, having spent the early part of the summer making ever larger webs as they themselves increase in size by shedding their outer skin (cuticle) whole. Their large September and October webs seem to appear overnight on almost every bush, bank, hedge, tuft of grass and group of flowers. If you can't find the spider itself sitting in the centre of its web, it will probably be lurking in its lair – perhaps a folded leaf to one side of the web – waiting for a victim.

The most familiar orb web builder – and one of Britain's largest spiders – is the garden cross, or diadem, spider (*Araneus diadematus*), so called because of the white crucifix-like pattern on the top of the abdomen, the ground colour of which varies from pale brown to reddish-brown or sepia. Common in gardens, along thick hedgerows and in open woodland glades, the web occupants are generally females, with bodies as big as a large pea. Adult male diadem spiders, recognisable by their smaller, more triangular abdomen and prominent palps, or mouth 'fingers', are less often seen, since directly after maturing they abandon their webs and spend their short lives visiting those of the females, eating virtually nothing in the meantime.

Courtship and mating are carried out with extreme caution among diadem and other orb

Above: Diadem, or garden cross (*Araneus diadematus*) spiderlings in a group. As in many species of spider, it is likely that these spiderlings disperse far and wide with the help of wind currents, on which they are wafted at the end of long silk lifelines. Although many orb web spiders mature at the end of their first summer, some individuals, and some other species as well, probably take two years to reach full size. Many are caught before maturity by predators.

web spiders for the short-sighted female is liable to attack all intruders even when they happen to be one of her own species.

Once arrived at the perimeter of the female's web, the male announces his presence by tweaking an outer strand, at the same time providing himself with an escape-line of silk in case of repulse. He may be chased away fiercely several times before the female responds to the special vibrations induced by his web-pulling, and allows mating to occur.

Mating itself takes place by means of the male's palps. Prior to the actual sexual encounter, the male discharges a quantity of sperm on to a special silk pad, then fills each of his palps, which act as reservoirs, with seminal fluid. Having temporarily subdued the female's aggressive tendencies, he then inserts first one and then the other palp into her genital aperture (epigyne), though he may have to retreat again after the first insertion. Mating over, the male retires, later seeking out another female. Many males, however, do not survive for more than one mating and either die of starvation or are killed by the female.

Egg-laying and hatching Some weeks after insemination, the female leaves her web and seeks out a hiding place where she produces a batch of several hundred eggs, which she covers with a double layer of yellowish silk. This cocoon may be fixed to the underside of a stone, beneath tree bark or perhaps in the corner of a garden shed. Here the eggs overwinter, hatching out the following May.

To start with, the spiderlings are very small, with abdomens scarcely as big as a pinhead, but they are distinctively coloured a rich yellow with a short bar of dark brown at the rear of the abdomen. The spiderlings occasionally attract attention by their habit of congregating in a tight ball on a base of silk. If you touch the ball with your finger, the little spiders scatter. The spiderlings remain in their ball until their next skin change, then disperse to make small individual webs of their own. Each spider may come to maturity at the end of its first summer but more usually

Construction of an orb web

All orb web spiders begin their web with a horizontal bridge line. A thread is secured at one end while the other is allowed to waft across a space until it adheres to a twig or leaf; the spider strengthens this bridge by passing over it several times, laying down more silk. Next the spider passes from one end of the bridge to the other, dragging a loose thread and fixing it at both ends. It then returns to the centre of this thread and descends on a further line which, after being pulled taut, is fixed to an outer point. The spider has now created the first three web radii and one frame segment in the form of a closed letter Y, the centre of the Y forming the web's centre. Further frame lines are added so as to make a multi-sided frame. By repeated climbing and dropping, further radii (up to about 40 in all) are constructed. The central hub, where the spider sits, is then completed, and an inner strengthening spiral added. Now, leaving a gap, the spider constructs the main outer web spiralling, using radii as footholds (but only as a temporary measure). Finally, the spider goes over the main spirals again, destroying them as it goes and replacing them with gum-coated lines that will secure the prey. Oil on the spider's feet prevent it being caught in its own web.

Above: The first line the orb web spider makes is a horizontal bridge secured at both ends and strengthened by silk strands.

Above: This closed letter Y, formed by the spider descending on a loose thread, establishes the centre of the web and one frame segment.

Above: The spider adds more frame lines and radii by a series of climbing and dropping manoeuvres.

Above: The completed web.

Some orb web spiders

Araneus diadematus

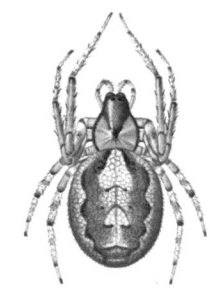

Zygiella x-notata

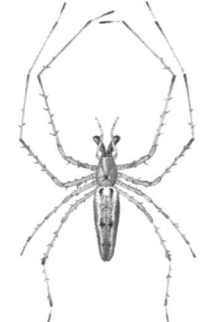

Tetragnatha montana

Meta segmentata

takes another year, dying soon after its own mating and egg-laying. However, this probably depends partly on the weather and the food supply.

Trapping prey in the web Spiders usually construct their webs in the evening or the early hours of the morning, commonly positioning them only 30-60cm (1-2ft) from the ground and at vantage points instinctively chosen to secure a steady stream of prey. In gardens they take a heavy toll of insects such as craneflies and daddy-long-legs whose low, blundering flight renders them especially prone to ensnarement. A wide variety of prey is taken, from small flies to grasshoppers, but the more violent or unpleasant tasting infiltrators are generally cut loose.

Only the larger, outer spirals of the orb web spider's web are sticky (viscid) and it is this region which traps the blundering insects. If the spider is lurking in its lair, it is given immediate notice of the victim's arrival by means of a line of silk connected to the web, which the spider holds in its forelegs. The spider then dashes across the web to bite the prey, injecting it with venom which also contains a digestive enzyme to break down the insect's tissues into liquid form, which the spider drinks. At the same time the spider swathes the captive in silk so it is powerless and can be stored for future use.

Despite its apparent delicacy, the spider's silk is remarkably strong and elastic. It is produced by six spinnerets, special organs situated at the hind end of the abdomen, each of which exudes silk in multiple strands that, by chemical reaction, coalesce and solidify as one as they leave the body.

The role of spiders in controlling the insect population is significant, but spiders themselves are not without enemies. Birds take toll of them, and many spiders are preyed on by robber-flies, ichneumons and hunting wasps as well as other spiders.

Some garden species Garden spiders belong to the family Argiopidae, of which there are about 40 species in Britain. All of them make orb webs, but few are as large and conspicuous as the diadem spider. One of the more secretive species is the rather sinister-looking *Araneus umbraticus*, which builds its web on old trees and outbuildings. Mot-

tled brown or near black, with a subdued crenellated pattern on its flat and somewhat dimpled abdomen, this spider spends most of the daylight hours in a crevice near its web, emerging at night to kill and collect prey. This spider hibernates in winter. *Araneus quadratus* is another large, related species, commoner on heathland in northern England. Its variably coloured abdomen bears a dotted pattern in the rough form of a rectangle.

Many other orb web spiders are much smaller, notably those of the genus *Meta*. *Meta segmentata* is a typical example. Often spinning on low vegetation in gardens, its web has a clear space in the centre and is usually set at a slight angle to the ground. Equally distinctive are the webs spun by the two commoner species of *Zygiella*. Each is identifiable by the omission of spiralling from two upper segments of the web.

Above: Some garden-dwelling orb web spiders; these are all females. *Tetragnatha montana* belongs to the Tetragnathidae family, not the Argiopidae like the others; its web is made of such fine silk that it is difficult to see it at all.

Opposite page: A superb view of *Araneus diadematus* as it sits in its web.

Below: Female *Araneus diadematus* with prey wrapped securely in silk. The spider revolves the victim in its legs, swathing it with strand after strand of silk until it is absolutely helpless.

AUTUMN MOTHS

The noctuids are one of the biggest families of moths–over 300 species breed in Britain! They are fast-flying, fat-bodied moths, active only at night when they sometimes come to lighted open windows.

By day noctuid moths hide away among leaves or on tree trunks, and nearly all are dull shades of grey and brown–excellent colours for camouflage. A few species, however, have bright red wing markings; all the species marked in this way are out and about as adults during the autumn months. Most of the red moths in other families (the burnets and tigers, for example) make themselves obvious by day and their bright colours warn birds to avoid them because they are poisonous. The red noctuids, on the other hand, are not poisonous and use their red colour for protection in other ways.

The red underwing moth (*Catocala nupta*) is the best known of all the red noctuids. It has a wingspan of up to 8cm (3in), which makes it the biggest British moth in the family. The adult hatches from its chrysalis in August and lives on well into the autumn– usually until late October. It uses its long tongue to feed on nectar from late-blooming flowers, and also on the sweet sap that runs from the damaged trunks of trees.

During the day the red underwing hides its 'red petticoats' completely as it rests on a tree trunk. The delicately patterned forewings camouflage the moth perfectly. If a bird should happen to peck at a resting red underwing, the moth flicks its forewings forwards and flashes its brightly coloured hindwings in the face of the attacker. This is a distraction display; it often scares the bird away and saves the moth's life.

The female red underwing lays her purple-brown eggs, a few at a time, in crevices in the bark of poplar and willow trees. The egg stage lasts right through the winter, the caterpillars hatching the following April.

Throughout its life–from April to July– the caterpillar spends the day hidden in a crevice on a tree trunk, climbing up the trunk at night to feed on the leaves. The caterpillars are long and thin, and in colouring match the tree bark exactly. The fully grown caterpillar usually spins a few dead leaves together with silk, and pupates inside. The brown pupa has a coating of bluish-white powder. The adults emerge in August.

The red underwing is fairly common in the

south and east of England, but becomes rarer in the north. Two of the red underwing's close relatives are much rarer. Both the dark crimson underwing (*Catocala sponsa*) and the light crimson underwing (*C. promissa*) have a similar life cycle to that of the red underwing, except that their caterpillars feed on oak leaves, not poplar and willow. Both species are hardly ever found anywhere in Britain except in and around the New Forest.

The herald moth is common, and more widespread than the red underwing, and can be found anywhere on the mainland of Britain and Ireland. Unlike the red underwing, the herald's red colour is on its forewings and is therefore always on view, even when the moth is trying to hide. The herald's shape makes it resemble a dead, shrivelled leaf, and the red colour, combined with the duller colours, helps to improve its disguise.

The herald moth is one of a small group of noctuids that spend the winter in the adult moth stage. In late autumn the herald flies around ivy blossoms, feeding on one of the

Above: A herald moth (*Scoliopteryx libatrix*) on sallow. It has a 4cm (1⅝in) wingspan. The antennae of the female are threadlike and not feathery like those of the male. Like the red underwing moth, the herald flies at night. If it is disturbed, this moth quickly falls to the ground. If you want to see the herald (and other moths) at close quarters, you can attract them by 'sugaring' tree trunks. Make up a mixture of sugar, treacle and rum and smear it on a suitable tree trunk in a place that is easily visible. The sweet mixture will attract the moths from twilight onwards.

Sound tactics

Many moths—including all the noctuids—have sensitive ears on the sides of their third (hindmost) thoracic segment, just below where the hindwings join the body. The ears are often hidden under the furry body scales, and the ear drum itself is set in a pit. Sounds make the drum membrane vibrate and this triggers the nerve impulses which reach the moth's brain and enable it to hear. The nerve impulses fire most strongly when very high-pitched sounds are heard. So the sounds that moths are best at hearing are those made by the moths' most dangerous night-time enemy: bats.

Bats hunt moths at night and they find their prey by making ultrasonic squeaks and listening for the echo as the sound bounces back from a flying moth. Noctuids are among the favourite prey of the larger British bats, but they have several ways of evading capture. When a noctuid hears a bat's sonar squeak it may just close its wings and drop to the ground (right), or

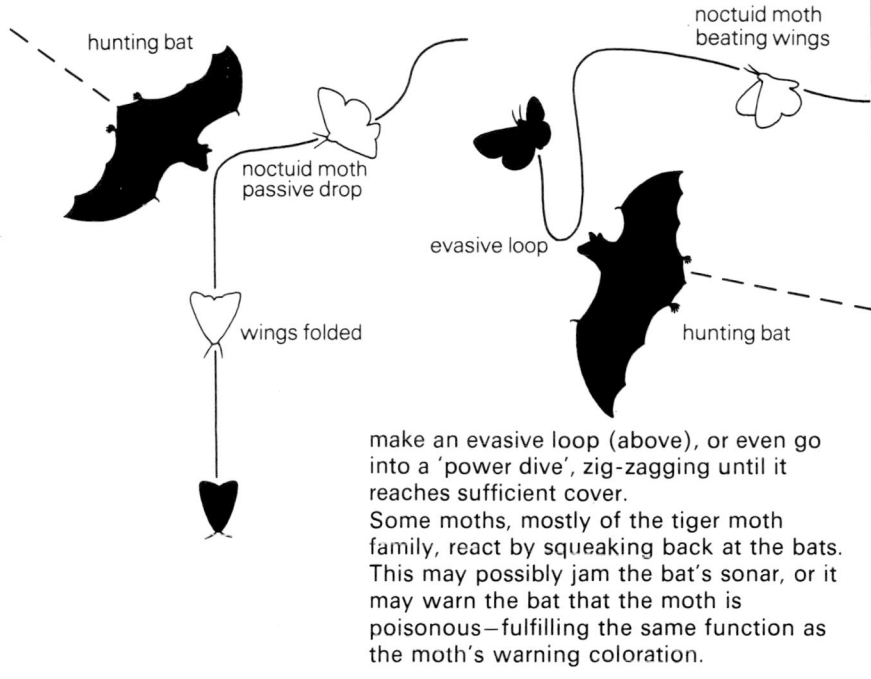

make an evasive loop (above), or even go into a 'power dive', zig-zagging until it reaches sufficient cover.

Some moths, mostly of the tiger moth family, react by squeaking back at the bats. This may possibly jam the bat's sonar, or it may warn the bat that the moth is poisonous—fulfilling the same function as the moth's warning coloration.

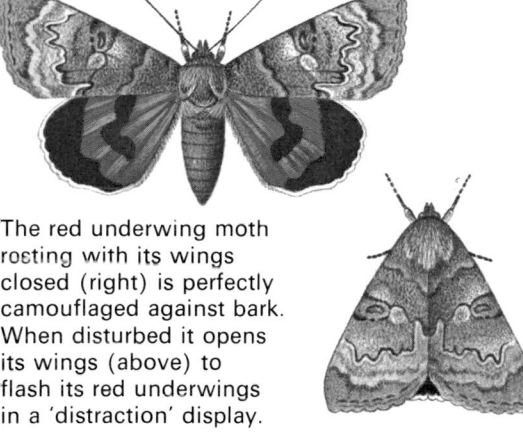

The red underwing moth resting with its wings closed (right) is perfectly camouflaged against bark. When disturbed it opens its wings (above) to flash its red underwings in a 'distraction' display.

Left: The greeny-grey red underwing caterpillar is very difficult to see as it rests during the day on a willow twig. At night it climbs up the twig to feed on the willow leaves.

Below: A red underwing showing its red 'petticoats'. The colour of its underwings make it one of the most handsome of all the noctuids in the British Isles.

last sources of nectar before winter sets in. It then finds somewhere sheltered to hibernate—in a roof loft, a shed or barn, inside a church, or perhaps a cave. When it hibernates in a humid cave, the moth often becomes coated with dew, but this seems to do it no harm. The furry scales on the wings probably prevent the water from penetrating.

In early spring the herald wakes up and searches for a drink from one of the earliest sources of nectar: pussy willow catkins. The female lays her eggs on willow, sallow and poplar trees, taking the opportunity to feed on nectar from the catkins produced by all these trees. The herald caterpillars feed on the same sorts of leaves as the red underwing caterpillars—but since they spend all their lives among the leaves, they are camouflaged green instead of a tree bark colour. The herald moth caterpillars feed from May to August, then change into black pupae enclosed in white cocoons. The adults begin emerging in August and are on the wing until October, after which they hibernate until the following spring.

PREDATORY LACEWINGS

Lacewings may be familiar in autumn, when they come into houses and sheds to hibernate.

There are about 54 different species of lacewings in Britain; they are known as Neuroptera or nerve-winged insects from the veined appearance of their wings. There are two common groups in this country–comprising about a dozen species of green lacewings and 29 species of brown lacewings.

Aphid eaters By far the most common and familiar of the British green lacewings is *Chrysopa carnea*. It is the only species to hibernate as an adult, the others spending the winter as full grown larvae in silken cocoons.

The adult's normal colour is yellowish-green with a white stripe running down the back, but during hibernation it becomes reddish in colour. Its wingspan is about 3cm (1⅛in) and it is about 1cm (⅜in) long. Both the adult and the larvae can be found on flowers and shrubs in gardens, woods and hedges throughout the British Isles as far north as the Shetlands. They consume large numbers of aphids and other small, soft-bodied insects such as small caterpillars and young scale insects. The larvae suck their prey dry, but the adults have normal chewing mouthparts and devour all parts of their prey.

Eggs on stalks A female lacewing lays approximately 500 eggs, each less than 1mm long and placed at the end of a thin stalk about 3-5mm long. These are laid singly, or in small groups, usually on the underside of leaves.

Above: *Chrysopa carnea*, a green lacewing, at rest on an aphid-covered lettuce leaf. An insect of the evening and night-time, it will fly during the day if disturbed, with a slow, fluttering flight.

Below: Lacewing eggs — each one quite separate and distinct.

The eggs hatch in one or two weeks into active, voracious, spindle-shaped larvae. They have six legs and prominent curved mandibles which, along with the second jaws (maxillae), make a pair of sucking tubes to extract the juices of their prey.

Camouflage tactics The larvae have a very interesting characteristic; they bear rows of hooked spines on their bodies to which they attach the skins of their prey and other debris as camouflage. The older larvae of *C. carnea* do not do this, but in other species, such as *C. ciliata*, all the larvae are camouflaged and use the debris as a shield.

Suitable pieces of debris are selected carefully and held in the jaws. The larva bends its head back and, with aid of its front legs, fixes the pieces to its curved hooks. The abdomen is anchored while this takes place by a false leg at its tip.

When the older larvae are about 8mm (⅓in) long they secrete silk through their anus for their cocoons, which they spin in the soil or in debris at the foot of trees and bushes. After three or four weeks the pupae, which possess strong mandibles, cut through the cocoon and climb out. They then walk some distance before undergoing their final moult to the adult form.

Tree-top relatives The brown lacewings, another common group, are rarely seen because they are smaller and more inconspicuous than the other lacewings, and spend much of their life high up in trees looking for the aphids on which they prey. Each species always seems to choose the same tree or trees for egg-laying. For example, *Hemerobius stigma*–a common species–always lays its eggs on conifers.

The female of this species cements her eggs between the scales at the base of pine needles (not on stalks). There is a succession of broods throughout the year, even in the winter, the eggs hatching in nine days in the summer but taking up to five weeks in winter.

The larvae are similar to those of the green lacewings, growing 7-8mm (⅓in) long, but they do not use camouflage. They have enormous appetites and can eat as many as 3000 newly hatched pine aphid nymphs before pupating. After a week or two in summer, but a little longer in winter, they spin silken cocoons among the pine needles. The pupae are active and the adults emerge after three weeks in summer. In winter, they may stay as pupae for some months, or emerge during a mild spell. Not all species of brown lacewing follow this life-cycle; most have just two broods in the year and overwinter as resting larvae or pupae, both protected in cocoons.

The adult brown lacewings are just as predatory as their green relatives. An adult female *H. stigma* kept in captivity for seven weeks is on record as having eaten no less than 17,500 pine aphid eggs and nymphs! The adult's stronger jaws enable it to eat the eggs and larger nymphs that are too tough for the larvae.

The biter bit Although both green and

Above: The larva of a green lacewing attacking an aphid. It sinks its jaws deeply into the victim, lifts it up if possible, then sucks it dry. Each larva consumes an average of about 100 aphids.

Left: The female *C. flava* makes the stalk for her eggs by touching the leaf with a secretion as the eggs are being laid. She then lifts up her abdomen so that a viscous thread is drawn out. The egg is left at the tip.

Below left: The giant lacewing (*Osmylus fulvicephalus*) can be found in numbers under bridges and also in bushes.

brown lacewings are predators, they are not without their own enemies. Parasitic wasps attack the larvae and pupae, and the larvae are also preyed on by ladybird and hoverfly larvae. They are even subject to attacks from their own relatives, the larvae of one species frequently eating the larvae of smaller species.

The largest lacewing The handsomest species of lacewing is the giant lacewing which occurs locally in colonies along woodland streams with dense bankside vegetation.

The male is unusual among lacewings in having scent glands which he uses to attract the female before mating. The female lays her eggs in May, June or early July on foliage near water. Only about 30 eggs are produced.

These hatch after three weeks into larvae of much the same shape as those of the other species, but with long, slender jaws that curve slightly upwards and outwards. The larvae use these to probe for the larvae of other insects, mainly midges, at the water's edge. They impale their prey, which quickly die from the effects of the poisonous saliva of the giant lacewing larvae.

The larvae overwinter before they are fully grown, finishing their growth in the spring. They spin their cocoons in April or early May when they have reached a length of 15mm (⅝in), and the adults emerge a month later.

FRUIT-LOVING SOCIAL WASPS

In autumn social wasp colonies begin to disintegrate and the old queens die. The new mated queens, however, and the surviving workers, spend their time feeding on ripe fruit and the nectar from late blooming flowers – particularly those of ivy.

Above: A German wasp feeding on a ripe plum in autumn. These insects make themselves a nuisance wherever there is ripe fruit to be had. By contrast, wasp larvae are fed mainly on meat – flies, caterpillars and spiders.

Social wasps live in annual colonies headed by a fertilised female (queen) whose offspring they are. There are seven species in the British Isles, the largest being the hornet which is uncommon and nests in hollow trees. The common, German and red wasps nest underground; the tree and Norwegian wasps choose aerial sites in hollow trees or bushes, while the seventh (lacking workers) is para-sitic on the red wasp. The common and German wasps are abundant, and most studies have been made of them, although all have similar life histories. Their bold yellow and black coloration and tapering abdomen make all these insects easy to identify.

Establishing the colony The wasp's year starts with the fertilised queen waking up from hibernation in early spring to seek a suitable nesting site. Common and German wasps look for places such as old mouse holes in banks, but other enclosed spaces such as attics and sheds may be selected. When she has found a site, the queen starts to build her nest, laying eggs in the cells as she builds.

The first eggs hatch five to six days after nest-building starts and the queen then spends part of the day bringing back nectar and insects she has captured to feed the young larvae. The larvae take about two weeeks to become full grown, when they spin a silk cap and lining to the cell. During their feeding stage they do not excrete any waste matter, but this is now done and the mass of waste is

Common wasps

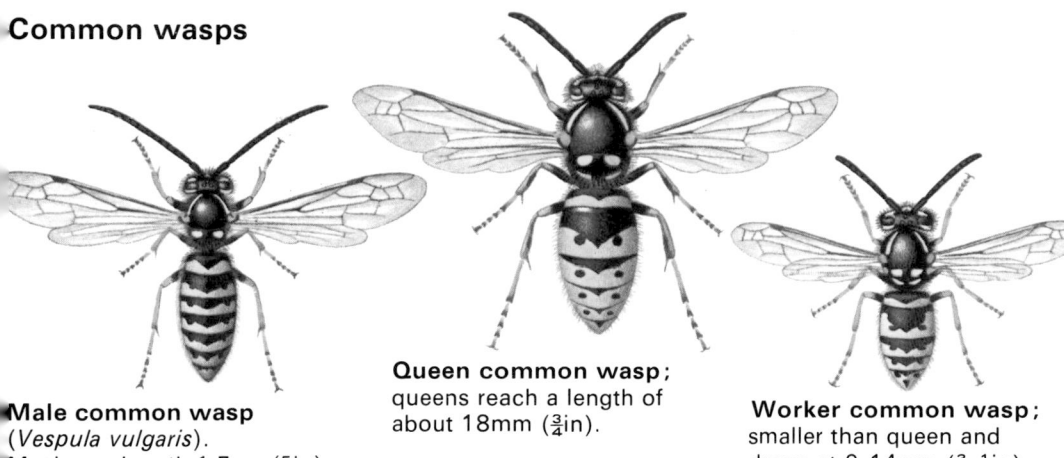

Male common wasp (*Vespula vulgaris*). Maximum length 1.5cm ($\frac{5}{8}$in).

Queen common wasp; queens reach a length of about 18mm ($\frac{3}{4}$in).

Worker common wasp; smaller than queen and drone at 9-14mm ($\frac{3}{8}$-$\frac{1}{2}$in).

Below: German and common wasps feeding on a windfall apple. You can distinguish the two species by the markings on the abdomen. The common wasp has a broad black triangle near the base, while the German wasp has a row of heavy black diamonds in the centre.
Although wasps are unpopular because they sting, damage fruit and spoil picnics, they are valuable to man because they prey on flies and other insect pests.

placed at the bottom of the cells, filling them up so that each cell can only be used two or three times. The larvae change to pupae and emerge as adult wasps after a further ten days or so, by which time the queen has increased the comb to 20 or 30 cells.

The young wasps at this time of the year are all small females (workers) and are subordinate to the queen, their mother. They gradually take over all nest operations, leaving the queen solely responsible for egg-laying. Later in the year workers lay some eggs, but as they never mate, their eggs are all unfertilised and produce males only. This is the rule in wasps, bees and ants and it seems, in some way not yet understood by scientists, that a mated female is able to decide whether to lay fertilised, female-producing eggs, or unfertilised, male-producing eggs.

As the number of workers increases, so do the nest size, the number of combs, thickness of the envelope and the number of larvae needing feeding. Ground-nesting wasps also need to enlarge the size of the hole containing the nest by carrying away balls of earth.

Foraging and feeding The main food of the adult wasps is carbohydrate in the form of nectar, but other sources include honeydew excreted by aphids, jam and ripe fruit, and they also rob honey bee hives of honey. Their mouthparts are adapted for biting, licking and chewing.

The adults need carbohydrates as a ready source of energy to maintain their active existence. The larvae are also fed on carbohydrate, but their principal food is flesh in the form of masticated bodies of other insects – and also meat from butchers' shops! The prey consists of flies, caterpillars and spiders.

When wasps are searching for prey they move much faster than usual, flying to hedgerows and other places that are frequented by insects. It seems that sight is the most important sense in finding prey. Once sighted, the wasp pounces vigorously and kills by biting into the victim's neck, often causing decapitation. It then bites off the legs and wings before carrying the prey back to the nest. By preference wasps choose prey that is resting. They sometimes use their

stings on large prey, or on bees.

Worker wasps have three main foraging tasks – bringing back pulp for building, collecting sugary liquids and capturing prey. The length of their adult life varies from two to four weeks. Compared with honey bees, wasps have very little ability to pass on information, having nothing to compare with the bee dance, for example, but they are very flexible in their foraging activities and soon learn the best places to seek prey. Larvae indicate hunger to the workers by scratching their cell walls with their mandibles.

The social organisation of the colony is maintained by a constant exchange of food

Worker tree wasp (*Dolichovespula sylvestris*); reaches a length of 1.2-1.5cm ($\frac{1}{2}$-$\frac{5}{8}$in).

Worker German wasp (*Vespula germanica*); smaller than common wasp. Makes its nest underground.

Worker red wasp (*Vespula rufa*). Same size as the German wasp. Nests in trees.

Inside a wasps' nest

A social wasp's nest is made of chewed wood mixed with saliva to produce a kind of papier mâché. This is laid down in narrow strips to form horizontal combs of hexagonal cells, supported by pillars and surrounded by a paper envelope. The cells open downwards. The common wasp and hornet use rotting wood and make a yellowish-brown, brittle paper; the German and other species use dead but sound wood that produces a grey, more elastic paper. The nests of the common and German wasps grow to about 25cm (10in) in diameter with seven or eight combs and 10,000 cells, though they sometimes grow even larger. A colony of common wasps usually has about 2000-3000 workers. The main spurt of activity takes place in July. The other species make smaller nests 16-21cm (6-8in) in diameter, with only three or four combs and a much

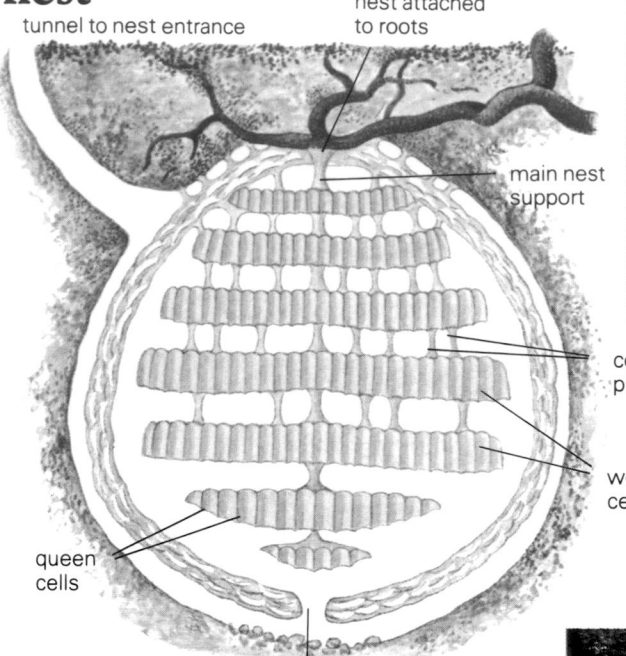

thicker envelope. The whole nest hangs from a support such as a root, with the entrance at the bottom. The combs are supported and separated by a central pillar and narrower pillars at intervals.

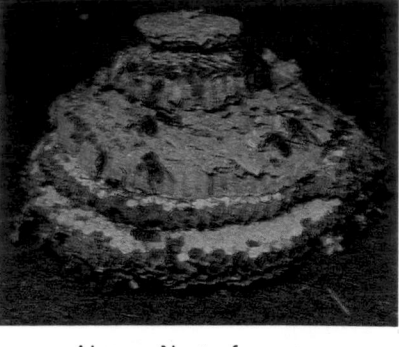

Above: Nest of common wasp dug up and exposed to show shape and structure. Note the large cells—for queens—at the bottom.

Below: Wasp grubs (larvae) in their cells. The capped cells contain the wasps that are pupating.

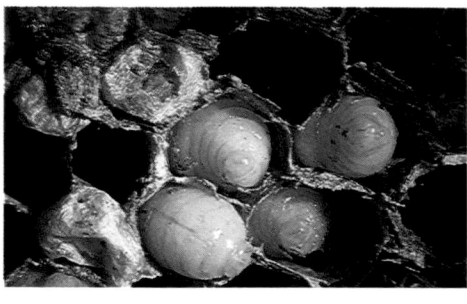

among the individuals, known as 'trophallaxis'. Adults continually elicit drops of fluid from larvae and also have mouth to mouth contact with each other. If any of this is prevented, the colony goes into a decline. It seems that the larvae can be stimulated to produce a drop of nutritious fluid which is eagerly sought by the adults. The queen imbibes large quantities which help her to maintain her egg output, and newly emerged adults feed on little else. The amount of the secretion seems to depend on the amount of fluid or food that the larva has had.

Adult wasps stimulate one another to pass food from their crops by stroking with their antennae. This is the way the queen obtains her food, supplemented by larval secretions. These exchanges probably contribute to colony odour, enabling members to recognise each other. The presence of a queen ensures a contented, normal colony; her removal results in changes of behaviour—for example the workers sit about in groups instead of flying out to forage. This suggests that the queen produces a substance which permeates the entire colony and helps maintain its coherence.

The new queens Later in the season, when the colony is strong, combs of larger cells are built at the bottom of the nest. These are destined to produce new queens; some of the larger cells are also built at the edges of the lowest normal comb. It seems that eggs

develop into queens because the larvae have more and better food and are placed in larger cells—male eggs in these cells also produce larger males. Males are produced at the same time as the queens, from unfertilised eggs placed in either type of cell and laid both by the queen and by workers. Males have longer antennae and their sole function is to fertilise the young queens. Each colony produces 1000 or more males and queens.

Mating takes place from late August, the males often congregating on sunny days, but it may occur near the nest without swarming. Following mating, the queen seeks out a hibernation site, often indoors. She does not always hibernate immediately after mating however, and may fly for a further six weeks. A hibernating queen clings on to a support such as a curtain or wooden beam with her mandibles and folds her wings and appendages in a characteristic way. Hibernation sites need to be well-insulated, with moderate humidity.

In late summer with the appearance of the new males and queens, the social organisation of the colony begins to disintegrate, and the old queen dies slowly, after which the workers desert the nest or die, as the males do when the weather gets colder. In the autumn the workers no longer capture prey as there are no larvae to feed, and they spend much of their time eating ripe fruit and nectar. They particularly favour nectar from ivy.

Hoverfly parasites

The space below the nest of a ground-nesting wasp in time becomes a kind of midden or refuse heap, laden with rubbish of all kinds as well as masses of dead larvae and adult wasps. It is a breeding ground for a number of flies, the best-known being hoverflies such as *Volucella pellucens* (below) that bear some resemblance to wasps and seem to enter the nest without being molested by the wasps themselves. Their larvae live in the midden and later on invade the nest to feed on the larvae and pupae within. The adults visit flowers for nectar and pollen.

TRANSCONTINENTAL BIRD MIGRATIONS

The British Isles are fortunate in seeing the arrival of a great many bird species in spring, but even more spectacular than this is their departure in autumn. The flights of finches, meadow pipits and skylarks down the east coast, and those of geese up the mountain passes of Scotland, are truly thrilling.

Those birds which migrate, rather than remain at home, do so for one simple reason – to find food. Birds which breed in the far north in summer come to spend winter in Britain because there is no food available in their Arctic breeding grounds. (In the Arctic tundra in summer there is a short-lived flush of insect life which, together with other sources of food, sustains the birds while they mate and raise young.) In the same way, there is not enough food in Britain in winter to supply most of our insect-eating birds. Such aerial species as swallows, swifts and martins have almost no chance of finding flying insects to feed on during the winter. Similarly, the warblers and flycatchers that de-

pend on the insects and other invertebrates which are plentiful during the warmer months, cannot rely on their being available during the winter. These birds therefore move south to winter in the tropics.

Perhaps the most interesting question is why do they ever return from their winter home – where there is plenty of food and nesting space? The answer is that there is a wide variety of local birds – including several species of swallow, for instance – that are specially adapted to a year-round existence in the tropics. There is no chance of a vast number of northern birds being able to breed and compete successfully for food in such a network of tropical species.

Above: Arctic terns in flight – perhaps on one of their incredible migratory journeys. These birds are the longest distance migrants of all birds. Those that breed north of the Arctic Circle spend winter close to the Antarctic pack ice, and so experience continuous daylight for up to eight months of the year. Several Arctic terns from Europe have been reported from as far away as Australia. The close of summer and the beginning of autumn is, therefore, an important time for them, as they prepare for their fantastic trip. It is essential that they have been able to feed sufficiently well during the summer, so that they are in peak condition for migration. This is necessary even though they are able to feed on the journey.

Summer migrants
(birds that come to
Britain in summer.)
Swallows winter furthest
south in Africa. Route
northwards in spring just
east of southern route in
autumn.
Swifts in Britain only in
May, June and July.
Winter in Malawi.
Lesser whitethroats
winter in east Africa.
Intermediate fattening
area in northern Italy,
also call in on Nile Delta.

Whitethroats migrate
south-south westwards.
Autumn fattening area in
N.W Spain; winter in
Sahel region of W. Africa.

Seabird and wader routes
(not illustrated).
Knots reach Britain from
Greenland and Canada.
Manx shearwaters
winter off Brazil.
Gannets migrate further
as juveniles than adults,
to tropics and
Mediterranean.
Ruffs from E Siberia to
Britain, winter in W
Africa, return via Italy.

Below: House martins
congregate on telegraph
wires before migrating on the
long trip to their wintering
quarters in Africa. Swallows,
also insect-eating birds,
migrate at much the same
time as the martins.

Summer migrations

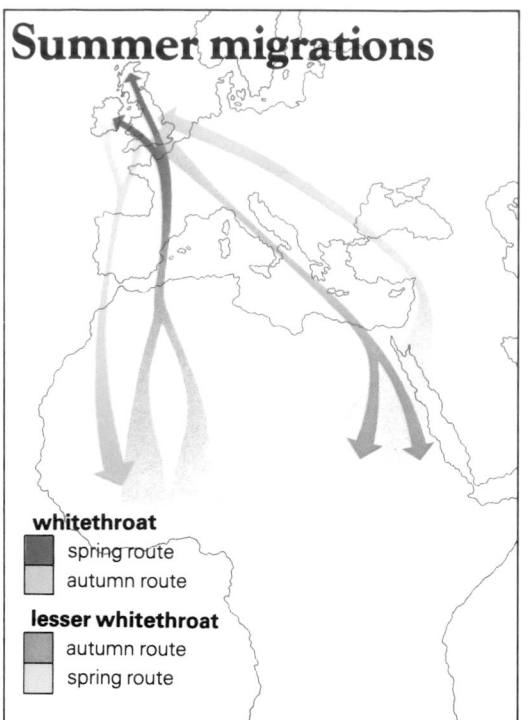

whitethroat
■ spring route
□ autumn route
lesser whitethroat
■ autumn route
□ spring route

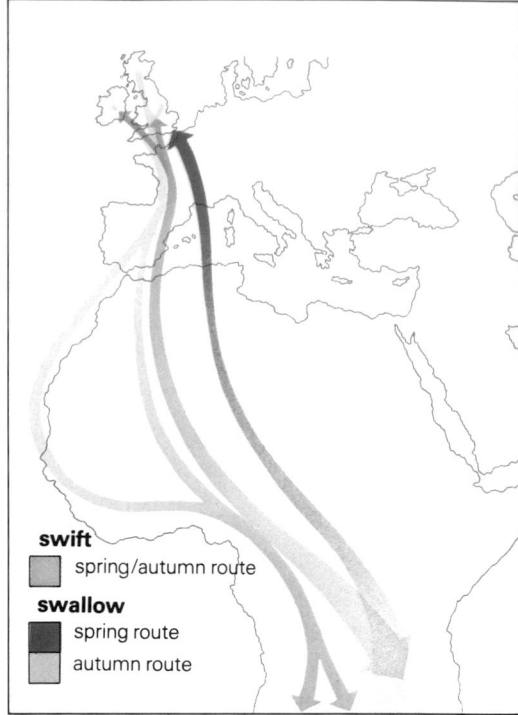

swift
□ spring/autumn route
swallow
■ spring route
□ autumn route

To feed or fly away During the winter months, British birds have two options: sit it out or move southwards. If they remain they must either exploit a new food source, or a specialised feeding style which allows them to feed in the same way. In the first case, species like the blue and great tits feed during the winter on dormant insects and their eggs that are hidden in the bark of trees, or on different foods like the tons of peanuts fed to them by bird-lovers. In the second case, birds such as wrens and dunnocks remain here, feeding largely on the arthropods which they prize out from shelters in thick cover.

Network of routes The journeys that bird migrants make vary enormously. Many people think of bird migration as something which just concerns swallows from Europe reaching southern Africa; but this is only a minute part of the web of migration woven round the British Isles. Not only do our summer birds leave here to winter in warmer areas, but our islands also play host to millions of birds spending their winters with us. The geographical position of the British Isles on the western flank of Eurasia, with the warming influence of the Atlantic and the subtropical water brought north-east to our shores by the Gulf Stream, makes them a welcome refuge for many species of waterfowl which spend their summers in Siberia.

The distinction between migratory and sedentary species is not clear cut because there are Continental populations of many resident British birds which are themselves migratory – some of them, like starlings and blackbirds, reaching Britain as winter visitors in large numbers.

Timetables of flights The timing of migration is crucial; in spring returning birds cannot afford to arrive too early. They would starve on arrival if their food supply was not available. On the other hand the individuals which arrive first, and manage to survive, are able to occupy the best territories.

In most bird species the males arrive first so that they can mark out territories and then attract the females to them. On the other hand some species, particularly ducks and geese, pair off in the winter quarters and migrate to the breeding grounds together. Sometimes the ducks which pair in the winter originate from very different areas but, once joined together, one will follow the other to unfamiliar territory. This phenomenon – called abmigration – accounts for some puzzling recoveries of ringed British-bred ducks in central Russia during the breeding season.

The main activity for most birds, which starts immediately they come to Britain in summer, is breeding. But for many birds this is followed by another crucial period–the annual moult–when they renew all their feathers. The timing of the autumn migration is also crucial: for the adult birds, the moult follows the busy breeding period, and for the young birds the autumn pre-migration period determines whether they will be able to build up their strength and survive.

Daylight trips Those birds that make their journey in daylight are called diurnal migrants. Generally the diurnal migrants make their trips in rather short bursts of a hundred or so miles at a time. Often their routes are greatly influenced by the local landscape, the birds funnelling through mountain passes or across short stretches of sea. In the British Isles the autumn flights of finches, meadow pipits and skylarks down the east coast, and the flights of geese up the mountain passes of Scotland, are an unforgettable sight.

These concentrations of diurnal migrants are responsible for the enormous congestion of soaring birds at the Straits of Gibraltar and the Bosphorus each autumn. Hundreds of thousands of white storks and birds of prey congregate at these places each year. Falsterbo, in southern Sweden, provides another concentration point for migrants moving southwards from Scandinavia. Britain is not endowed with such spectacular sites, but you may see high numbers of diurnal migrants at many south and east coast headlands during the autumn–Portland Bill and Selsey Bill, Beachy Head, Dungeness, Gibraltar Point and Spurn Head are all good vantage sites.

Night-flights Those bird migrants that travel at night–nocturnal migrants–are not always as easy to see when they migrate; but you can infer their movements by watching any suitable area and recording the fluctuating numbers. This is particularly easy on offshore islands or coastal headlands where migrants that would never normally be seen in such barren areas may appear in large numbers. Bird observatories dotted around the country, have been operating for up to 30 years and carefully record the birds which pass through. Their records show what the common birds do each year as well as the activities of rare visitors.

In contrast to the short steps generally made by the diurnal species, nocturnal migrants may fly non-stop for more than three days–in some cases regularly for 80 or even 100 hours. With an air speed of about 25 miles per hour this means that many can fly 2500 miles in one stretch. The birds which do this, such as sedge warblers, store fat under their skin (subcutaneously) to use as fuel on their flight. They may well double their weight before migrating. Sedge warblers take off from southern England in the autumn weighing about 22g ($\frac{3}{4}$oz), fly for four days and land in Senegal, south of the Sahara,

four days later weighing about 10g ($\frac{1}{3}$oz). Other species, like the closely related reed warbler, do not make such long single trips, but stop off on the west coast of Portugal to refuel.

How do they navigate? Such long journeys are not without their hazards. Even if the bird has fuelled up adequately it must still be able to find its way properly. Birds navigate by referring to the sun and stars (which implies some inbuilt timing mechanism), and to the earth's magnetic field. They also rely on an inbuilt homing device to give an indication of direction. They have evolved their migratory routes simply because these routes work. It is certain that the newly hatched warbler, for instance, has within its genetic make-up the information it needs to accomplish its migration.

Perhaps the one aspect that makes bird migration such a fascinating part of ornithology is the tremendously varied habitats that one individual bird visits and lives in during its year. For example, the black-headed gulls which take bread from the

Winter visitors (to the British Isles).
Wigeons wintering here breed across Scandinavia into Siberia.
White-fronted geese in Ireland and west Britain come from Greenland; those in south and east England (also Slimbridge) are from northern Russia.
Redwings, common birds in Britain in winter, come from Iceland (where there is a distinctive species *colurni*), and from Scandinavia and Russia. Many travel even further south to Spain, Italy and as far as Greece and Turkey.
Chaffinches resident here have brick-red underparts.

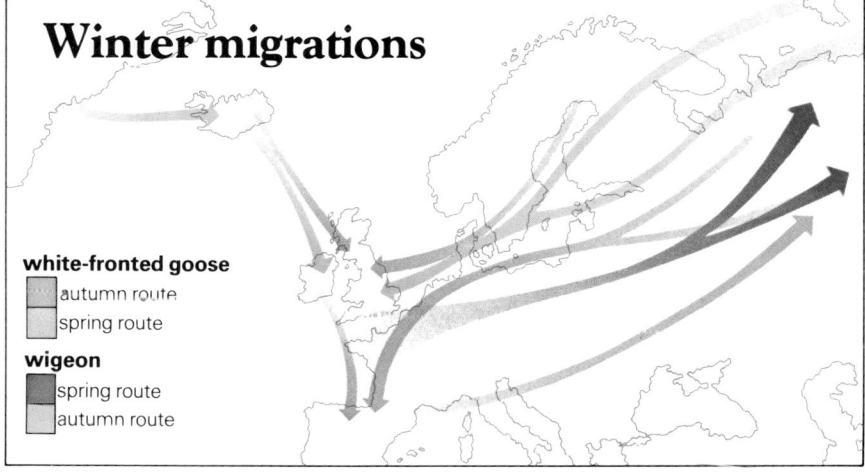

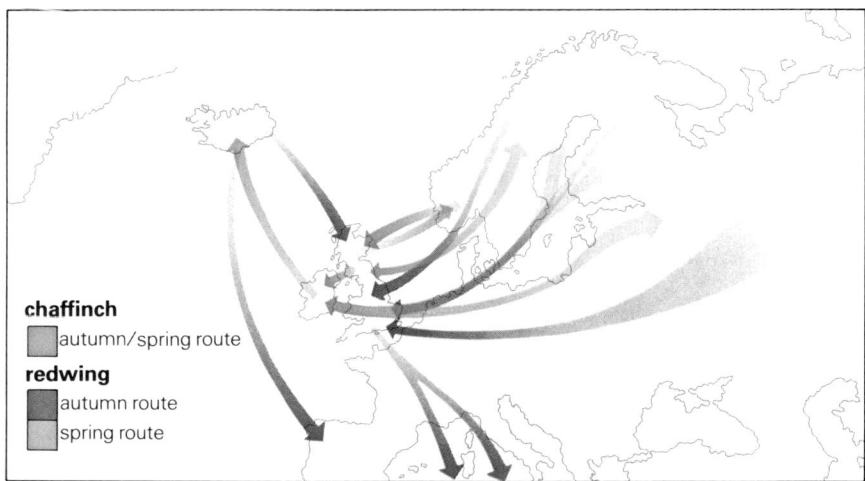

tourists on Westminster embankment include individuals bred on marshes in Poland, Czechoslovakia and Scandinavia. The swallow nesting in your garage may have been feeding among the debris of a South African gold-mine last winter, and will have passed over the Sahara during March.

Above: Most people forget that many geese and ducks migrate to Britain to spend the winter. Redwings, too, come from Scandinavia to Britain to escape the icy cold of their northern breeding grounds.

WHITEFRONT GEESE FROM THE ARCTIC

Every autumn whitefront geese arrive on our shores to escape the harsh winter of their Arctic breeding grounds, and to graze on our marshes.

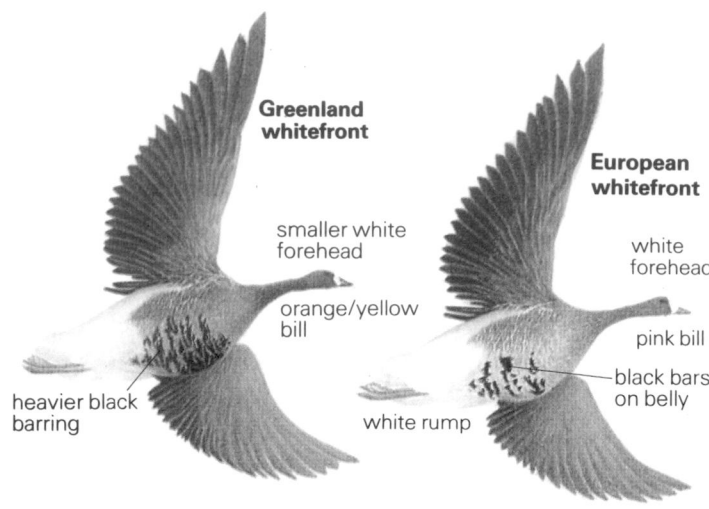

Greenland whitefront
- smaller white forehead
- orange/yellow bill
- heavier black barring

European whitefront
- white forehead
- pink bill
- black bars on belly
- white rump

The whitefronted goose is a generally grey-brown bird, whose main distinguishing features are a white forehead, a white rump and undertail area, and black bars on its belly. Birds in their first year lack both the black barring and the white forehead, though most show some indication of the latter by late in their first winter. Males and females have similar plumage but the former are a little larger.

In flight whitefronts appear entirely dark except for the white rump. Their wings are longer and narrower than those of other grey geese and they have a high-pitched laughing call.

Different races Whitefronts breed in the Arctic almost right around the globe, from north-west Russia, through Siberia to the

European whitefront (*Anser albifrons albifrons*). Winter migrant from western Russia to southern Britain. Grey-brown plumage with white markings. Pink bill. Length 66-76cm (26-30in).

Greenland whitefront (*Anser albifrons flavirostris*). Winter migrant from Greenland to Scotland and Ireland. Slightly darker grey-brown plumage. Orange-yellow bill. Length 66-76cm (26-30in).

Below: A whitefront goose, showing the conspicuous barring on its belly.

Pacific coast, and then in Alaska, Arctic Canada and western Greenland. They winter quite far south, from western Europe, including Britain, around the Black and Caspian Seas, in China and Japan, and in California, Texas and Mexico. Throughout this very large range five different races have been identified: the European, the Greenland, the Pacific, the Interior and the Tule whitefronts.

Only two of these, however, are seen in Britain—the European race, which breeds in the western half of Russia and winters in western and southern Europe, and the Greenland race, which breeds in western Greenland and winters in Scotland and Ireland. These two species can be distinguished from one another by the colour of their beaks—the European whitefront has a pink beak and the Greenland race an orange-yellow beak – and the generally rather darker plumage of the Greenland whitefront.

Winter haunts In north-west Europe, the European whitefront winters in the Netherlands, West Germany, Denmark, Belgium and Britain. Over the last 20 years the numbers in Europe have been increasing very markedly, from about 60,000 in the late 1960s to the present 250,000. The great bulk of these have always wintered in the Netherlands, and nearly all this massive increase has taken place there, with numbers in the other countries staying the same or even dropping slightly. It seems that in terms of protection and quantities of food the Netherlands are ideal.

In Britain, European whitefronts are found in only a few localities—all in southern England and South Wales. The largest flock (3000-4000) is at Slimbridge on the river Severn near Gloucester. Other flocks, usually numbering some hundreds, occur on the river Towy near Carmarthen, by the river Avon in Hampshire and on the Isle of Sheppey in Kent. There are a few other scattered flocks.

The peak number of whitefronts found in Britain has rarely been above 5000 in recent years, though in the late 1960s it was up to 13,000. The decline has less to do with worsening conditions in Britain, where in fact protection has been improving, than with the excellent conditions the birds find in the

Netherlands.

With the Greenland whitefront, the entire population winters in the British Isles. Its principal haunt is the Wexford Slobs in southeast Ireland. More than 7000 birds occur here – one third of the total population of 21,000 birds. Other smaller flocks are scattered over much of central Ireland. In Scotland the main wintering grounds are on the island of Islay in the Inner Hebrides where between 3000 and 4000 birds spend the winter.

Nests in the tundra Whitefronts nest on the marshy Arctic tundra, making their nests on slight hummocks or mounds, raised just a little above the general level of the surrounding bog. Alternatively, they may nest on dry slopes or banks above pools and rivers. Unlike many Arctic-nesting geese, whitefronts are not colonial but nest apart.

The nest is little more than a shallow depression, around which the female places any pieces of vegetation she can reach, building up a low rim. She lays five or six eggs at daily intervals and then, when the clutch is complete, begins the four-week incubation. After egg-laying she insulates the eggs with down plucked from her breast. She also pulls the down and other nest material over the eggs when she leaves the nest to feed and drink.

Flight to distant lands After the young have hatched both parents look after them, leading them to the best feeding areas. The young birds need to grow as fast as possible, in order to be fully grown before the Arctic winter sets in and they must head southwards. Normally the young can fly about 42 days after hatching, and a few weeks later they set out on their first migration.

The migratory journey south, on which families embark together, may take some weeks, although bad weather can force the birds to move more quickly and cover longer distances. On arriving at the wintering grounds in Europe the family parties remain together in the flock. If you are watching whitefronts feeding, it is quite possible to pick out these family groupings as they move around together within the flock. They return to the Arctic around April, fully replenished for the breeding season ahead.

Above: Migrating whitefronts. Many families from the same area combine for the migration, with individual families remaining together in the same flock. In this way the young birds learn the route from their parents.

Right: The distinction between the European and the Greenland race is not always clear. This Greenland whitefront has a pinkish tinge to its bill.

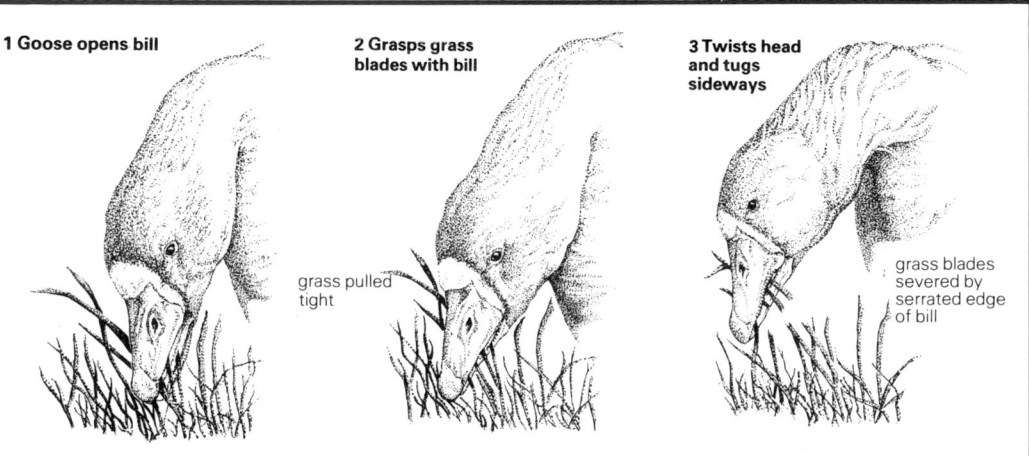

Grazing geese

Whitefronts are entirely vegetarian, feeding on plants in marshy areas and farmland. When grazing they open their bills (**1**) and seize grass blades with their beaks (**2**). They then twist their heads and tug sideways (**3**). The serrated edges on their beaks sever the tightly pulled grass easily. They also probe the ground with their bills for roots and other vegetative matter.

1 Goose opens bill

2 Grasps grass blades with bill

grass pulled tight

3 Twists head and tugs sideways

grass blades severed by serrated edge of bill

LOOKING FOR HARVEST MICE

As long ago as the 1930s people were suggesting that the harvest mouse was in imminent danger of extinction, and the boom in the number of combine harvesters in the 1950s was said to herald its demise. But recent evidence is far more encouraging.

In the last century harvest mice were frequently seen living in cereal fields, where they built their nests among the forest of stems. At that time cereals were an ideal habitat for harvest mice. Many crops were hand sown, which resulted in the plants growing in clumps rather than being evenly spaced, and these clumps of stems gave the mice extra cover. Many of the fields were full of weeds and insects, both of which supplied ample food for the mice before the crops were ripe in late summer.

The crops were harvested by hand, and the cut cereals stood in stooks in the fields, giving the mice plenty of cover to protect them from the rooks and other predators following the harvest. The stooks were later stored in large cereal ricks, which were not threshed until much later in the winter. In the meantime, the mice were either carried to the ricks in the stooks, or migrated there themselves, where they probably continued to breed. So by the time threshing came round, usually after Christmas, large numbers of harvest mice were to be seen – they were a

Above: The harvest mouse, our smallest rodent, runs easily up stalks of corn to find food, using its tail for extra support and to brake as it slides down again. It is the only British species with a truly prehensile tail that can be wrapped several times round a fixed object, so supporting the weight of the animal.

Right: The harvest mouse builds its breeding nest 30-40cm (12-16in) above ground, among tall grasses, reeds or corn. It is a firm, dense ball 8-10cm (3-4in) in diameter with a round entrance hole to one side. It takes about five to ten hours to complete.

common sight.

Today's harvest mice The changes in agricultural practice, especially since the 1950s, made cereal fields less desirable as a habitat. Harvest mice do not begin breeding until mid-May and the majority of litters (75%) are born in August and September. Most cereals grown today are early ripening varieties that can be harvested in June or July, and so are not available as a breeding habitat when the harvest mice need them. In wet summers, however, when the harvest may not be completed until the autumn, numerous nests may be seen in cereal fields, reminiscent of the sights of the last century. Perhaps one of the biggest hazards facing any harvest mice that do venture into modern cereal fields is the practice of stubble burning the day following harvest.

No one really knew how the harvest mouse had fared, and so in the 1970s the Mammal Society organised a survey to find out. Since the mice themselves are so rarely seen, some easy technique was needed whereby large areas could be covered in the search without resorting to labour-intensive trapping sessions. Since harvest mice rarely enter traps, trapping is not a very useful survey technique anyway. However, harvest mice build nests which are very characteristic, easy to recognise and fairly easy to find. So the Mammal Society's survey was based on finding nests.

Nest building Harvest mice build two kinds of nests: large ones for breeding and small ones for shelter. The breeding nests are 5-10cm (2-4in) in diameter, or even larger, and are nearly always built above ground level among the stems of any species of grass. Each spring as soon as the grasses have grown tall enough the harvest mouse climbs among the stems to find a suitable site to build its nest. It then sits on a stem holding on with its

Above: A typical harvest mouse nest built in reed-grass, showing how the leaves are shredded but left attached to the grass stems. The nest hangs freely between the stems rather than being built around them. Occasionally one or two stems may be accidentally engulfed by the nest, but they do not play any role in supporting the nest. Harvest mice nests are robust and in most years survive for much of the winter, despite rain, frost and snow.

Above: The two species that most frequently build nests in the same habitats as the harvest mouse are the reed warbler (top) and the dormouse (above). The reed warbler's nest is deep, cylindrical and cup-shaped, woven around the upright stems of plants, usually reeds. It is made from grass stems, flower-heads, leaves, down and even spiders' webs. The large breeding and shelter nest of the dormouse is domed, rather untidy and without any definite entrance. It is usually made of hedgerow plant species and the grass is not shredded.

Right: A harvest mouse nest in sedges—the mice have shredded the very long tough leaves. The nest is built over standing water.

Far right: A nest built in grasses among kale in a field. Sometimes the nests are in the heads of the kale or, as in this case, among the stems.

hind feet and prehensile tail, so leaving its fore-feet free for building.

The mouse takes a nearby grass leaf and fastens its incisor teeth around the outermost rib. Working from the middle to the end, it splits the leaf by jerking its head backwards, while still holding it in its fore-feet. The leaf splits along its length; with long leaves the mouse may have to repeat the exercise two or three times to split off one strand. This is continued with the next vein, then the next, until the free end of the leaf has been shredded into a number of strips. These strips are all still attached to the bottom half of the grass leaf, which in turn is still attached to the grass stem.

A narrow leaf may be split into six or eight strips; a wide one, such as a reed leaf, may be torn into 20 strips or more. Staying in the same position, the harvest mouse repeats the process with 20 or more leaves, first shredding them and then weaving them into strips to form the framework of the nest. The leaves are usually living and green, and the nest is perfectly camouflaged. As the leaves are left attached to their stems, the nest hangs freely at the end of the shredded grass leaves. It is very rarely built around the grass stems, and then only one or two stems may be accidentally engulfed by the nest; they do not play any role in supporting the nest.

To complete the nest, the mouse continues to work from the inside. It pulls more leaves through the nest wall and either shreds them in a similar manner or finely chews them. The innermost part of the nest is packed solid with finely chewed grass or thistledown. Any central chamber develops later from use.

Obviously this method of nest building is totally dependent on the use of grass leaves. Broadleaved plants, with their branching and reticulate veins, will not split in the same way as grass leaves, with their long, parallel veins. This is why harvest mice are always found in grassy areas during the breeding season. From the harvest mouse's point of view, grasses are of two basic types. Some have tall, flowering stems with leaves all the way up the stem. These include reeds, reed-grass, cereals

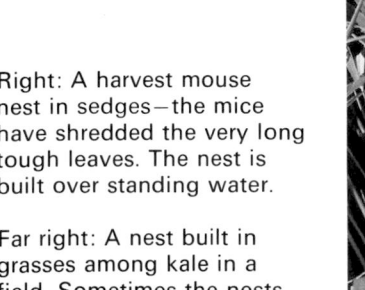

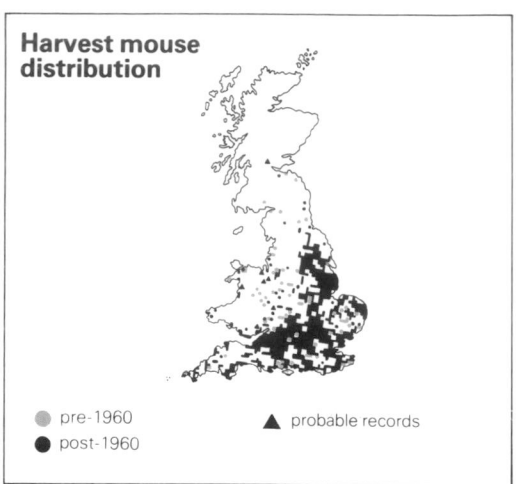

Left: In the last few years we have learnt much about the harvest mouse; we now know that many of our old ideas about its being rare or declining are false. But there is still more to learn. For many areas of the British Isles we do not know how common harvest mice really are, and so we need more records from throughout the country. In particular we need to know if the mouse is really so rare in northern England and Wales, and if it is really only found in one part of Scotland.

and many hedgerow species. The second type, such as the familiar cock's-foot and purple moor-grass, have shorter flowering stems that lack leaves.

Many smaller shelter nests are also built. They are usually 5cm (2in) or less in diameter, much more flimsy, often not lined, and usually built in similar situations to the breeding nests or in the base of grass tussocks, close to the ground. They provide cover for one mouse for not more than a few days and can be built in an hour or two. The breeding nests take at least a night to prepare and require some practice before the mice become competent nest builders.

While shelter nests are built all year round, breeding nests are only built from mid-May until late September, after which time the nests are slowly destroyed by winds and rain. In exceptional years, if the autumn is warm and dry, breeding may continue into late November or early December, but this is very rare. With the onset of inclement weather, the harvest mice spend much less time climbing in the grasses, and live in the base of grass tussocks, hedgerows and similar situations. If the mice have spent the summer nesting in wet, marshy areas they will migrate to a dry situation to overwinter.

Looking for nests The time to start looking for harvest mice nests is from late September onwards when the mice have finished breeding. It is then safe to start trampling the habitat and parting the grasses in a search for nests. If you are worried that a nest is in use, carefully insert a finger through the nest wall. If young mice are present, leave the nest and surrounding area well alone.

Harvest mouse nests are fairly robust and in most years will survive through most of the winter, and so there are at least three or four months in which to search for nests. No other nest can be confused with those of the harvest mouse, although the two species most frequently found nesting in the same habitats are the reed warbler and the dormouse.

Once it was established that nest hunting was a reliable survey technique, the Mammal Society used it to good effect. Far from confirming that the harvest mouse was rare or

Below: A harvest mouse in a less common habitat – raspberry canes. The mice eat such fruits as raspberries, blackberries and rose-hips.

declining, the survey found that it was much more widespread than previously supposed. In fact, the mouse has literally gone unnoticed for decades and is common even in south and east England. From the North York Moors and Cheshire northwards it is very rare, but is still found as far north as Edinburgh. In Wales records are few, and it would seem that the mouse is widely distributed but rare in the coastal belt of Wales.

The survey also showed that harvest mice can be found in a wide variety of habitats. The most popular sites for nests were hedgerows (13% of records), followed by bramble patches (11%), field edges (10%), ditches and reedbeds (both 9%). In fact 1205 records were collected from 43 different habitats, including gardens, rubbish tips, potato and kale fields. Some were on the edges of motorways, and one nest was on a rubbish tip close to the centre of Exeter. Of the grasses used for nest building, cock's-foot was easily the most popular (21%), followed by reedgrass (14%) and reeds (10%). Nests were recorded from 38 species of grass.

THE DISPERSAL OF THE RED FOX

As a family of fox cubs grows up, the links between them diminish. They soon start to travel alone in search of food and by late autumn or winter all young dog foxes have left home, some of them on journeys of up to seven miles from their birthplace.

Above: A fox cub, newly emerged from the earth, assesses his surroundings by sniffing the air carefully. When young foxes are making excursions from their birthplace they may exhibit an extraordinary sense of direction. In studies in Oxfordshire, juvenile foxes have been radio-tagged and followed into countryside apparently unknown to them; then they have suddenly turned to head unerringly for home.

The social organisation of red foxes is varied and flexible, and local differences are probably a consequence of varied food supplies, and different levels of mortality, much of it at the hand of man.

Irrespective of the adult group size in early spring (probably a single dog fox and between one and four adult vixens), it is swollen in summer by the annual addition of cubs. By late summer and early autumn, as these cubs mature, a new set of social pressures arises within the fox community. The home range that previously supported a couple of foxes must now sustain two or three times that number.

Growing up As a family of cubs grow up,

the links between them diminish, and the extent to which their activities are concentrated around the earth also declines. Cubs are born in late March, and by the end of July they are already travelling throughout their parent's range. Initially it is not uncommon to see a single youngster trotting at an adult's side, sniffing to investigate everything that catches the adult's attention. Later in summer cubs travel alone, sometimes returning to lie up near the earth, but sometimes focusing their movements on small ranges within the parental territory. As summer draws into autumn you may see small parties of foxes lazing together in the warming rays of the dawn sun. These will probably be sisters which grew up together and may remain in the group throughout the winter, and perhaps for years. However, for some young vixens, and almost all young dog foxes, the autumn of their first year sees the break-up of family ties and the start of their dispersal.

Leaving home Nobody knows exactly what prompts young foxes to leave home, but they can disperse over enormous distances, with males generally travelling farther from their birthplace than females.

Once a fox leaves its home range it may behave in a variety of different ways. Sometimes a young dog fox weaves its way across the countryside, travelling far in one night, then spends a few days in one area before

151

moving on. In this way he may criss-cross the locality, perhaps even ending up again, even temporarily, back where he started.

Other young foxes that have been radio-tracked have moved in a much more determined fashion: striking out from home in remarkably straight lines and being deflected only by major obstructions such as towns or rivers. Yet others seem to edge cautiously into dispersal; they make excursions from their natal range either in a variety of directions or to the same place. Then after several days or weeks of these short excursions they may move to the new site that they seem to have been prospecting.

Approach of winter With the end of autumn some mature foxes may also make excursions out of their previous territories. Dog foxes may go in pursuit of vixens on heat, while throughout the year even resident foxes will occasionally make excursions in search of extra food. Young dog foxes always disperse during their first winter. Popular opinion asserts that this is because their fathers drive them out, but of the radio-tagged foxes that have been studied, there is only fragmentary evidence that their departure was precipitated by an attack from the father. The timing of the departure is probably influenced by a combination of mounting pressures, ranging from parental aggression to diminishing food supplies in early winter.

The problem of securing adequate food in the cold months is not just a problem for juvenile foxes before they have perfected their hunting techniques; it is perhaps especially acute for animals which, like the fox, are opportunistic in their lifestyle. They hunt whatever is around but, as their prey species are finely adapted to avoid their predators, on some nights a fox may fail to catch anything. A string of such nights can add up to

Above: Foxes do not despise insects as food. This fox is searching the grass for invertebrates such as beetles.

Right: This fox has been fortunate enough to catch a hare. In addition to such live prey, foxes eat carrion and fruit, such as blackberries, strawberries and rose hips.

Opposite page: A young fox exploring its home territory – soon it will leave home and learn to live and hunt by itself.

Below: Adolescent foxes must find the abundance of fruit in autumn a boon while they are still perfecting their hunting skills, but they relish sweet things in general.

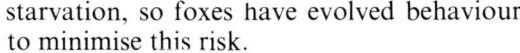

starvation, so foxes have evolved behaviour to minimise this risk.

Fox larders Foxes try to acquire surplus food while the going is good, and they store it for future use. Since much of the fox's food is highly perishable it can only be stored for a short time, but in an opportunistic life this temporary insurance policy may make all the difference.

The fox digs a small grave, into which the food is carefully nosed. With delicate sweeping strokes of its snout the fox then covers the hoard, pushing down the soil with jabs of its nose. Sometimes it uses its snout to push displaced grass stalks back into position and so further conceal the cache. It has a precise memory for where it has made its food stores, returning to them unerringly.

This behaviour probably underlies the phenomenon of foxes killing more than their immediate requirements. They are 'programmed' to seize whatever surplus arises, and caching ensures that they make the best use of it.

DEER SIGNS

Deer have been studied for centuries, so much is known of their behaviour. Autumn – the mating season for deer – is an excellent time to watch them.

There are seven species of wild-living deer in the British Isles but only the red and roe deer are native. The fallow deer was probably introduced from Asia Minor by the Romans,

and the other species – the sika deer, Chinese water deer, muntjac and reindeer – have been introduced at various times during the past 300 years.

Deer are mainly social animals, living in groups or herds. They are active at dawn and dusk, coming into the open from mainly woodland retreats to feed on grasses, shoots, leaves, berries, root crops and cereals.

Male deer – known as bucks or stags depending on the species – have antlers which are grown before the rut each year and then shed. Of the female deer, only the reindeer has antlers. The breeding season usually begins in early autumn and the young are born to coincide with the best feeding time

Above: A young fallow deer. Fallow deer are widely distributed in parks and woodland areas throughout the British Isles. Like red deer, they are highly attached to traditional rutting stands and will return to them year after year. Many feral herds also exist, formed from escaped park animals.
The best way to watch deer is to stalk them or to wait for them in a high seat or hide. Dawn and dusk are the ideal times.

for the mother–the summer of the following year. The muntjac is an exception–it breeds throughout the year.

Watching techniques There are two basic ways of observing deer at close range: either by stalking them on foot to try to get closer, or by waiting in a hide or high seat for the deer to come to you. As with all mammal watching, wear drab, waterproof clothes, preferably brown or green. Wellingtons are suitable in woodland, but for stalking deer on hills stout walking boots are more comfortable. At close or medium distance deer can be watched with binoculars, but for long range viewing–possibly of highland deer a mile or so away–a telescope is useful.

Deer parks are the easiest places to see deer at close quarters. These deer–usually red, sika and fallow–are used to public gaze and may allow a close approach on foot. Don't attempt this in the breeding season as you may provoke an attack from an irate stag or buck. At this time of year, or with shyer park deer, watching is best done from a vehicle. Even wild deer, which can sometimes be observed from roadsides as they feed, do not associate a vehicle with danger, but will soon disappear if you open a door or leave the car.

Deer that live in woodland, such as the roe, are best watched from a high seat or hide near their regularly used runways or feeding areas. Hides can be purchased, or constructed from canvas or tarpaulin draped over a wooden framework and anchored with cord or twine. Purchased hides are not very durable and should not be left in the open for too long.

There are several drawbacks to hides: they tend to concentrate human scent in one place, vision is limited, and sitting in a small canvas box for long periods can be uncomfortable.

Above: These branches have been cut down to help the deer feed in winter; a spot like this is a good place to wait to see deer.

Below: A family party of sika deer. This species is mainly found in thick woodland with dense undergrowth, and sometimes in marshy areas. The New Forest is an ideal place to watch the rut in September and October.

In well visited areas hides can attract the attention of vandals. It is better to use hides on undisturbed private property, or take advantage of natural hides such as trees, rocks or ruined buildings–objects with which the deer are already familiar.

A better method of remaining undetected is to make a high seat. These can be bought, but a far cheaper method is to fit a wooden platform securely to the branches of a tree, several feet above the ground. The platform can be reached by a ladder, and it gives an unrestricted view, keeping your scent well above the animals. It is also above their line of vision and any noise at that height is unlikely to frighten them.

Stalking Getting close to deer by stalking is more of a challenge, and a greater sense of achievement is felt if you can approach, then leave, without being spotted. Deer have excellent sight and hearing, and an acute sense of smell. To avoid detection needs care and a little forward planning. Always keep downwind. Test the direction of the wind at every opportunity by throwing grass or crumpled dry leaves into the air, or by holding up a handkerchief (out of sight of the deer). Remember that in woodland wind tends to eddy and a freak current of air may take your scent to the deer.

If you know where the animals are congregating, perhaps at a feeding area or rutting ground, approach quietly, using cover and stepping carefully to avoid cracking twigs or fallen branches. During the breeding season, the sound of the bellowing stags or bucks will help you locate the rutting area. The males will be concerned with herding the females, but look out for the does or hinds, especially one that may be a little way from the main group but is still very much on the alert.

If you see a group of deer in the trees, continue to walk and allow them to see you. Do not stop when you first notice the animals – if they have spotted you they will quickly move into cover. When you are well out of their sight and smell, test the wind direction and then double back and approach the deer carefully.

Stalking away from the cover of woodland is more difficult and you must be prepared to get down on your knees or stomach and to crawl for long distances. Red deer, especially, are a challenge to the stalker, for during summer they spend much time high in the hills on exposed terrain. When you first spot the deer, and before they have detected you, get out of sight and test the wind direction. If the deer are a long way off and the wind is not in your favour, you may have a great detour to make before a safe approach is possible.

Deer can spot a figure silhouetted against the skyline at great distances, so only walk upright if the contours of the land allow you to remain hidden. When cover is lost and you

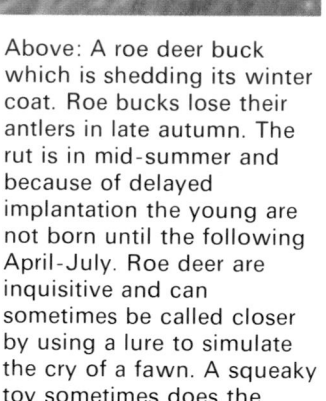

Above: A roe deer buck which is shedding its winter coat. Roe bucks lose their antlers in late autumn. The rut is in mid-summer and because of delayed implantation the young are not born until the following April-July. Roe deer are inquisitive and can sometimes be called closer by using a lure to simulate the cry of a fawn. A squeaky toy sometimes does the trick.

Below right: Red deer damage to trees may be as high as 3m (10ft).

Below: A cast antler which has been chewed by deer for its calcium. The antlers of fallow deer are the most commonly found.

have to move over open ground, lie flat on your stomach and only move when all the deer have their heads down. Freeze when a head is raised or a deer looks towards you. The stalk will end when you are close enough to have a good look through binoculars, or if the deer spots you, or if you run out of cover and any further movement will give you away.

Female deer are most easily watched when they have young calves or fawns. A doe or hind will not move far from her offspring lying in cover, and if she barks a warning and runs round in circles you can be fairly sure of being near the hiding place. Never handle a young deer, even if you think it has been abandoned. In all likelihood the mother is nearby and will return when you have gone. Although a handled deer is unlikely to be rejected by its mother because of human scent on its body, overhandling may cause it to leave cover and try to follow you.

Looking for signs You can learn about the habits and behaviour of deer before you begin watching them by studying the signs they leave in their territory. The regular runways or paths are most obvious in woodland where the deer have been moving through thick cover, or during snow. You will see droppings and tracks – they vary enormously with species, age and weathering, and you may be able to detect the musky smell of scent deposited by the males on trees and bushes during the breeding season. At this time of year, too, the males make scrapes with their forehoofs at the base of trees and beside bushes and other landmarks, and thresh young trees and tall plants with their antlers. Roe deer make rings around a stone, tree stump or small tree or bush during their rut in July and August. The rings are usually circular, sometimes a figure of eight, and are formed when the buck chases the doe prior to mating.

During the rut you may also find a fresh wallow, a wet or muddy depression where red

deer stags have been rolling to enhance their scent. These wallows are used by both sexes at other times to help rid the animals of their old winter coat. Traces of hair may be found around wallows in late spring. At the end of the breeding season male deer shed their antlers, which are mostly eaten by the deer and provide a valuable source of calcium for the expectant females. Newly formed antlers are covered in thin skin or 'velvet' which is removed by being scraped on vegetation. This is known as fraying and young trees used for this purpose, worn and damaged about two feet above the ground, may have traces of velvet attached. More serious tree damage is caused by barking–the stripping of the

Above left: The droppings of roe deer are a helpful indication of the animals' presence nearby as they are usually found near bedding areas.

Above: A red deer scrape is often found by tree trunks or stumps. Groups of deer paw and stamp the ground as they play around the tree. This behaviour is also particularly common among fallow and roe deer.

outer layer for food.

Look too for signs of the ways different species feed. Roe are browsers, chiefly feeding on low leaves and shoots. Sika are mainly grazers of fields and open moorland. Other species, such as the fallow and the muntjac, are both grazers and browsers.

A good field guide will be able to tell you where the various deer species are distributed in this country. It is a good idea to do some research into the habits and behaviour of the deer you want to watch before undertaking any practical observation. Apart from the naturally wild red and roe deer and herds of fallow deer in the ancient hunting forests, most deer you see are escapes from parks.

Looking out for deer

Tracks–¼ natural size

muntjac deer

roe deer

sika deer

fallow deer

red deer

pig

goat

sheep

cattle

Deer tracks at speed

fore

hind

walk or trot

canter or gallop

cleaves

dew claws

Droppings–⅔ natural size

red deer stag
light brown-black, pointed at one end

fallow deer
usually black, in lines or piles

sika deer
small green-black depending on age, often in heaps

muntjac deer
black and shiny, faceted with point at one end, usually single pellets

roe deer
dark brown-black, glossy, may be near bedding area

sheep
dark brown-black, left in large masses

brown hare
brown, round, scattered

goat
brown, shaped like date-stone, in groups

rabbit
brown-black, large numbers in regular latrines

Winter ~ life in the cold season

On a frosty day in mid-winter a sinister beauty etches the land, embalming it in a hard glaze of ice. Although many of the plants have set seed and withered, and many animals have migrated or are in hibernation, there is still a surprising amount of activity in the countryside, especially on milder days when the sun is shining.

In the British Isles it is hard to determine when winter truly begins yet, after the trees have shed the last of their leaves in mid-November, the change seems to jar. The richness of autumn is soon forgotten, and it becomes as difficult to recall vividly the soft green pelt of a woodland canopy as it is in June to imagine a leafless glade. In a sense this is a bonus; if our memories were more perfect, the drama of seasonal change would be much diluted.

Within the season of winter itself, the British Isles experiences a variety of climatic conditions, the result of its location between the Atlantic to the west and the Continent of Europe to the east. Constant waves of deep Atlantic depressions force chill moist air over the countryside, bringing with it icy rain, sleet and snow. This pattern is most evident in December, often the stormiest month of winter. In January and February high pressure over northern Europe often gains ascendancy and, while it fends off the Atlantic onslaught, it clamps a pall of still-freezing air over the British Isles. The sea is now at its coolest; the sun's meagre warmth is rapidly lost to clear blue skies, and temperatures typically hover around zero all day.

Our severest winters are generally associated with such high pressure located above the polar regions. In the record-breaking winter of 1981-2, temperatures plunged to extreme lows, reaching minus 20-25°C (−4-13°F) overnight. The depressions which penetrated this frozen still-life from time to time disgorged heavy falls of snow and drifted it into deep scalloped waves wherever obstacles arrested the force of the wind. Such conditions greatly stretched the survival capabilities of wildlife.

In these extreme winters, shrubs and trees, such as the holm oak and sequoia redwoods, introduced from warmer climes, suffer badly Our native trees, evolved to withstand such conditions, also wilt, but less so. As they shed their leaves, they turn to a state of virtual hibernation. Blizzards may blow harmlessly through the bare wood—if the trees retained their leafy canopy they would crack and topple under the dead weight of entrapped snow. Conifers evade winter's bite by evolving needle-like leaves which minimise the surface area through which vital moisture would otherwise be lost.

The foliage of trees is such a gift of shelter

Left: Food is always scarce in our bleak, snowy mountain areas in winter.

Below: Hoar-frost coats the remnant of summer's leaves and ferns with white.

and food in summer that it is hard to imagine any species profiting by its loss in winter. The bare limbs of trees, however, bathed in moisture and wan sunlight, provide ideal conditions for the lowly single-celled alga *Pleurococcus*, which now spreads upwards, dusting trunks and branches with a thin emerald sheen. These limitless vertical pastures are welcome food for herbivorous invertebrates – notably woodlice and millipedes, which are active through the winter months. They ascend the trees, mainly by night, to scrape a living from the rich algal bloom on the bark. *Pleurococcus* thrives best on deciduous trees, shunning the more acidic surface of conifers and also birches, which is why this species retains its silvery white gloss all year.

The remarkable survival powers of some other insects are equally evident in the depths of winter. Wherever the shelter of a hedge or wall offers a haven of still air, especially if it is warmed by a shaft of sunlight, swarms of winter gnats dance in apparently perpetual motion. The jigging clouds, comprised entirely of males, are curiously conspicuous, which serves them well, for the purpose of this communal aerial display is to attract females with which the dancers can mate.

The winter moth also chooses the grimmest season to mate and lay eggs. Scientists have noted about six females to every square metre of oak canopy. Each insect lays about 150 eggs, so paving the way for a mass emergence of defoliating caterpillars in the spring. Many adults are snapped up by hard-pressed tits in the cold light of dawn, but with their eggs safely jettisoned, the moths have ensured the survival of the next generation.

Most insects, however, lie dormant, buried in whatever nook or cranny offers them the best protection from cold and predators. Many moths and butterflies overwinter as pupae, though some adults, such as those of the brimstone and tortoiseshell butterflies, also overwinter successfully. The key to the survival of many so-called 'cold hardy'

insects lies in the conversion of blood sugar to glycerol which acts as a dilute anti-freeze, protecting vital tissues against prolonged sub-zero temperatures.

Some animals of the cold north, notably the Soay sheep on St Kilda, are thought to find a different source of anti-freeze by eating more moss in winter. Many mosses are rich in fatty acids which, when absorbed, may help to keep limb joints mobile in low temperatures. This may explain why the reindeer, a herd of which is now well established in the Cairngorms, paws laboriously at the snow crust to expose moss, even though it provides little in the way of actual food.

Equally ingenious adaptations are shown by such hibernating mammals as hedgehogs, dormice and bats. The surplus food they so feverishly gather and devour in autumn is converted into a thick layer of brown fat which produces a third as much energy per gram as normal body fat. To enable it to tap this source slowly through the winter, the hedgehog drastically reduces its heartbeat and breathing rate, so that up to 15 minutes may elapse between successive breaths. Simultaneously its blood thins to prevent clotting and its body temperature drops to near that of its surroundings. If the hedgehog becomes too cold, it automatically shivers to generate a little extra heat. A mild spell in mid-winter can prove fatal, spurring hibernators into energy-sapping activity and leaving them with depleted fat stores if freezing conditions suddenly return.

Others cope better with fluctuating temperatures. A mild day coaxes out some bats, no doubt to the detriment of any flying insects. Badgers are exceptionally hardy and readily emerge from semi-hibernation on warmer days.

Deep snow, however, is a major hazard for those mammals, active all winter, who may have to travel further afield for food, so burning up valuable body reserves. Scottish red deer ultimately abandon snowbound hills to graze on lowland pastures, while roe deer demolish bramble thickets and strip the bark of saplings wholesale. Small mammals such as voles and shrews are better off, mining tunnels under the snow to escape the hostile conditions above.

The covert existence of small mammals in winter also affords them protection against such predators as foxes and weasels which stay active throughout the year. In Scotland, however, the stoat regains some of the advantage by moulting into a white coat in winter, adding the weapon of camouflage to its hunting strategy. Prey species such as the mountain hare and ptarmigan likewise abandon their brown summer coat for a white one and so make themselves less conspicuous to stoats and other hunters, notably the golden eagle.

Birds are especially vulnerable to the famine conditions imposed by a blanket of snow and ice. In harsh weather red grouse have been seen entering farmyards to pilfer chicken-feed; curlews and water rails – normally among the wariest of birds – venture into gardens, and even snipe have been seen at bird tables.

Although it occasionally freezes over in the hardest winters, the coast is usually an invaluable refuge for many birds we typically associate with inland haunts. Freshwater birds such as herons and kingfishers are often seen by the shore in winter, especially when rivers and streams are icebound. Kingfishers adapt remarkably well, plunging into rock pools in search of small fish and crustaceans.

Indeed, birds travel vast distances to escape inhospitable conditions. Normally quite sedentary birds of all kinds may join in spontaneous 'hard-weather movements', roving widely around Europe in spectacular flocks. First to move are often the lapwings, skylarks, redwings and fieldfares. Radar studies have shown that if severe conditions alternate between the British Isles and Europe, lapwings often commute back and forth across the Channel several times each winter. Some winters also bring exotic immigrants, notably waxwings and crossbills when their native Scandinavian food crops fail to support them.

The short winter days give birds little time in which to meet their food requirements. It then becomes vital to conserve as much energy as possible during the long, cold over-night vigil. Small birds are especially vulnerable to heat loss at night, and some, such as wrens and long-tailed tits, huddle together in groups to share body warmth in a snug recess, such as a tree hole or old nest.

Some species, however, breed so early in the year that winter is a time of intense advance preparations. Male tawny owls stake out their breeding territories in November, proclaiming ownership with their familiar hooting call. By December pairs are firmly established in their own domains, and the male begins courtship-feeding of the female, principally offering her voles and mice. By late February or March the female will be fortified for egg-laying and the role of incubation which she alone performs for upwards of a month.

Another famous early nester is the golden eagle which not uncommonly incubates its eggs stoically in a snowbound mountain eyrie in March. While seasonal fluctuations in their prey favour late winter nesting in these two raptors, it is close association with man-made food supplies that enables the diminutive collared dove to nest, albeit in small numbers, throughout the winter months.

As spring draws near we traditionally look to the plant kingdom for more obvious signs of stirring activity. Few plants are equipped to flower or fruit in winter, although gorse may flaunt the odd bloom in December, and the winter-toadstool, 'velvet shanks', with its dense clusters of yellow caps, adds welcome colour to bare deciduous woodland. Even by January, however, there is a gentle but perceptible quickening of pace; the blooms of snowdrops and winter aconites emerge, looking all the bolder for their pallid fragility. In sheltered corners of woodland, elder slowly uncurls its first leaves, and hazel extends its pollen-laden catkins to the first drowsy flying insects, while high in the bare treetops a mistle thrush practises its song for spring.

FLOWERS: SUMMER'S REMNANTS

Many of our herbaceous plants persist in some form well into the winter months, providing striking evidence of a summer long gone, even when the snow is on the ground.

The winter months are often thought of as the drab time of year. The colourful berries and fruits of autumn have either been eaten or have become dry and shrivelled. Most of the spring flowers have yet to appear, and leafless trees and dead vegetation contribute to the starkness of the landscape. Yet many interesting plants can still be found, especially when the weather has been crisp and dry.

Grasses and reeds The flowers of grasses, sedges and rushes are small and individually insignificant, but the inflorescences (whole heads of flowers) provide some of the most eye-catching features of the winter countryside.

The confusingly named common reed, which is in fact a grass, reaches up to 3m (10ft) in height, often forming large stands. The cane-like stems are topped by large, silvery, plume-like inflorescences which toss and bend in the wind, shining in the winter sunlight.

Most grasses are smaller and more slender than the common reed, and in winter their dead flowering stems are beaten down and broken by wind and heavy rain. However some, such as the barren brome with its elegant, pendulous flower spikes, may remain unscathed. Cotton grass may also survive. This is not a grass at all but a relative of the sedges, named for its seedheads which look like balls of white cotton-wool. These delicate, fluffy heads, dancing in the slightest

Above: Preserved here under a covering of frost and snow, the seedheads of the bulrush start to lose their smooth, cylindrical appearance by February or March as fluffy seeds are released and dispersed by the wind.

Below: The basket shape of the flower heads of the wild carrot. As the ripe fruits are shed, they often fall into the centre of the basket, where their spines interlock to form a solid mass of fruits.

breeze, are a bright feature in the otherwise sombre boglands in which the plant grows.

Another relative of the sedges is the bulrush, sometimes wrongly called the reedmace. This majestic plant grows in swampy ground at the fringes of lakes and ponds and in slow-flowing water, often covering extensive areas. The stem may reach 3m (10ft), and from July onwards supports a seedhead which looks like a thick, brown, furry cylinder made up of thousands of tightly packed seeds.

Fruits and capsules Many of the summer left-overs are fruits, or the structures associated with fruits. The white, feathery fruits of traveller's joy (*Clematis vitalba*) which is a vigorous climber and fruits prolifically, begin to ripen in September or even earlier, but remain attached in globular heads for several months. As the trees and shrubs shed their leaves, these fruits become much more noticeable.

Wood avens (*Geum urbanum*) is a slender, erect perennial with hooked fruits gathered into dark, burr-like heads. Protected by the hedgebanks and woods in which it grows, it may survive the rigours of winter weather. Woodland and hedgerows may also conceal the striking fruits of the gladdon or stinking iris (*Iris foetidissima*). It has a dull brown capsule which splits into three parts to reveal a mass of bright orange-red seeds that remain attached to the capsule segments until spring. Another orange-red fruit of hedgerows and waste ground is the Chinese lantern (*Lycium chinense*), which has become naturalised in Britain. The familiar papery lantern is formed by the inflated calyx (fused sepals) of the flower, which contains an orange berry.

Capsules Parts of plants that are frequently found in winter are the tough, woody stems and seed capsules of herbaceous perennials. These plants are very slow to break down and rot, and remain as relics until spring, when they are replaced by new growth from the rootstock.

Poppies produce some of the most familiar seed capsules. They normally cease flowering by August, but individual plants may continue to flower for several months after this and their capsules can be found quite late in the year. They are easily recognised by their pepperpot construction and the different species are so distinctive that they can be identified by the shape, ridges and hairs of the capsules. Field poppy (*Papaver rhoeas*), for example, has rounded, hairless capsules, while those of the bristly poppy (*P. hybridum*), are, as the name suggests, very bristly. In contrast, the capsules of the pale poppy (*P. argemone*), are long, narrow and oblong, with few bristles.

Bracts and flower heads Members of the daisy family bear their fruits and flowers in heads protected by a cup of overlapping bracts. After the fruits have been dispersed, the bracts remain. The spiny heads of thistles are remarkably persistent, drying to a papery consistency and retaining the shape of the head long after the dispersal of the fruits. The carline thistle (*Carlina vulgaris*) in particular may retain its heads for many months, and when used in floral decorations lasts for years.

Hardheads (*Centaurea nigra*), a close relative of the thistles, is a common roadside plant in chalky or limestone areas. The bracts are not spiny, like thistle bracts, but have a soft, fringed upper half. In old heads, this fringed upper portion bends outwards, giving the heads a rather open, cone-like appearance.

The tough, toothed stems and familiar prickly flowerheads of the teasel also last right through the winter. Their stark, black outlines are a common sight, particularly on otherwise bare motorway verges.

Silhouettes of stems Some of the most familiar roadside sights of winter are provided by the tall, stiff, silhouettes of members of the parsley family such as hogweed, cow parsley and wild angelica. As the leaves die and the ripe fruits fall, the hollow stems become brown and brittle. Finally, only the upright, bleached stems remain, supporting the rays of the characteristic umbrella-shaped flower head with perhaps an occasional fruit remaining attached. The wild carrot is also common in fields and on grassy roadsides and has very dense flower heads with numerous rays that curve inwards to form a basket shape.

Above: In autumn and winter, the seed clusters of traveller's joy form a feathery white blanket over twigs and branches, hence its other name of old man's beard.

Right: The distinctive capsules of the opium poppy (*Papaver somniferum*) are large, woody and globe-shaped, with a fluted cap.

Below: Ice crystals have formed on the dead flower heads, making this solitary specimen of hogweed a spectacular winter sight.

HOW PLANTS OVERWINTER

Even though January and February are winter months, it is still possible to find some flowers in bloom – especially if the winter has been mild. The secret lies in the way each plant has stored food.

When a flowering plant overwinters, the foliage dies away to leave an underground food-storing structure, ready to produce new flowers and foliage in the spring. Although structures vary, they have similarities reflecting such common problems as cold and lack of sunlight faced by all overwintering plants.

Lifespan However, not all flowering plants are adapted to overwintering. Annuals are plants that live and die within a single year, relying totally on seeds to ensure their appearance the following year. Because only a fraction of the seeds produced is likely to germinate, annuals such as the rosebay willowherb produce vast quantities of seeds and tend to grow in bare or disturbed ground where the chances of survival are greatest.

Biennials last for two years, having the capacity to survive one winter. They do not flower in their first year, which is spent in storing up enough food to enable them to produce flowers and seeds in the second.

Perennials, on the other hand, are able to live for many years because of their adaptations for overwintering. They are often found in environments such as woodland, where thick ground cover and lack of wind makes it difficult for a seed-producing plant to establish a new generation.

If they are to live through the winter, plants must be able to cope with a number of problems, not least of which is the cold. To help them do this, the root, stem or leaves of the plant are modified to form distinctive underground overwintering structures.

Root structures The minimum modification to be found among perennials is the rootstock, which is the name given to a toughened stem base and root, capable of overwintering and storing food. It is a very basic structure, found in cultivated roses as well as wild primroses, but it is not always totally effective in combating the rigours of our winter climate.

Another simple overwintering structure is the root tuber, which is found in both biennials and perennials. Biennials, being most abundant in dry grassland, often have a long tap root for extracting scarce supplies of

Above: Clusters of snowdrops appear in woodland from January until March, very often while snow is still on the ground – hence the alternative name of 'snow-piercers'. The flowers are protected by a leaf-like structure, which envelops them as they force their way upwards.

water, and into which food is passed during their first year of growth. The food causes the root to swell and form a root tuber as in the wild carrot or wild parsnip. (This is the part that has been developed by growers to provide us with the more familiar cultivated vegetable forms.)

Stem structures The most commonly found

Right: The early purple orchid possesses a mass of fibrous roots, which enlarge to store food and become root tubers. As with many of the flowering plants that overwinter rather than grow from seed, they appear early in the year, often in April, in woodland. Dog's mercury (in the background), which grows from a rhizome, may be seen as early as February.

modification for overwintering in perennials is the rhizome. This is really no more than a creeping stem that grows horizontally underground and can be used to store food material. It may appear in different forms: in Solomon's seal and dog's mercury the rhizome constitutes the main body of the plant, annually sending up an aerial flowering shoot. The rhizome of the iris family, and of many grasses, is dominated by a terminal cluster of leaves and tends to lie closer to the surface of the soil.

The corm is a more complicated modification of the stem, which is shortened to an extreme to produce the stout, rounded body so familiar in the crocus. If the papery, brown scale leaves are peeled off the terminal bud, (which produces the main flowering shoot), the axillary or lateral buds (which produce the foliage leaves) can be seen quite clearly within.

Food manufactured by the plant during the year is passed down to its base where it develops into a new corm directly upon the remains of the corm from the previous year. This would mean that over the years, corms would eventually form so close to the soil's surface that they would be in danger of freezing. This problem, which also affects bulbs, is largely overcome by the presence of special 'contractile' roots, whose function is to draw the structure back into the ground. In the case of the meadow saffron (a species of lily and not a crocus), the new corm develops alongside, rather than on top of, the previous year's remains.

Rhizome—a creeping, swollen stem normally growing underground, sometimes seen on the surface.
Root tuber—swollen part of the root; stores food and lasts only one year.
Corm—fleshy underground stem; lasts only one year. New one grows from the old.
Rootstock—swollen stem base used to store food.
Bulb—constructed of fleshy leaves surrounding next year's flowerbud.

Leaf modifications The most familiar overwintering structure of all is the bulb, which is typical of most members of the lily family, including the tulip, daffodil and onion. Outwardly similar to a corm, it is formed from a greatly condensed shoot of stem and leaves. Unlike the corm, however, it is the leaves, rather than the stem tissue, that are modified for overwintering and food storage. This can be seen by cutting an onion in half, revealing the closely packed, overlapping leaves which have become thick and fleshy with stored food in the form of sugar. The tough, brown outer skin that protects the bulb is composed of the withered remains of the old leaf-bases. If it is left for any appreciable time in the light, a green flowering-shoot develops from the centre of the bulb, which provides all that is needed for the initial growth of the plant.

Above: The flower most associated with spring is probably the primrose. Small clumps of the yellow flowers are seen in woods and hedgerows throughout the British Isles from March onwards—even earlier after a mild winter. Once abundant, its existence is threatened in some areas, particularly near towns, as a result of over-enthusiastic collection.

How flowering plants spend the winter

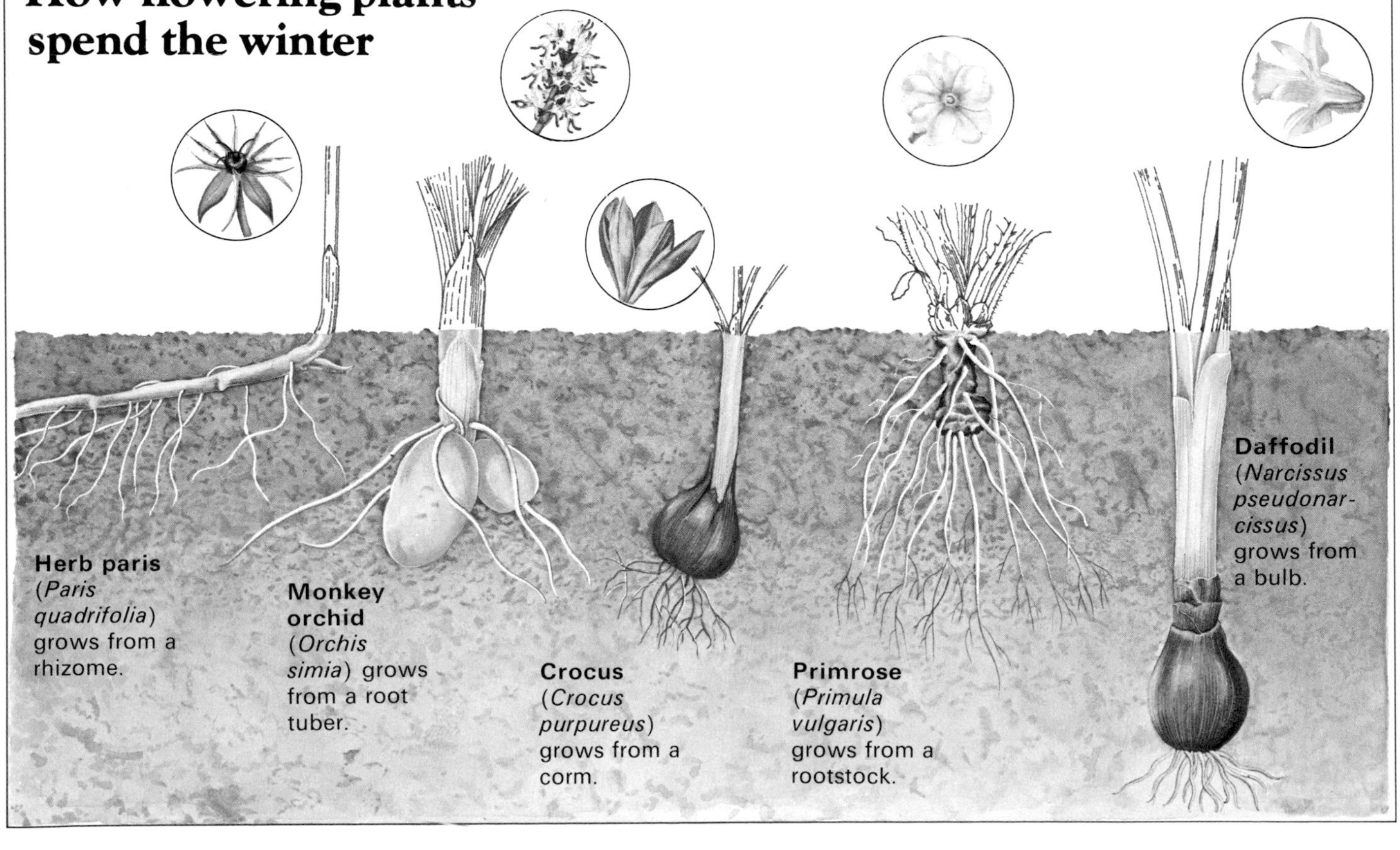

Herb paris (*Paris quadrifolia*) grows from a rhizome.

Monkey orchid (*Orchis simia*) grows from a root tuber.

Crocus (*Crocus purpureus*) grows from a corm.

Primrose (*Primula vulgaris*) grows from a rootstock.

Daffodil (*Narcissus pseudonarcissus*) grows from a bulb.

WINTER FLOWERS

The greys and browns of the winter landscape epitomise the bleakest time of the year in terms of nature. But a few flowering plants flourish despite the conditions and introduce a much needed splash of colour. Why do they come out now and how do they survive?

It is very unusual in the plant world for flowers to bloom only in the middle of winter. Out of about 2,000 species of flowering plants native to the British Isles, only a couple of dozen have a true flowering season in January and February.

Some plants will flower spasmodically all year round given favourable weather conditions – plants like shepherd's purse, chickweed or Buxbaum's speedwell – but their peak comes in the warmer months when they are growing most vigorously. To most people the true winter flowers are the snowdrop and the winter aconite: the first obvious flowers of the new year, they provide a very welcome sight.

Snowdrops begin to flower as early as Christmas in a mild winter, but if it is very cold they will wait until well into March. They were once rare in Britain, found only in the damp woods of western England, but today they are much more widespread, probably having escaped from gardens into surrounding woods. The flowers close at night and when they open the next morning, usually around ten o'clock, the petals start to ooze out nectar. If you touch the tip of your tongue inside a snowdrop after it has been open for a few hours it tastes slightly sweet. Because the petals droop the nectar is protected from rain. The flower is a powerful attraction to the few early insects about at this time of year. Honey bees are sometimes seen to land on one of the spreading sepals and, by clinging to this with their hind legs, they delve into the flower for pollen and nectar.

Spring snowflakes are rare relatives of the snowdrop and they too are more often found as a garden escape than as a true descendant of plants of our primeval forest. Similar to a large, robust snowdrop, the spring snowflake is easily recognised by its bell-shaped flowers with green tips to the petals. They come out a little later than snowdrops and are sometimes produced in pairs on the stem.

Winter aconites come into flower at about the same time as snowdrops, their flowers expanding in sunny weather to reveal curious tubular petals which again hold droplets of nectar. Each flower is surrounded by a leaf-

Above: The first yellow flower of the new year, the winter aconite opens its shiny sepals in the sun when the temperature reaches 10°C (50°F).

Structure of flowers

The first job of any flower is to produce seeds, which it usually does by attracting insects for pollination. The barren strawberry has a simple flower structure and insects are drawn to the nectary within the flower. The winter aconite is one of many variations on this theme: its sepals, resembling petals, attract insects, and the petals have evolved into nectar cups.

like ruff, but the true leaves, which are highly poisonous, emerge from the ground only after the flowers have withered. Introduced from Southern Europe 400 years ago, the winter aconite has become widely naturalised.

Barren strawberry By far the commonest of our winter flowers, if not the most spectacular, is the barren strawberry, so called because it superficially resembles the true strawberry, but its fruit is hard and inedible. It too produces nectar (from a small five-sided nectary, a pad between its stamens and ovaries) and this is drunk by flies and beetles and even the occasional small tortoiseshell butterfly that has woken early from its hibernating sleep.

Winter survivors Most plants are dormant

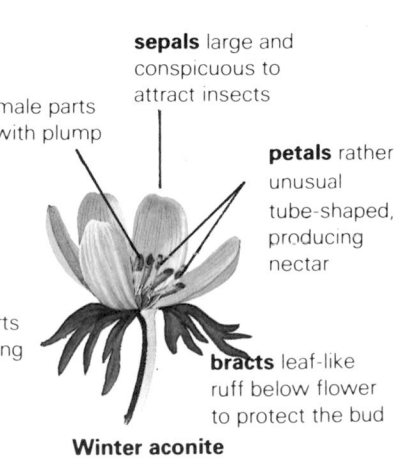

sepals green, resembling small leaves, protect bud before flower opens

petals conspicuous, often with faint lines to direct insects

stamens male parts of flower with plump sac at tip containing pollen

pistils female parts of flower containing ovule which later forms seed

Barren strawberry

sepals large and conspicuous to attract insects

petals rather unusual tube-shaped, producing nectar

bracts leaf-like ruff below flower to protect the bud

Winter aconite

in mid-winter and wait until later to flower, when pollinating insects are abundant and the milder weather encourages growth. Although winter flowers have a monopoly of any insects such as bees or flies that may be about, this is scarcely sufficient reason to flower early.

So why do these particular plants expose their flowers to the rigours of winter? Partly it is because they do not depend entirely on insect pollination for reproduction and each plant can be fertilized by its own pollen. They also have root structures which can multiply and produce new plants. (Winter aconites have tubers, snowdrops and snowflakes have bulbs, and barren strawberries have runners.) However, plants only 'improve their stock' if one flower is fertilized by the pollen of another, and with both these 'do-it-yourself' methods of reproduction the new plant is usually identical to the parent. If cross-pollinated, the next generation turns out slightly different from the parents, and consequently some plants are perhaps better adapted to their environment.

The original environment of these plants may be another clue to their winter flowering. They occurred in the woodland which once covered Britain and Europe and adapted to this habitat by growing and flowering early in the year before the trees cut out their light. The temperature of woodland soil is considerably higher than that of the surrounding exposed land, and moss and dead leaves also act as insulation.

Anti-freeze or central heating? For years botanists have been researching ways in which some plants survive intense cold. In some species flower buds as much as five degrees warmer than the surrounding air have been recorded and you may notice places where plants have melted the snow immediately around them. These higher temperatures are generated by rapidly growing plant tissues although if the plant were to keep up these growth rates to withstand a prolonged frost it would quickly use up its food reserves and starve.

Some plants, such as garden dahlias, die immediately there is a frost while hardy plants such as snowdrops can freeze solid and then recover when they thaw. They do this by closing up to protect the reproductive parts and withdrawing water from their cell structure into the minute intervening air spaces. Here ice crystals can form without causing any harm.

On thawing, even hardy plants can wilt; starved of water, the plant may be horizontal for a couple of hours before recovering and resuming its former vitality.

Although not flowering as early as the winter flowers, the early dog violet (below left) and ground ivy (below centre) soon follow them in March.

Spring snowflake (*Leucojum vernum*) flowers Feb-April in damp woods in SW England, very rare. Ht. 25cm (10in).

Early dog violet (*Viola reichenbachiana*) flowers March-May in woods on calcareous soil. Ht. 15cm (6in).

Barren strawberry (*Potentilla sterilis*) flowers Feb-May in open woods. Ht. 15cm (6in).

Snowdrop (*Galanthus nivalis*) flowers Jan-March in damp woods. Ht. 20cm (8in).

Ground ivy (*Glechoma hederacea*) flowers March-June in woods, hedges, open ground. Ht. 25cm (10in).

Winter aconite (*Eranthis hyemalis*) flowers Jan-March in woods in S. England. Ht. 15cm (6in).

HOW DO FISH SURVIVE IN THE WINTER?

Most of our sea-going and freshwater fishes can survive the normal temperatures of British winters very well simply by searching out deeper, warmer water. Only in extremely cold winters, such as that of 1962-3, are any significant casualties reported in Britain.

Fishes are cold-blooded animals, and most of them are unable to regulate their body temperature which is not maintained at a more or less constant level as man's is, for example; instead, their body temperature is influenced by their surroundings. This means that fishes living in Arctic seas in winter have a body temperature very close to the freezing point of fresh water, while others living on tropical coral reefs have a temperature around the level of a tepid bath. Not surprisingly, no species of fish occurs in both habitats.

Change of habit The ability to live with a body temperature the same as that of their surroundings has several important consequences for fishes. In temperate areas, like Britain, the temperature may vary greatly during the year. A minnow living in a small stream may be in water just above freezing point in winter, but at 20°C (68°F) in summer.

This change in temperature greatly affects the fish's body metabolism. In winter, the minnow is sluggish, probably lying close to a boulder in the stream bed or hiding in the

vegetation at the edge of the bank, hardly moving, breathing slowly and not feeding. The same fish in this stream in summer is very active. All its internal systems function at their peak and, as a result of the abundant food, the fish grows – something that does not happen in winter. In lakes and ponds fishes behave similarly, and in a severe winter they tend to live quietly in deeper parts of the lake.

Water and ice Water is an unusual substance in the way it reacts at very low temperatures. It contracts as it cools, until it reaches a temperature of 4°C (39°F), when it begins to expand. It continues to expand until it reaches freezing point.

In a very severe winter the surface temperature drops, the water contracts, its density increases and it sinks from the surface to the bottom. However, once the surface temperature drops below 4°C (39°F), the water expands instead of contracting. It becomes less dense, and therefore stays at the surface. Eventually ice forms at the surface and,

Above: In severe winter conditions, ice will form even on large areas of water. To survive, fishes and other aquatic life seek out the deeper parts. Here they are relatively safe since the water under the ice eventually settles at a uniform temperature above that of freezing point. Occasionally you may see fishes frozen in deep ice on ponds; they almost certainly died because ice crystals formed in their bodies, breaking down the cells of vital organs.

Right: This map of British waters shows where certain sea species – namely the tunny, blue shark, cod and sole – move to in winter when the temperature of the water drops due to severe cold conditions.

although it gradually becomes thicker the longer the frost lasts, the water beneath stays unfrozen and between freezing point and 4°C (30°F) for weeks on end.

Fishes can thus survive in this unfrozen water through long periods of hard frost, although they do so by reducing their life activities to a very low level in response to the low temperatures.

Casualties Fish mortalities due to ice cover are rarely high, except in certain ponds which are either very shallow or have a dense plant growth on the bottom. In the latter case, if the icing over of the pond is followed by a snowfall, light is cut out and the plants produce more carbon dioxide than oxygen. In these cases, the water in the pond may become deficient in dissolved oxygen and, if there are a lot of fishes present, many may die. Fortunately, this happens rarely in Britain and then mainly in ornamental lakes in parks and gardens.

Deep retreat Most wild fishes, however, succeed in avoiding the worst of winter by retreating into deeper, and thus warmer, water. In rivers in very cold winters the fishes tend to accumulate in deep pools, where the water stays marginally warmer, or they move downstream, which often brings them into deeper water and even into the upper estuary. Similarly, in very severe weather the fishes in large natural lakes tend to quit the cold small tributary streams and shallows and move into deeper water.

Easier at sea Sea fishes are much less vulnerable to the adverse effects of severe cold, mainly because of the vastness of the sea, which retains its warmth and rarely becomes as cold as rivers and lakes. The sea also has the advantage of a much lower freezing point than fresh water, due to the salt that it contains. However, in exception-

ally severe winters, there is a mass migration of fishes from the shallow inshore waters and river mouths into deeper water to avoid the cold.

The most severe impact of prolonged cold is on those fishes, like the blennies and gobies, that live mainly between the tide-marks and in very shallow water. While many of them migrate into deeper water, some may not find suitable habitats, and so die. Severe cold can also affect the fishes' food supply by reducing the quantity of invertebrates and marine algae available.

Even in deeper water not all the fishes are safe. During the intense cold of the winter of 1962-3, North Sea trawlers caught large numbers of dead soles, among other fishes. These flatfishes are particularly sensitive to cold and they tend to congregate in the deeper parts of the southern North Sea.

Fishes generally live through winter by lying low and making fewer demands on their environment by being inactive and feeding less. It is this that allows them to survive in an environment that appears inhospitable to us.

Above: Species like the salmon *(Salmo salar)*, spawn in winter, laying their eggs among gravel, often in shallow, running water. The eggs survive and develop in water temperatures down to freezing point but development is slow and mortalities increase at very low temperatures. A positive consequence of the long growth period is that the fry are born at a time to take advantage of the abundance of food animals that appear in the spring.

Below: Conger eels *(Conger conger)* are near the northern extremity of their range in British waters. This probably makes them more sensitive to the cold: they suffered many casualties in the 1962-3 winter.

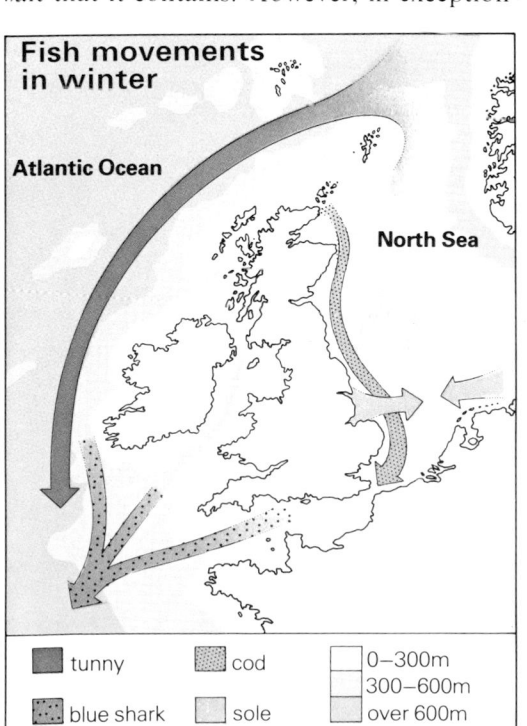

Fish movements in winter

Atlantic Ocean

North Sea

- tunny
- blue shark
- cod
- sole
- 0–300m
- 300–600m
- over 600m

MOTHS OF LATE WINTER

Geometer moths have superbly efficient camouflage colouring; adults, about at the beginning of the year, look like bark, while the caterpillars which hatch in April imitate twigs.

The moths you are likely to come across early in the year, all members of the large Geometridae family, have a special feature in common – the females are flightless and can only crawl feebly about on trees and in the undergrowth. The female spring usher and early moths have only vestigial remnants of wings, while the dotted border has stunted, ragged-looking and quite useless wings; female pale brindled beauty, March and mottled umber moths are devoid of wings and look like six-legged spiders. The females never have any need to fly since the winged males will seek them out by scent when the time comes for mating.

Cryptic camouflage The males are night-flying moths which spend most of the day resting in foliage, or on a branch, post, paling or tree trunk. The 'cryptic' streaks, lines and spots on the wings camouflage the moths perfectly, particularly when the wings are in the closed resting position, and are designed to deceive predators. You may well have to search quite closely to find them. The colouring of the male spring usher, mottled umber and pale brindled beauty varies considerably, and light, dark or mottled individuals can be found; the March moth may appear in a dark, smoky coloured form in parts of the north of England. At night the males are attracted to light, so you may have more luck in seeing them if you leave a window open in a lighted room. The females are even more difficult to find since they often hide in a crevice in bark or under leaves.

With the exception of the mottled umber, you can see these moths from the beginning of the year to mid-April. The mottled umber is the odd one out, flying from October through to January or February.

Looper caterpillars Male and female moths mate soon after they have emerged from the chrysalis towards the end of the winter and the females lay their eggs on twigs or in bark crevices soon afterwards. The caterpillars which hatch from the eggs belong to the group known as loopers. They have only two pairs of claspers or false legs (instead of the usual five), situated on the sixth and tenth segments of the abdomen, and they move along a twig or leaf by stretching out at full length, securing a firm hold with their true legs, then arching the body and drawing the claspers up in a loop almost to the point held by the thoracic legs. The true legs are then thrust forward and take a firm hold again, in preparation for the next loop. It looks as though the caterpillar is measuring the ground with its body – hence the group name geometer which means ground measurer. The caterpillars often stand upright on their claspers and look like sticks.

Food plants Spring usher caterpillars feed only on oak leaves, but the caterpillars of the other species will feed on hawthorn, birch, sallow, blackthorn and other trees as well as oak. March and mottled umber caterpillars sometimes become so numerous that they reach plague proportions and are largely responsible for the nearly leafless condition of some trees, particularly oak.

Early hibernation The caterpillars feed throughout most of April and May, but in late May or early June they crawl down the tree trunk to the ground (or drop down on a thread of silk) to pupate. The mottled umber, spring usher and early moths pupate in flimsy silk cocoons on the ground surface or in leaf litter under their food plant; the dotted border, March and pale brindled beauty burrow just below the soil. And there they stay till the following spring (or till October in the case of the mottled umber).

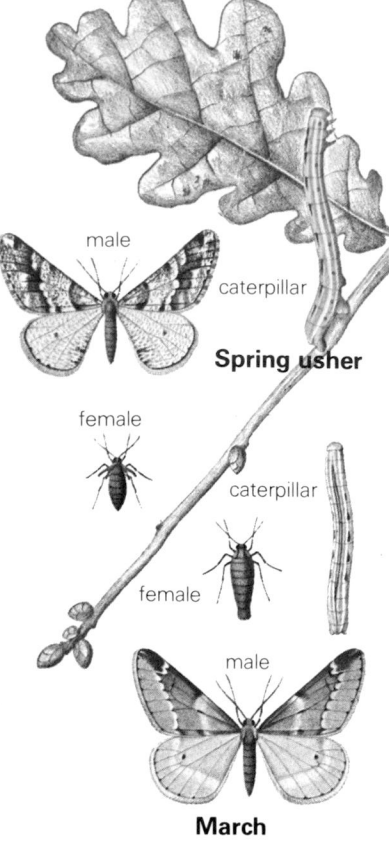

male
caterpillar
Spring usher
female
caterpillar
female
male
March

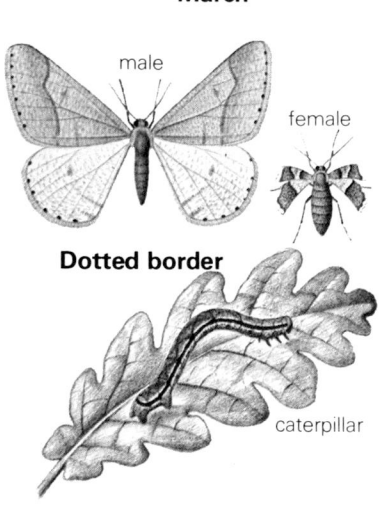

male
female
Dotted border
caterpillar

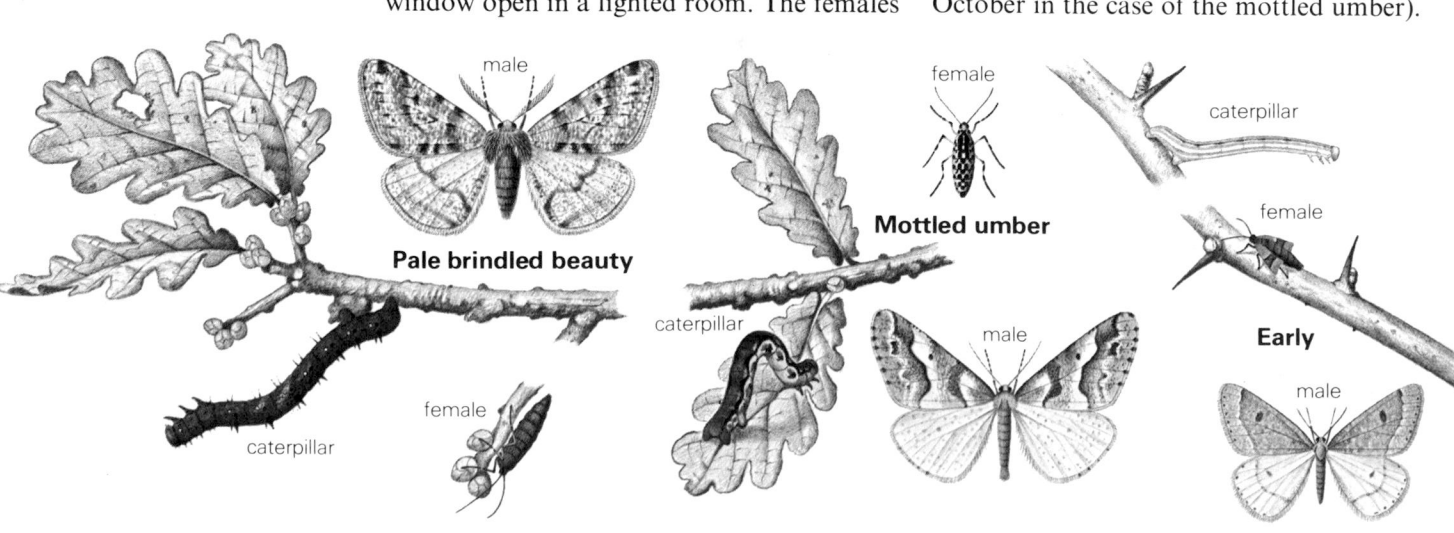

male
Pale brindled beauty
female
caterpillar
female
caterpillar
Mottled umber
caterpillar
female
caterpillar
male
Early
male

WINTER VISITING THRUSHES

Of our six species of thrush, two are mainly winter visitors – the redwing and fieldfare. Their chief breeding grounds are in Scandinavia and Siberia.

No matter where you are in rural Britain, if you are out of doors on a calm, clear autumn night you are likely to hear, high overhead, the sounds of the winter visiting thrushes as they arrive: either a thin 'seep' or a dry, throaty chuckling call. These visitors are the redwing and the fieldfare (most of our breeding thrushes belong to four species: the song and mistle thrushes, the ring ouzel and the blackbird).

These thrushes begin their migration in Scandinavia or further east in northern Siberia. They fly along the European coast of the North Sea until they reach the Netherlands. From here a proportion cross the sea to England. Smaller numbers make the long crossing direct from Scandinavia to northern England and Scotland. The birds set off at dusk. If conditions are calm, those flying to southern England arrive well before midnight; those coming direct from Scandinavia make their landfall in the small hours or even at dawn.

If there is a full moon, it is possible to see these birds by looking through binoculars at the moon. Any birds that pass before the white face of the moon are clearly visible as

silhouettes. From the numbers seen in this way, birdwatchers estimate the volume of migration at different times and on different nights.

The redwing The 'seep' sound is the commonest flight call of the redwing. This bird is fractionally smaller than the song thrush, which has a similar call. Some song thrushes from the Continent join our resident song thrushes for the winter, and so it is necessary

Above: A fieldfare in a thicket. Migrant fieldfares begin to arrive in Britain in autumn, as soon as the weather turns cold in Scandinavia. They may arrive as early as September, but migration may continue as late as December. Often they continue westwards, and some reach Ireland.

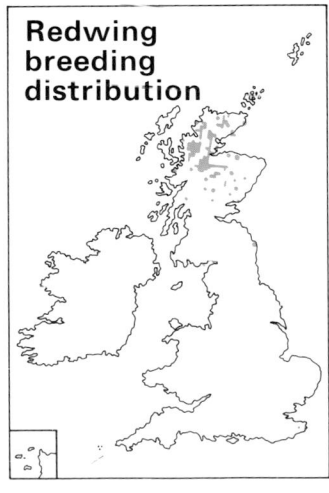

Redwing breeding distribution

Left: Redwings experience difficulty in finding enough to eat during snowy periods. Here they are feeding on some rotten pears left out for them.

to distinguish the redwing from this species. With a little practice you can tell the calls apart: that of the song thrush is a rather sharper 'tsip'.

These two birds even look similar. If you see the birds in flight, a glimpse of the redwing's rich russet-red underwing makes its identity clear, for the song thrush's underwing is a pale sandy beige. If you see the birds on the ground in daytime, there are some more obvious differences. In winter, song thrushes are usually seen in ones and twos, rarely far away from the nearest bushes, whereas redwings tend to occur in flocks, often widely scattered, over open grassland and fields. The redwing always has a darker back than the song thrush–particularly the race *coburni* which breeds in Iceland and winters in Scotland, occasionally straying further south. More important, a fringe of russet is visible where wing and flanks meet. Just as characteristic is the redwing's bold eyestripe, which is either white or yellowish-white.

Unusual migration pattern The vast majority of redwings seen in Britain and Ireland are spotted during the winter months, and are mostly migrants from Scandinavia and further east, where they breed in the northern pine forests, the birch woods and the stunted willow scrub as far north as the fringe of the Arctic tundra. Their pattern of migration is a most unusual one, for birds seen (say) in Britain in one winter may spend the next winter in southern Europe, and vice versa. In some years the numbers leaving Scandinavia are vast, and for a few days or weeks in autumn eastern Britain may seem full of redwings dotted across every suitable damp grassy field, until they gradually disperse to the West Country and Ireland.

As the smallest of the true thrushes, redwings suffer severely in cold winters, and any prolonged snowfall results in large numbers of underweight redwings struggling to find enough food to keep warm and stay alive.

Redwings breeding in Britain It may be that our breeding population of redwings owes its origin to one, or several, of these huge autumn influxes of Scandinavian birds, but an alternative theory suggests that they originated from the returning spring migration of birds that had wintered in southern Europe. Some of these redwings may have been blown off-course to the west, settling where they found a suitable habitat.

The first proven breeding was in Scotland in 1925; sporadic attempts continued until a big increase occurred in the mid-1960s; in 1968 there were 20 pairs in Wester Ross alone. Most of the British breeding stock, probably now several hundred pairs strong, is to be found in northern Scotland. Their choice of habitats is wide, including birch and oak woodland, birch and willow scrub, alder carrs and lines of alders along streams, and the shrubberies of houses with large gardens. Elsewhere in Britain, a few pairs breed in the

Visitors from Scandinavia

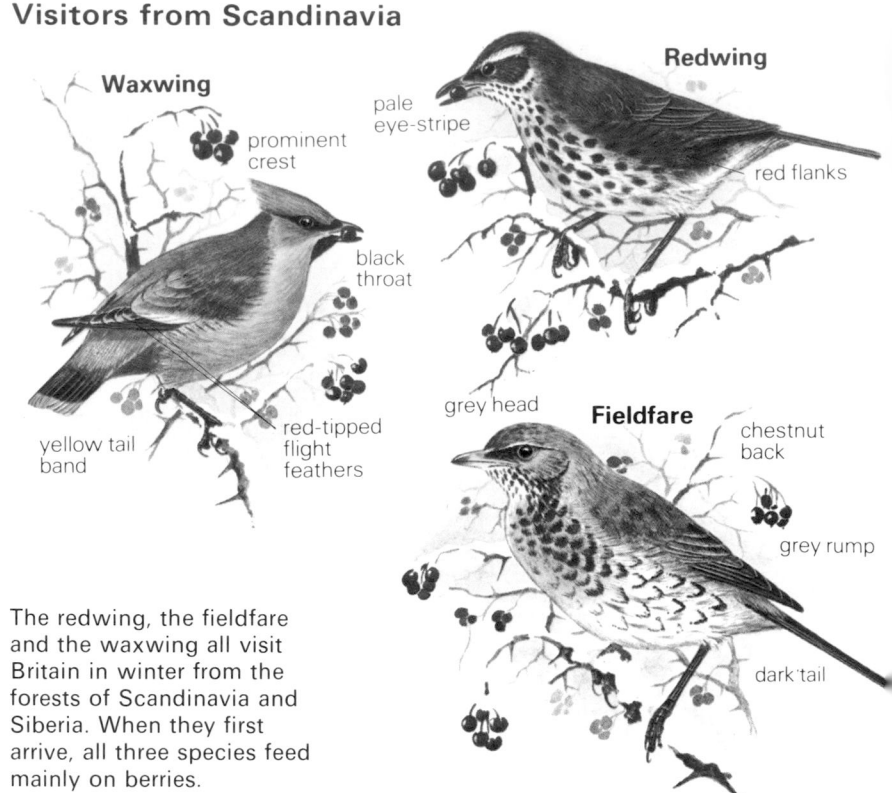

The redwing, the fieldfare and the waxwing all visit Britain in winter from the forests of Scandinavia and Siberia. When they first arrive, all three species feed mainly on berries.

Border Country, and others, astonishingly, as far south as eastern Kent.

The nest has much the same appearance as that of a song thrush, built of coarse grasses with a mud core. Unlike the song thrush, the redwing puts an inner lining of fine grasses within the mud cup.

The fieldfare This is a much larger bird than the redwing–more likely to be confused, at a distance, with the mistle thrush, especially as both present a long-tailed appearance in flight. A closer view, however, reveals the true beauty of the fieldfare's plumage. A grey hood extends to a rich russet back, which in turn leads to a pure grey rump. The tail is black. In flight or perching overhead, the fieldfare

Fieldfare (*Turdus pilaris*); winter visitor; a few pairs breed in Scotland and England. European range expanding. Sexes alike. Length 25cm (10in).

Redwing (*Turdus iliacus*); winter visitor; small population of a few hundred breeding in Scotland. European range expanding. Sexes alike. 21cm (8¼in).

Below: A redwing on its nest. Nesting begins in May, and there are normally two broods each summer.

reveals that its breast is cinnamon coloured, with dark brown spots, fading to white on the belly.

Even more characteristic than its plumage is the fieldfare's cackling laugh of a call: an easily remembered phrase even for those with a poor ear for bird voices. The summer song is less distinctive and not in keeping with the general musical quality of thrush family songs: a harsh, poorly formed jangle of notes.

Spreading south In Europe the fieldfare is a bird of northern forests with a distribution closely similar to that of the redwing, stretching as far east as Siberia. In Scandinavia, from whence most of our migrant fieldfares come, they nest in farmland, open woodland and even in suburban parks and gardens. For more than a century the fieldfare has been extending its range slowly westwards and southwards. When the birds reached Denmark their new colony expanded rapidly; but the same has not happened with the small British population (to date). The first British breeding pair was reported in Orkney in 1967, with further pairs in Shetland in 1968. They now breed on the Scottish mainland in a number of localities, and in England as far south as Derbyshire and Staffordshire, but the annual breeding total remains extremely small – perhaps ten pairs or less.

Fieldfare breeding season The fieldfare builds a nest similar to that of the mistle thrush. It is often sited in a tree fork, but in northern areas, where suitable trees or bushes are absent, it is situated on the ground. A foundation of thick dry grass stems, and also occasionally twigs, is lined with grasses and a thin-walled mud cup. The innermost lining, within the mud cup, is of very fine dry grass blades.

On their Continental breeding grounds, fieldfares tend to be loosely colonial, but there are hardly enough of them in Britain for this to be apparent.

Above: A fieldfare disturbed while feeding among a rich crop of berries. This photograph was taken early in the autumn, before the main plundering of the berry crop by such birds as redwings, fieldfares, song thrushes and mistle thrushes.

Left: A redwing fluffs out its feathers to keep warm on a winter's day. Any spell of cold weather may bring fresh hordes into Britain from across the North Sea; or the cold may cause those already here to migrate further westwards, in search of slightly warmer conditions.

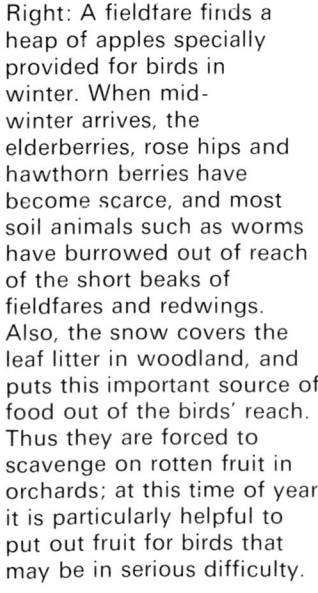

Right: A fieldfare finds a heap of apples specially provided for birds in winter. When mid-winter arrives, the elderberries, rose hips and hawthorn berries have become scarce, and most soil animals such as worms have burrowed out of reach of the short beaks of fieldfares and redwings. Also, the snow covers the leaf litter in woodland, and puts this important source of food out of the birds' reach. Thus they are forced to scavenge on rotten fruit in orchards; at this time of year it is particularly helpful to put out fruit for birds that may be in serious difficulty.

their crossing of the North Sea. They were busily replenishing the energy stores used on the journey by devouring the cotoneaster berries.

A handsome visitor The waxwing is a strikingly handsome bird, about the size and build of a starling. Its flight silhouette is in fact very similar to that of a starling, with long pointed wings and a short square-ended tail. If a waxwing flies low overhead, you can see that its bill is noticeably shorter than that of the commoner bird, while the tip of its tail carries a bright yellow band. Although it does not often call, the waxwing's voice can also betray its identity, for its usual note is a thin, high-pitched trill (its Russian name–'sviristel' –means 'reedpipe bird').

When seen perched or feeding, the waxwing is unmistakable. The general colour of the head, breast and belly is pinkish-brown, but the back is a darker brown. The rump and tail are grey, the latter shading into black with a conspicuous yellow tip, while the under-tail is a rich, dark chestnut. The chin is black and a black line extends round and behind the eye. The forehead is chestnut, shading into pink-ish-brown on the top of the head, where the feathers are elongated into a remarkably long crest.

The flight feathers are mainly black but carry white markings. The bird's name is derived from the red tips to the inner flight feathers (secondaries); the webs of the feather tip are fused to the shaft, resembling bright red sealing-wax.

Britain invaded Despite this conspicuous appearance and the bird's tendency to form flocks (sometimes large, like the one in Aberdeen), the waxwing is unfamiliar to most people because it is an irregular visitor, whose arrival follows irruptions from its breeding areas (Scandinavia and northern Russia) in the manner of crossbills and the much rarer nutcracker and Pallas' sandgrouse. These irruptive species visit our shores infrequently, but when they do arrive, they tend to occur in substantial numbers.

A flock of over 1000 waxwings was seen near Louth in Lincolnshire during the early days of an invasion in the autumn of 1965.

Above: A waxwing in winter. Note the yellow tail band.

Waxwing (*Bombycilla garrulus*). Irregular winter visitor from Scandinavia and northern Russia, appearing in 'irruptions'. Length 18cm (7in). Sexes alike.

WANDERING WAXWINGS

The waxwing does not breed in Britain, for its home lies in Scandinavia and the north of Russia. It visits us only in winter, but even then its appearances are unpredictable.

One morning in early December 1970 a roadside bank in Aberdeen was suddenly transformed from brilliant scarlet to a subtle pinkish-brown. The scarlet had been an almost total cover of cotoneaster berries, upon which had settled a flock of over 400 waxwings, colourful and bizarre immigrants from Scandinavia which had just completed

Waxwing irruptions
When Britain plays host to these northern invaders, many other European countries– normally far south of the birds' range–also receive wandering birds. During large irruptions waxwings may range as far south as Italy, Spain and Portugal (shown on our map in a dotted line), but in most years they are able to spend the winter on their northern nesting areas. The solid lines on the map indicate the main advances of the birds in an irruption year.

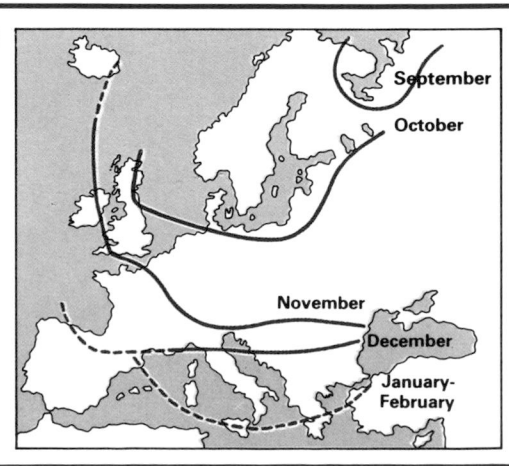

Irruptive invaders

Waxwing
from N Europe and Asia

rowan berries

Nutcracker
from Central European mountains

Arolla pine seeds

Pallas' sand grouse
from SE Europe and Asia

grain

Crossbill
from N Scandinavia

spruce cone seeds

Blue tit

British populations swollen in winter by irruptions from N Europe

beech mast

Great tit

Such large flocks are typical of the early arrivals and therefore tend to occur along the east coast. As the birds move further into the country, these large flocks break up so that later in the winter, and the further west one goes, the smaller the flocks tend to become. Nevertheless, flocks of a hundred or more do occur occasionally in Ireland.

The number of birds that arrive in Britain during an invasion can vary widely from a few tens to several thousands. Equally variable is their time of arrival. In 1965 the earliest birds appeared in September, while in the much smaller invasion of the 1956-7 winter waxwings were not seen until February.

Once an invasion of Britain occurs, they move from their initial landing places on the east coast and spread to other parts of the country, but the extent to which more westerly areas receive visitors depends to a certain extent on the size of the irruption. When numbers are small, the waxwings may remain near the east coast, but after a large immigration, as in the 1965-6 winter, the westward spread during the early part of the invasion is followed in the spring by a return to the east of the country as the birds that have survived our winter prepare to return to their breeding grounds. Most waxwings have left Britain by the end of April.

Population and food supplies This unpredictability over the waxwing's arrival in Britain and southern Europe is ultimately related to the bird's diet. In spring and summer waxwings do in fact eat insects, but at other times of the year they are vegetarians. In fact they are among the relatively few species that can, if necessary, survive on a diet consisting solely of plant material. Within the vegetable realm, however, waxwings prefer berries and it is this specialisation which forces them to vacate their breeding areas

periodically.

Most fruiting trees do not produce large crops every year, rather they crop heavily every second year, but even this heavy crop can be quite variable. In the vicinity of the breeding areas rowan, hawthorn and juniper are the waxwing's main autumn and winter foods. If a series of good breeding seasons coincides with reasonable winter berry crops, the waxwing breeding population increases over successive years and may extend the breeding area southwards Once a high population level has been attained, a failure of the berry crop will force these birds to emigrate in search of sufficient berries to survive the winter.

Above: Besides the waxwing, other bird species arrive suddenly in Britain from time to time. When their populations have become large—this coinciding with a failure of the fruits or seeds upon which they depend—they leave their normal areas in search of food to keep them alive over winter. This is called an 'irruption'.

Below: Cotoneaster berries, and also those of rowan, hawthorn and juniper, provide the waxwing's main food in the winter.

175

SWANS FROM THE FROZEN NORTH

Two swans that arrive here in winter can be told from the familiar mute swan by their black and yellow bills. They are whooper and Bewick's swans – migrants from the far north. Apart from the intricate patterns on their bills, they look very much alike.

Bewick's swan (*Cygnus bewickii*). Winter visitor, mainly to southern Britain, where it inhabits shallow estuaries, lowland lakes and flooded grassland. Length 1.2m (4ft) from bill to tail.

Whooper swan (*Cygnus cygnus*). Winter visitor, mainly to northern and central Britain, where it can be found in the same habitats as the Bewick's swan. Length 1.5m (5ft).

Each October, flocks of wild swans migrate to Britain from their summer breeding grounds far to the north. Some reach us from Iceland, while others come from much further away – from northern Scandinavia or even the tundra of Arctic Siberia.

For hundreds of years people thought that these swans all belonged to the same species, and were called whooper swans. Then, in 1830, a perceptive ornithologist called William Yarrell realised that there were two quite different species present. He named the smaller of the two Bewick's swan, in memory of the famous naturalist and wood engraver, Thomas Bewick, who had died two years before.

Telling them apart Yarrell was able to distinguish the two species by closely examining dead birds and museum specimens. In more usual conditions, however, it is not always easy to tell them apart, especially for the birdwatcher observing swans on a distant lake.

Both species are white, like the more familiar mute swan, but differ from the mute in having a long straight neck and a black and yellow pattern on their bills. The mute swan has a curved neck and an orange bill, with a black knob at its base. Trying to tell the whooper from the Bewick's swan is much more of a problem. If you can get close to the birds then the best way is to look at the pattern on the bill. On the whooper the yellow patches extend down the sides of the bill, coming to a point beyond the nostril. On the bill of the Bewick's swan the yellow patches normally have a rounded end and never extend as far down as the nostril. However, the pattern on the Bewick's bill is variable.

Such fine distinctions are useful if you can get close enough for a good view. If not, then you must rely on other more subtle differences. The whooper swan is bigger than the Bewick's – it is at least 25% heavier – but this is not always apparent, even when you are lucky enough to have both species present for comparison. The best feature to look for is the relative size of the neck and head. The

Above: A whooper swan flapping its wings as a part of preening. The other swans in the picture are also whoopers. The name 'whooper' comes from the bird's distinctive trumpet-like call, which can be heard a great distance away.

Above right: It is often difficult to distinguish a whooper swan from a Bewick's swan. If the bird is too far away for you to see its bill pattern, the best guide is the neck. Both species have straight necks, unlike the mute swan's which is curved, but the whooper's neck is much longer than that of the Bewick's. The bird shown here is a whooper.

Right: A group of Bewick's swans preening themselves. The Bewick's is the smallest species of swan found in Britain, though size is not a reliable guide to identification, even when a Bewick's swan can be compared directly with a whooper.

yellow patches joined across bill

Bewick's swan

yellow patches separated by a black line

yellow patches separated by a third yellow patch

yellow patches extend beyond nostril

Whooper swan

Left: The bill pattern provides a clear distinction between the two species. On a Bewick's swan the pattern can be classified into three main types, but in all three the yellow patches never extend as far down the bill as they do on a whooper.

whooper, as well as being larger, has proportionately a longer neck and head. In general, a swan with a really long neck, no matter how large or small it seems to be, is almost certainly a whooper swan.

The two species can also be distinguished by their calls, particularly in flight. The whooper has a deeper, more trumpeting call than the Bewick's, but there is a lot of variation. This applies only to the adults; the young of both species have a high-pitched squeaky call.

Winter and summer distribution Whooper and Bewick's swans are winter visitors to Britain; they do not breed here. Both species inhabit shallow estuaries, lowland lakes and flooded grasslands. They are sometimes seen in mixed flocks, but more often only one species is seen at a particular locality.

In the summer their distribution is completely separate. The breeding ranges of the two species are determined by the length of time each needs to complete the cycle of egg-laying, incubation and fledging. The whooper swan, being larger, needs $4\frac{1}{2}$ months, whereas the smaller Bewick's swan can

group of Bewick's swans disputing territory

defending pair

intruder

Above right: The shape of the yellow patch on their bills indicates that this pair of birds are whooper swans. Both whooper and Bewick's swans pair for life.

Left: A Bewick's cygnet. The nest of a Bewick's swan consists of a large conical mound built from moss and lichen. Usually four creamy-white eggs are laid and incubated for about 30 days. The young are tended by both adults and take about six weeks to fledge.

Below: A pair of whooper swans with cygnets. The nest of a whooper is similar to that of the Bewick's, but the incubation and fledging periods are longer. Whoopers usually lay five or six eggs.

manage the cycle in just under three months. This difference allows the Bewick's to breed in the northern Arctic regions of Siberia where the summers are short, while the whooper swan has to breed in the more southerly regions of Russia, in Iceland and in Continental Europe.

Whooper swans The majority of whooper swans that winter in Britain – numbering over 7000 – come from breeding grounds in Iceland, where they nest by the larger lakes throughout most of the country. Breeding pairs are strongly territorial and do not tolerate other swans entering a large area around their nests. Non-breeding birds – composed of young birds and adults who have failed to breed – flock together for the summer on shallow coastal lagoons and large inland waters.

In the second half of October, the whooper swans migrate across the north Atlantic to Scotland and Ireland, covering the 600–800 miles in a single flight. Once in Britain, they gather into large flocks, occasionally over a thousand strong, on various lochs, notably Strathbeg, Grampian, Leven and Tayside in Scotland, and Foyle in Northern Ireland.

The swans feed on vegetation in the water and also fly out to the surrounding farmland in search of spilt grain from harvested corn fields and broken pieces of potato in harvested potato fields.

As the winter approaches, the large flocks break up and the birds disperse more widely. Many swans move from Scotland into Ireland, and others fly further south into England. Whooper swans can be found as far south as Norfolk and Cambridgeshire.

Summer in Scotland The departure of whoopers for their breeding grounds begins in March and continues throughout April. However, a few birds remain behind for the summer in Scotland, usually because an injury prevents their making the return flight. Occasionally, a pair of Scottish birds breeds. This happened recently on a Hebridean island. It is not known whether this pair was injured, but it is possible that the birds were perfectly healthy. Several species of northern breeding birds have begun to colonize Scotland in recent years, and the

Above: A flock of Bewick's swans flying across a field. As well as feeding on marshland vegetation both Bewick's and whooper swans fly out to nearby fields to graze and feed on morsels left after harvesting.

whooper may be joining their numbers.

Bewick's swans The Bewick's swan arrives in Britain from Arctic Siberia. Its journey is mainly overland, and the birds have a number of regular stopping places, where they can break their journey. The whole trip may take several weeks, with birds stopping for long periods until forced by the weather to move further south and west.

They begin arriving in Britain in October, and further arrivals take place right through until January. Most Bewick's swans are found in the southern half of Britain, at sites

such as the Ouse and Nene Washes, Slimbridge in Gloucestershire, the Somerset Levels, and several sites in Ireland.

Learning about Bewick's One of the main wintering sites in Britain for Bewick's swans is the headquarters of the Wildfowl Trust, at Slimbridge in Gloucestershire. Over the years, much has been learned about the life of these swans. Each pair brings their young with them on migration in the autumn and the family stays together throughout the winter. In this way, the young swans learn the migration route.

Despite the loss of its natural habitats to drainage and reclamation schemes, there has been a steady increase in the wintering population of the Bewick's swan since the 1960s. This is largely due to its adaptation to feeding on root vegetables left in arable fields.

Five miles high A study of swans has shown that they prefer to wait for a tail wind before setting off on a migration. A remarkable example of swans picking up a tail wind occurred one December. A radar operator spotted what he thought was a flock of birds on his screen. There happened to be an aircraft near by, and he asked the pilot if he could identify them. The astonished pilot reported that it was a flock of about 30 swans (later identified as whoopers) flying at a height of about five miles. It was later discovered that these birds had the benefit of an 80mph tail wind, but they were also having to put up with a temperature of $-48°C$ $(-55°F)$ and an atmosphere containing only about 40% the amount of oxygen found at sea level. Clearly, these birds are superbly well adapted for high-altitude flight.

Migration routes

Most whooper swans arrive in Britain from Iceland. A few reach us from Scandinavia and Russia, where they breed in wooded regions south of the tundra, but most of this population winter on the Continent or in Turkey or Southern Russia.

Britain's population of Bewick's swans all come from the open wastes of the tundra in the far north of Russia. In autumn they slowly make their way south-west, stopping to rest for quite long periods until forced by the approach of winter to move on. They arrive in Britain between October and January.

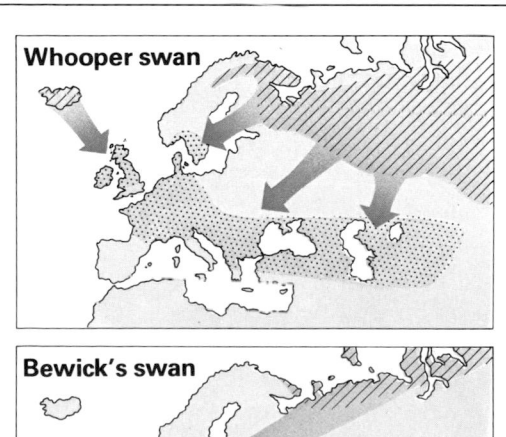

Whooper swan

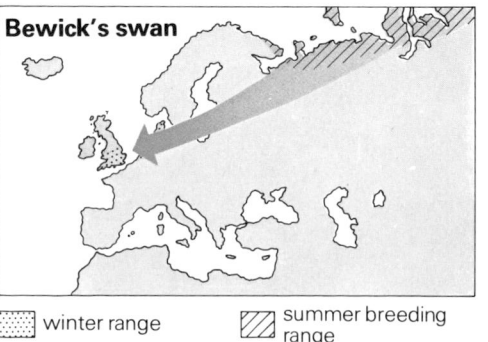

Bewick's swan

⋅⋅⋅⋅ winter range   ▨ summer breeding range

HIBERNATING TO SURVIVE WINTER

Our hibernating mammals—hedgehogs, dormice and bats—literally 'switch off' in winter when food becomes scarce. So ingenious is the technique that scientists have been considering how to induce hibernation in deep-space astronauts.

Some animals solve the problem of living through the winter months, when food is scarce or unavailable, by hibernating. Only a few British species in fact hibernate; they are hedgehogs, dormice and bats. Many cold-blooded creatures such as frogs, snakes and snails become torpid in winter, but it is only the warm-blooded animals that change from their warm state, with a constant body temperature, to a cold state, in which their body temperature fluctuates with the surrounding air.

Switching off Hibernation is usually compared to a deep sleep; but it is more than that. The body's processes re-adjust completely: the heart beat slows, breathing almost stops and the body temperature falls to within a few degrees of freezing. These changes ensure that the body uses minimal amounts of energy to maintain life. For example, a fall of 20°C (35°F) in body temperature reduces by three quarters the rate of chemical reactions in the body and the consumption of stored food reserves. In hibernation the body barely 'ticks over' in a state of suspended animation. The animal is stiff and cold, almost dead.

There has been considerable scientific interest in the mechanisms of hibernation because, if they could be applied to humans, astronauts could make long-duration flights without needing to carry several years' supply of food. During hibernation, physical damage is less traumatic to an animal's body, so there is also medical interest in hibernation as a way of improving the human body's tolerance to major surgical operations.

Hibernating animals are thus virtually 'switched off' for the winter, with the great advantage that they do not need to feed at the very time that food is unavailable. The price they pay is that they are totally immobile and therefore vulnerable to climate and predators. So it is essential for them to choose a protected place in which to hibernate.

Choosing sites Dormice and hedgehogs try to gain protection by building a special nest called a hibernaculum. The common dormouse chooses the bottom of a hedge or the base of a coppiced hazel. Hedgehogs may use old rabbit burrows, but usually construct a

nest under brushwood or brambles, or tucked up against a log. The hibernaculum of the hedgehog is a sturdy construction made of tightly packed leaves. These form an insulating layer which maintains the inside of the nest at between 0° and 5°C (32°–41°F) for most of the time. This is the best temperature range for hedgehogs to hibernate efficiently. The nest also keeps the occupant dry and protects it from snow and frost.

The hedgehog is totally dependent upon its nest for the three or four months passed in hibernation. These hibernacula are so snug that other animals—such as bees and mice—often move in when the hedgehog has left. Sound construction means nests may last for up to 18 months; but hedgehogs do not usually reoccupy old nests. In fact they may build several in the space of a few weeks—almost as though they were practising the art—and then use only one of them. These spare nests may be useful if the chosen hibernaculum is destroyed or flooded out during the winter.

Where bats hide Most of the 16 species of British bats are solitary hibernators, although a few spend the winter in small groups. Bats often select a humid cave, cellar or hollow tree in which to hibernate—two species always hibernate in caves and six prefer to use these dark, undisturbed dwellings if possible—because they offer a relatively constant temperature and a high humidity. These conditions are particularly favourable because

Above: This tiny hibernating dormouse is oblivious of the fact that it has been taken from its winter retreat. Hibernating mammals should not be disturbed from their deep sleep, since arousal forces them to use up precious reserves of fat unnecessarily.

Below: This chart illustrates how our hibernators solve the problem of winter food shortages. They switch off their central heating and allow body temperature and heart and breathing rates to fall. Their cold, torpid bodies just tick over, relying on the energy stored in the reserves of fat.

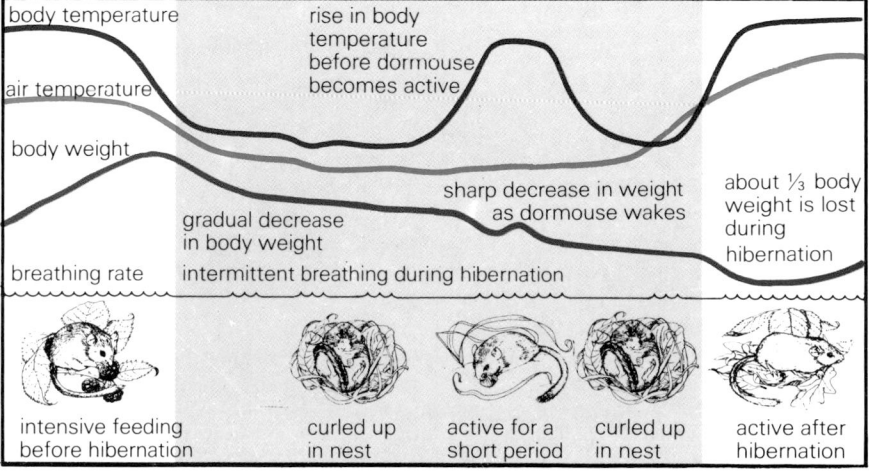

body temperature

air temperature

body weight

rise in body temperature before dormouse becomes active

gradual decrease in body weight

sharp decrease in weight as dormouse wakes

about ⅓ body weight is lost during hibernation

breathing rate — intermittent breathing during hibernation

intensive feeding before hibernation

curled up in nest

active for a short period

curled up in nest

active after hibernation

Making a hibernaculum

In autumn the hedgehog carries the fallen leaves of deciduous trees to a sheltered place under some brambles. When a large pile has been gathered, the hedgehog crawls inside and moves round and round until the loose leaves have become tightly packed against the bramble branches. This secure, weatherproof nest will be its home —hibernaculum—during the cold winter.

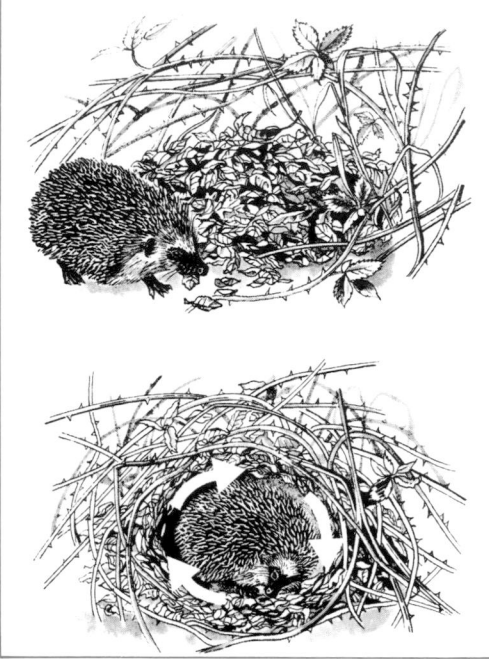

Above: True hibernators, such as this hedgehog, do not always sleep right through the winter uninterrupted. It is quite common for hedgehogs to move to another nest if they wake up before spring.

they prevent the bats losing water by evaporation. (Some bats, however, will select areas as near to freezing point as possible to conserve energy.) Constant conditions are also helpful because bats do not then need to cope with unusual warmth or cold, or climate changes. Old mines and large roof spaces such as in barns and attics are therefore also good locations for bats.

Bats hang upside down (some believe this is to reduce the stress on their hind legs) and where they roost varies according to the individual species. The horseshoe bat hangs from the roof of a cave, while the Daubenton's bat squeezes itself into crevices in cave walls or may burrow among loose material on the cave floor. Other species of bat hibernate in trees or buildings, but if the weather gets very cold they will move into caves. Perhaps for bats hibernation can be seen as a strategic alternative to migration.

Interruptions Hibernators are at risk if the air temperature falls too low. Below 0°C (32°F) there is a risk of ice crystals forming in the animal's blood; this would be fatal. Hibernating mammals usually allow their body temperature to fall and match that of their surroundings, fluctuating as the air temperature goes up or down. But if the environment cools below 1°C (33°F), the animal's body functions 'switch on' again and either keep the body ticking over at just above freezing or arouse the animal to activity.

Most people think of hibernation as an unbroken event, deep sleep from November till March. In fact arousal is frequent during that period. This is why bats may be seen flying in mid-winter and hedgehogs are killed on roads in January and February. Experiments show that hedgehogs wake up every couple of weeks or so and it is rare for a hedgehog to stay in the same nest for the whole winter. Bats stir naturally too, while with dormice the periods of unbroken slumber are probably quite a lot longer. Animals will also stir if disturbed.

Living off fat Hibernators have large stores of white fat (similar to the fat on joints of meat). This substance forms the body's 'fuel', to keep it ticking over. Some hibernators, such as pet golden hamsters, store food in the form of caches of nuts and seeds; but hedgehogs and bats cannot do this and so they must store a whole winter's energy requirements, in the form of white fat, in their bodies. Masses of it accumulate under the skin and around the body during the early autumn. By the time hibernation begins, fat may account for over a third of the animal's total weight. All this food reserve may be used up in the course of four months' hibernation.

Clearly it is essential that enough fat is stored away before hibernation starts. In some years, bad weather in late summer or early autumn makes this very difficult to do because insects and other food are in short supply.

The hedgehog's nesting material
The hedgehog prefers to use the leaves of broadleaved trees to make its protective nest (hibernaculum). These trees are found as far north as latitude 60, which corresponds to the approximate northern limit of the hedgehog's range. It may well be that the survival of the hedgehog depends on the availability of suitable leaves with which to make a winter nest. More support for this idea comes from the fact that hedgehogs are rarely found in coniferous forests, where suitable leaves for nesting material are scarce.

Waking up is not a simple matter. The main problem is to raise the body temperature through 30 degrees or more to the normal active level. This is done by using a special tissue called brown fat, which forms orange-brown lobes in the body, especially in the shoulder region (often called hibernating glands). The sole purpose of this fat is to generate heat when required. Warmth is circulated round the body by the blood stream; when the muscles are warm enough, they begin to shiver and produce more heat. It may take half an hour for a small bat to rouse itself fully; larger hedgehogs could take over twice as long.

Every time a hibernator wakes up, it consumes quantities of brown fat. So it is important not to disturb hibernators unnecessarily because this will reduce their chances of getting through the winter on their remaining fat reserves. Bats are particularly sensitive to disturbance in winter and their chances of survival are diminished if they are aroused, especially by intruding cavers stumbling unwittingly into their retreat.

Knowing the time It is not known exactly what causes an animal to begin hibernation or end it. It is likely that hibernation ceases when the average air temperature rises above a certain level in spring. Should a period of cold weather then return, the animal will resume hibernation until conditions improve. The stimulus for a bat in the shelter of a deep cave, where the temperature hardly changes, must be much more subtle than that for the comparatively exposed dormouse in its leafy nest.

Temperature is also crucial at the onset of hibernation, but in this case it is only one of a complex of factors which warn the animal to begin hibernating. For example, if captive hedgehogs are kept well fed, they will refrain from hibernating even in quite cold conditions. If their food is stopped, however, they will hibernate while it is still comparatively warm. In fact hibernation is probably triggered off by a combination of weather conditions and food shortage, which normally occur together in autumn.

Without their ability to hibernate, it is doubtful if bats and hedgehogs (and probably dormice too) could find sufficient food during our winters to survive. Although often successful, this strategy is not, however, without risks of its own. The major re-adjustments that the animal undergoes are a severe challenge to the body's machinery. The reliance on stored fat reserves is also something of a gamble. Will there be enough to last? What if spring comes later than usual? Hibernating animals cannot defend themselves against predators, either. So it is scarcely surprising that many die each winter, especially animals hibernating for the first time. Between 30 and 60 per cent of hedgehogs and bats never live to see their first birthday.

Below: Greater horseshoe bats — one of the largest and rarest species in Britain — hang in a cluster upside down in a cave. In the cool, steady temperature of the cave, loss of water is minimised — a very important factor for the survival of the bats. By clustering together in this way, the bats are able to conserve body heat while they hibernate.

THE STRUGGLE FOR WINTER SURVIVAL

The unpredictability of our weather makes winter a hard time of year for all animals. The sudden falls of snow, heavy rain, frost, high winds and storms – and the occasional surprisingly warm day – tax the physical resources of the hardiest of mammals.

Above: There is not much to eat for a red deer hind and stag in the New Forest in winter. Shortage of food sometimes forces deer to move on to farmland to forage, where they often damage root crops and vegetables.

In winter mammals need to use more energy than usual to keep warm. But food is scarce and the daylight hours required for hunting are shorter; plants are lying dormant, not producing nourishing green shoots; and there are no flying insects about for the insect-eaters. Survival through to spring is achieved only by those mammals that are fit, strong and able to endure exposure to the cold and a shortage of food.

There are three ways in which mammals can solve this annual survival problem. The first is to move to more hospitable territory; the second is to hibernate – to sleep through the winter; the third is to fatten up in autumn, setting aside a standby larder when there is more than enough food about, and also to search harder for food. However, the inescapable fate of many British mammals in winter, especially of our smaller species, is death. They are simply unable to get through the months of food shortage and severe weather.

The long sleep Bats, like birds, have the necessary equipment for migration by flight, but they usually take a less strenuous course of action by going to sleep in winter. By the end of autumn, each bat has fed well on the flying insect population and has built up a thick layer of fat that almost completely covers its body under the skin. This fat provides the necessary energy for the bat's reduced metabolism (in hibernation it uses about one hundredth of the oxygen it normally breathes). From October to April the bats congregate to roost. The greater horseshoe bat hibernates in caves or buildings, hanging upside down from wall or roof with its wings folded around it, while the pipistrelle prefers a sheltered dark place such as a barn or perhaps an attic.

Bats are not complete hibernators, however; should the night air temperature reach 10°C (50°F) or more they may wake up from their torpor, and even fly around their winter quarters.

The long winter sleep of the dormouse may also be interrupted; then it will eat some of the store it has laid by in its nest. Like the bats, the dormouse becomes very fat in autumn; it settles in its winter nest (usually a burrow in the ground or a hole in a tree) and rolls up into a ball with its head bent down, chin resting on its stomach. Here it stays for six months. Its body temperature becomes so low that it feels cold to the touch.

The hedgehog is possibly the lightest sleeper of Britain's mammalian hibernators. It may sleep for only a few days at a time until well into winter. Then, from about December to March or April, it retires to the bottom of a hedge or a hollow under tree roots and curls up among the leaves, grasses and moss. Here it is secure from frosts until spring.

Squirrels are also able to live through short spells of severe weather in a lethargic

Above: The hibernating dormouse, supposedly secure and hidden among leaves and twigs, is not safe from foxes, or from badgers, weasels and stoats. Four out of five sleeping dormice may well be eaten each winter by hungry carnivores.

Below: A stoat in its white winter coat. Like foxes and weasels, this animal is out and about all winter, relying on its hunting skills to find food and its thick fur to keep warm.

state, but they do not hibernate. Heavy rain, mist and strong winds, rather than low temperatures, keep them in their dreys.

Always on the move Most mammals live in the same territory or 'home range' all their lives, but the long journeys made by whales mean they live a settled life only at each end of their migrations. Some whales journey towards our temperate waters in winter. The common dolphin frequents the English Channel and is also found off the Irish coasts, coming from a south-westerly direction in autumn and leaving for the open Atlantic in the spring. The yearly migrations of shoals of mackerel and, off Cornwall, of pilchards may be a reason for the dolphin's movements.

For most whales, migration is linked to feeding and breeding needs. The fin-whale, or common rorqual, which can be seen at sea off our western coasts in spring and autumn, and the dumpy humpback whale, have similar feeding and breeding migratory habits. The Atlantic right whale, normally found in the north Atlantic, makes regular winter migrations to Spain, Portugal and North Africa, returning to the west of the Hebrides and further north in summer.

The seals, too, move round the coasts of Britain. The common seal, found all round our shores on sand and mud banks, moves away from the British mainland in winter. The larger grey seal, on the other hand, comes to our shores in winter to breed and bear young.

Seasonal struggle for survival For those mammals that do not migrate, or hibernate, successful survival through the cold months depends on a combination of factors. All mammals have coats of hair or fur which can be fluffed out in low temperatures to create an insulating layer of air and they can build up layers of fat beneath the skin during the summer which act as a shield against the cold climate ahead. Many mammals also hoard food as a precaution against the days when snow and rain make it impossible for them to forage and, to make fewer demands on their bodies, they slow down their pace of life in general.

The badger, for example, reduces its

Above: Grey seals come to our stormy, rocky shores in winter, gathering in their breeding colonies on northern and western coasts from the Scilly Isles to the Farne Islands. Most of their pups are born between September and December.

Below: Not all mammals hibernate – the badger and the squirrel are active all year round. Those animals that do hibernate sleep for different lengths of time. Hedgehogs can still be seen in November and are active again in late March, while dormice hibernate in October and reappear at the end of April. Bats may wake up in late February.

activity in winter, spending more time in its sett. It can go without food for a fairly long time since much fat is stored under its skin, and it may remain below ground for several days at a time. However, even on the coldest days, some badgers are active. The fox is another mammal that is active all year round. A great opportunist, it readily comes into towns to scavenge. In autumn and early winter it is mainly active at dusk, whereas at the end of winter it may be about at any time of the day or night.

Fruits, berries and seeds are in great demand by many winter-active animals. Deer, essentially woodland dwellers, eat leaves, grass, berries, shoots and ferns, but also forage on farmland when times are hard. In winter red deer hinds and their families move down from the mountains in Scotland to lower ground where the land is more sheltered from wind and snow. The roe deer moves into denser parts of the woodlands and plantations during the cold months.

Plant seeds are an important food for the ground-feeders, such as the mice. The long-tailed wood mouse gathers seeds, berries and roots to set aside as a winter store in a side room or nest-chamber of its burrow. This mouse has been known to graze at night on winter cereals growing next to a wood, causing considerable crop damage in the process. The aggressive mole, whose whole life is a feverish hunt for food, also puts by stores for times of scarcity. To survive, it must consume its own weight of food every 24 hours. In winter, earthworms make up at least 90%, if not more, of its diet. After a sudden frost, when the movement of worms through the soil is restricted, the mole is able to eat its fill and still have enough to store. To do this, it injures the front end of each worm so that it cannot escape, and then stores it in one of its underground tunnels.

The losers Many small mammals do not succeed in the struggle to live throughout the winter. Unable to escape from the cold, and without enough food to keep the body warm, they soon perish. The small muntjac, a fairly solitary deer of woodlands in central England, starves to death in severe seasons, while rats have a mortality rate of about 91–97% per year. High death rates occur among the shrews, mice, voles and rabbits as well.

Few small mammals ever survive more than one winter; because of this they are sometimes called 'annuals'. It is thought that the majority of adult shrews die in the autumn, leaving only the young animals to carry the species over the winter to the next breeding season. This means that each individual shrew lives about 14 to 16 months. It survives only one winter, that immediately after birth, and has only one breeding season, that of the year following its birth. The life history of mice and voles is very similar.

	J	F	M	A	M	J	J	A	S	O	N	D
badger												
squirrel												
hedgehog												
dormouse												
bat												

WINTER TRACKS AND SIGNS

Mammals are, on the whole, secretive creatures. Often, the best evidence of their existence comes from tracks and trails; these are especially easy to spot in winter.

Winter is an excellent time of year to look for signs of a mammal's activity, especially after a fall of snow on a windless day. In snow which is a couple of centimetres thick and hardened by frost, tracks are clean and sharp. Most mammals stay hidden during the worst of the weather, but once it has improved there is a lot of feeding activity and footprints are made in many places.

Imprints also show up well in mud and sand. Damp, slightly muddy earth by a woodland path, a ditch in a forest or a hedgerow are good places to look for tracks. The wet sand on a beach at low tide or even the damp sand on the dunes are other surfaces where you can expect to see clear trails.

It is as well to know what mammals are about during the winter and therefore what tracks to expect to see. The dormouse hibernates during the cold months, and so does the hedgehog, although it is a lighter sleeper—it wakes only when it is relatively warm so it is not about when snow is on the ground. Weasels tend to make tunnels and holes in thick snow rather than travel over it. The tracks of the small lightweight stoat are usually indistinct as the foot pads are covered with hair.

Rabbit and hare tracks are commonly seen during winter. They are quite similar in appearance except that the hare's are slightly larger and more widely spaced out. It is easy to tell the two apart, however, with the aid of

Above: A fox foraging in the snow for food. The tracks it makes are similar to those made by a dog, but the pad marks of a dog are closer together, giving a more compact track. This fox is probably creeping along on the scent of a small rodent.

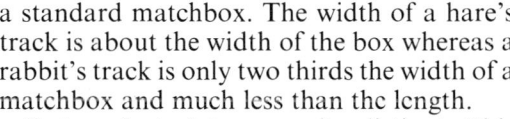

Below: Stoat prints in wet, muddy sand at the edge of a lagoon near Southwold, Suffolk. The closeness of its prints suggests that the mammal was running.

a standard matchbox. The width of a hare's track is about the width of the box whereas a rabbit's track is only two thirds the width of a matchbox and much less than the length.

Badger footprints are quite distinct. This animal moves with a heavy tread, the hind foot usually registering in the print of the forefoot. The large tracks are square in shape with a very broad heel pad.

Deer slots Identification of individual slots is based mainly on size. The largest are made by the red deer stags which have footprints 8cm (3in) long. Next in size is the fallow deer buck with slots 7cm (2¾in) long, then the sika with prints 6.5cm (2¼in), the roe 4cm (1½in) and finally the muntjac slots which are 3cm (1¼in) long. It must be remembered that male slots are proportionately larger than those of females.

Caches of nut shells are give-away clues to the presence of small mammals—hazelnuts being the favourite food of many. Their thick hard shells make them difficult to deal with but each animal has its own particular way of tackling the problem and in doing so leaves individual toothmarks on the smooth brown shells.

Mice and voles gnaw a hole in the shell to get at the kernel inside. Lodging their upper incisors in a part of the shell that is slightly rough they are able to gnaw with the lower incisors. The wood mouse gnaws in such a way that it leaves an untidy hole with tooth-

Most of our mammals are shy creatures and are not often seen during the day. Evidence of their whereabouts, habits and homes are usually betrayed by their tracks, trails and other signs, such as droppings, that they leave behind after a night's activity. Winter is a good time to search for these signs since snow, mud and damp ground show up clear trails and footprints very clearly.

run

trot

Badger Tracks distinct due to heavy tread. The five toe pads lie close together and the long claws of the forefeet are clearly visible. The faeces are deposited in specially dug latrine holes.

Above: Tell-tale footprints to and from an opening identify the sett of a badger. This mammal does not hibernate, but will stay in its sett in very cold weather for days without eating. In milder periods it leaves its sett at night to search for food.

Naming footprints
Several terms are used to describe the different types of mammal footprints.
Track refers to a single footprint in the ground, or two if they have registered.
Trail means a pattern or succession of tracks left by a moving mammal.
Registering is when the tracks of the hind feet almost, or completely, overlap those of the forefeet.
Slot is the individual footprint of a deer.
Cleaves are the two halves of a cloven hoof.
Splaying is the term used when the cleaves spread out in soft ground.

marks both on the inside and outside of the shell whereas the bank vole leaves a shell with holes that have toothmarks on the inside only.

The squirrel splits the shell lengthwise into two clean halves. First it holds the nut with its forefeet and gnaws a groove across the top to make a small hole. Putting its lower incisors into the hole it presses the nut down until it cracks open.

Pine cones are another favourite food of these same mammals. Cones stripped with a frayed base and left lying out in the open are the work of squirrels. Cones stripped by mice and voles are left with a smooth, round base. They are less likely to be found as these animals drag the cones into the safety of their underground runs to eat.

Bark, twigs and buds are important sources of food for mammals during the winter, especially deer. These relatively large mammals leave quite noticeable feeding signs on trees. Deer have no upper jaw incisors, so that they tend to break or tear off, rather than bite, shoots and twigs, leaving frayed, uneven ends behind. When deer attack a tree it is said they 'bark' the tree. They strip the bark upwards with their bottom incisors leaving long bare patches of trunk. Usually a mature tree is barked on one side only and does not die. Young trees, however, may suffer so much damage that they do not recover. Considerable damage is also done to young trees by the bark-gnawing activities of voles in winter.

Mammal droppings are very informative clues to an animal's life. Each individual species tends to produce its own characteristic droppings. The plant-eaters eat large quantities of food to obtain sufficient nourishment. As a result they make frequent droppings that are usually small and round. The flesh-eaters do not eat in such quantity, as a small amount of meat gives lots of nourishment and energy. They produce fewer faeces and these are often cylindrical with a point at one end. Some mammals such as rabbits drop their faeces at random while others such as the badger and fox use special latrines.

Heaps of rabbit droppings are often found on ant hills and mole hills where they are used to mark out territory. The droppings are about 10mm ($\frac{3}{8}$in) in diameter. The hare's are slightly larger, 15-20mm ($\frac{3}{4}$in) in diameter, and are pale brown or yellow-brown in winter. They are often found in small piles a short distance away from the hare's form. Squirrels leave dark brown or black droppings in the winter. They are quite short, less than 5mm ($\frac{3}{16}$in) long, almost spherical with one flattened and one pointed end.

Deer droppings are called fewmets. They are usually short, black and cylindrical often with a small point at one end. They are usually deposited in quite large heaps or clusters at the feeding places. The roe deer often defaecates while it is moving so the droppings are scattered along its trail.

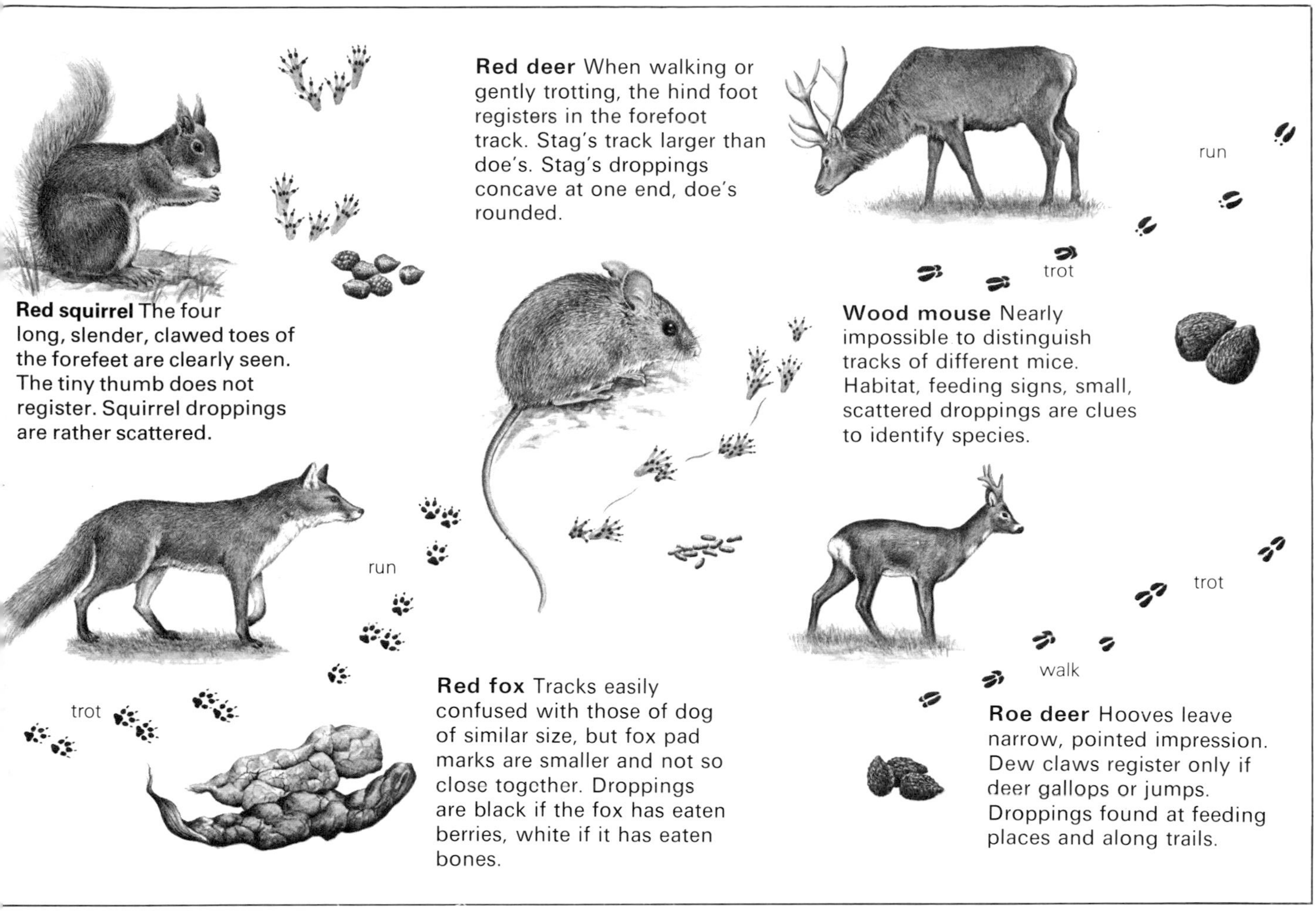

Red squirrel The four long, slender, clawed toes of the forefeet are clearly seen. The tiny thumb does not register. Squirrel droppings are rather scattered.

Red deer When walking or gently trotting, the hind foot registers in the forefoot track. Stag's track larger than doe's. Stag's droppings concave at one end, doe's rounded.

run

trot

Wood mouse Nearly impossible to distinguish tracks of different mice. Habitat, feeding signs, small, scattered droppings are clues to identify species.

run

trot

Red fox Tracks easily confused with those of dog of similar size, but fox pad marks are smaller and not so close together. Droppings are black if the fox has eaten berries, white if it has eaten bones.

trot

walk

trot

Roe deer Hooves leave narrow, pointed impression. Dew claws register only if deer gallops or jumps. Droppings found at feeding places and along trails.

The badger scrapes out a special latrine—often near its sett—about 10cm (4in) deep in which to deposit its droppings. It does not cover it over after use, but uses it time and again. The faeces may be either like those of the fox or semi-liquid, depending on what the animal has been eating.

Fox faeces are like those of a dog but smaller, usually 8-10cm ($3\frac{1}{2}$-4in) long. They are cylindrical and have one end twisted into a point. They vary in colour from black to grey and often contain the bones of small mammals and birds.

Scent marking is used by many mammals as a way of claiming their territory or of keeping a pair together. Our sense of smell is poorly developed and we are unlikely to detect these signals.

Within their home territories the mammals lead regular and well-organised lives. Each tends to have a system of well-worn paths and runways between home and feeding ground and these are clearly seen in winter when the ground cover is less dense. Other signs to look for are the homes themselves. The mole's hills are unmistakable, and so too is the sett of a badger. Freshly trodden earth around the sett entrance means it is inhabited. Lack of spiders' webs across the mouth of the hole also means that the animals are coming and going frequently. Steam rising from the entrance on a cold winter morning is proof that the badger is at home.

Right: Tree damage caused by a fallow deer in the New Forest during its rutting season. The bark is completely stripped, so this young pine tree will not recover.

Below: Squirrel 'table'. Both the grey and red squirrel feed on pine cones. An unstripped cone is taken to a favoured feeding place, such as a tree stump, and the scales are gnawed off one by one so that the squirrel can obtain the seeds lodged inside.

INDEX

The entries listed in **bold** type refer to main subjects. The page numbers in *italics* indicate illustrations. Medium type entries refer to the text.

ACKNOWLEDGEMENTS

Photographers' credits: A-Z Collection 70, 71, 123(bottom), 125(bottom): Heather Angel 13(top), 14, 19(top, bottom), 20(middle, bottom), 23, 26(top, bottom), 28(top left), 29, 32, 34, 36(left, bottom right), 37(top right), 60, 62(bottom), 65(bottom), 71(bottom), 72(bottom), 73(bottom), 75(top, bottom), 78(bottom), 81(middle), 84, 86(bottom), 88, 93(top), 97(top), 110(top), 116, 117(bottom), 118(top), 120(top, bottom), 123(top), 128, 129(bottom), 130(top), 131(bottom), 132, 136, 138, 149(top left), 164(top, bottom), 165, 166, 169(bottom), 182, 184: Aquila Photographics/J B Blossom 146; A J Bond 77; P T Castell 94(bottom), 97(bottom); Wayne Lankinen 174; T Leach 80(bottom); A T Moffat 91(top); E K Thompson 147(bottom); D S Whitaker 45(top); M C Wilkes 111(bottom): Ian Beames 8(top, lower middle), 30(top), 109, 189: Biofotos/G Kinns 57, 156(top); Jeremy Thomas 82: Bruce Coleman Ltd/N G Blake 173(middle); E Breeze-Jones 54; Jane Burton 143, 163(bottom); Bruce Coleman 103; Eric Crichton 78(top); S Dalton 46, 48; Dennis Green 49; P A Hinchcliffe 55; Gordon Langsbury 113; John Markham 134; R K Murton 100; Hans Reinhard 18, 52, 95, 108(top), 169(top); Kim Taylor 139(bottom); E Dusher 15(bottom), 178(middle): Vaughan Fleming 61(left), 62(top): Bob Gibbons Photography/R Fletcher 56-7, 154; Bob Gibbons 91(bottom), 157(left): Dennis Green 171(bottom), 177(bottom): Derek Hall 156: Tim Halliday 41: Stephen Harris 148(left, right), 149(bottom left, bottom right): G E Hyde 140: E A Janes front cover (grey squirrel), 22-3: John Mason 31; 67(top): Richard Mills 44(bottom), 92, 173(top): Colin

Molyneaux 8(bottom), 10: P Morris 142: Natural Image/R Fletcher 154: NHPA/J M Bain 76; A Bannister 20(top); Joe Blossom 53; N A Callow 87(top); L Campbell 122; G J Cambridge 63, 118(bottom); W R Caulton 135; S Dalton 107, 126(top); F Greenway 106; B Hawkes 16(top), 131(top), 145; E A Janes 12(bottom), 67(bottom); W J Murray 188; K G Preston-Mafham 30; Philippa Scott 178(bottom), 179; M W F Tweedie 85, 141; George Wall 172: Nature Photographers Ltd/ S C Bisserot 12(top), 21(middle), 89(middle, bottom), 124, 137(bottom); F V Blackburn front cover, 16(bottom), 28(bottom), 42(bottom), 43, 64(top), 96, 98(bottom), 102(top, bottom), 105; D Bonsall front cover (chaffinch nest); B Burbidge 6-7, 67(middle), 126(bottom), 129(upper middle), 162(top); A A Butcher 69; Kevin Carlson 187(bottom); David Callam 153(bottom); N A Callow 133; A Cleave 35(bottom), 64(bottom left), 86(top); T Ennis 17; Robert Gillimore 111(top); M Gore 15(top); Michael Grove 13(middle); C Knights 42(top); Chris and Jo Knights 176; Owen Newman 107, 151, 153(top), 185(top); W M S Paton 11(middle), 153(middle); D Sewell 156(bottom); D Smith 44(top), 45(bottom), 175; P Sterry front cover (blackberries), 68(middle); Roger Tidman 64(bottom right), 173(bottom); Anthony Wharton 126(middle): Planet Earth Pictures/Geoff du Feu front cover (poppies); John Lythgoe 112-13: Premaphotos Wildlife/K G Preston-Mafham 38, 39(top, bottom), 65(top), 66, 68(top), 71(top), 72(top), 74, 79, 89(top), 117(bottom), 129(top, lower middle), 162(bottom): Press-tige Pictures/D Avon and T Tilford 104; T Howes 163(middle): M King and M Read 171(top): M King and M Read/Geoff Doré 158, 159; M King 156(bottom right), 157(top right); M Read 147(top):

Richard Revels 80(top), 81(top, bottom), 83(top, bottom), 137(top): John Robinson 8(upper middle), 11(bottom), 21(top), 36(top right), 50, 51, 90(top), 94(top), 149(middle), 156(bottom left), 180, 181: D A Sutton 73(top): Barry Tebbs 163: M W F Tweedie 139(top, bottom): Universal Natural History Agency/P Morrison 68(bottom): Wildlife Services/ M Leach 150, 152:

Photographers' credits Stephen Adams 80, 81: Graham Allen/Linden Artists 53, 107, 110: Norman Arlott 47, 50: Bob Bampton/The Garden Studio 69: Russell Barnett 75: Lindsey Blow 99(line): Robert Burns/Drawing Attention 186: Catherine Constable 146, 147: Sarah De'Ath title page, 104: Eugene Fleury 96, 99(line): Wayne Ford 44-5, 101, 105, 172, 175, 177, 178: Hayward Art Group 9, 33, 40-41, 48, 50(map), 54, 76, 77, 78, 166, 167, 181, 182: Richard Lewington/The Garden Studio 83, 86, 89, 90, 133, 135, 137(centre), 141, 142, 170: Josephine Martin/ The Garden Studio 74(colour): David More/Linden Artists 61, 119: Paul Nesbitt 131: Denys Ovenden 92, 93, 157: Liz Pepperell/The Garden Studio 165: Sandra Pond 65, 99(birds), 125, 127, 188, 189: Richard Revels 137(top): John Rignall/Linden Artists 24-5, 58-9, 114-15, 160-1: Gordon Riley 39: Colin Salmon 16, 17, 35, 99(map), 101(map), 103, 110(map), 144, 145, 150, 169, 171, 174, 179: Helen Senior/Groom & Pickerill 27, 31, 62, 70, 71, 111: David Sutton 74(line): Colin Walton 99(blue line):

Distribution map data on page 54 courtesy of The Biological Records Centre/The Mammal Society.

Index compiled by Richard Raper of Indexing Specialists, Hove, East Sussex.

Typesetting PHOTOCOMP LTD, BIRMINGHAM; Printing & Binding PRINTER INDUSTRIA, GRÁFICA S.A. BARCELONA;
Separations YORK HOUSE GRAPHICS, HANWELL; COLOURSCAN OVERSEAS CO PTE LTD, SINGAPORE;
Paper KNP MILL, HOLLAND